T0306492

Dear Chester, Dear John

Chester Himes and John A. Williams, Alicante, Spain, May 1969

Dear Chester, Dear John

Letters between Chester Himes and John A. Williams

Compiled and Edited by
John A. and Lori Williams

With a Foreword by Gilbert H. Muller

WAYNE STATE UNIVERSITY PRESS DETROIT

AFRICAN AMERICAN LIFE SERIES

*A complete listing of the books in this series
can be found online at wsupress.wayne.edu*

Series Editors

Melba Joyce Boyd
Department of Africana Studies, Wayne State University

Ronald Brown
Department of Political Science, Wayne State University

12 11 10 09 08   5 4 3 2 1

Library of Congress Cataloging-in-Publication Data

Himes, Chester B., 1909–1984.
Dear Chester, Dear John : letters between Chester Himes and John A. Williams / compiled
and edited by Lori and John A. Williams ; with a foreword by Gilbert H. Muller.
p. cm. — (African American life series)
Includes index.
ISBN-13: 978-0-8143-3355-6 (hardcover : alk. paper)
ISBN-10: 0-8143-3355-9 (hardcover : alk. paper)
1. Himes, Chester B., 1909–1984—Correspondence. 2. Williams, John Alfred, 1925—
Correspondence. 3. Authors, American—20th century—Correspondence. 4. African
American authors—Correspondence. I. Williams, John Alfred, 1925– II. Williams, Lori
(Lorrain) III. Title.
PS3515.I713Z48 2008
813'.54—DC22
2007030927

Grateful acknowledgment is made to the Coleman A. Young Black Diaspora Publication
Fund, the Department of Africana Studies, Wayne State University, for generous support
in the publication of this volume.

Photographs are from the John A. Williams Papers, Rare Books and Special Collections,
University of Rochester, and the personal library of Lesley Himes.

∞

*Designed and typeset by Maya Rhodes
Composed in Adobe Garamond Pro and Dear Theo 2*

MY WIFE, LORI, AND I DEDICATE THIS WORK TO RICHARD PEEK, director of Rare Books and Special Collections, University of Rochester Libraries, Rochester, New York. Director Peek's invaluable suggestions and overall support contributed greatly to the development of this project. We have been fortunate in having such a knowledgeable and energizing collaborator and friend.

Contents

Foreword

Foreword

The correspondence between Chester Himes and John A. Williams provides readers with an opportunity to appreciate more fully two important writers and also to
explore a unique period in American literary culture. Edited by John and Lori Williams, the letters and related documents begin in 1962 and end in 1987, tracing the
friendship of Himes and Williams against the backdrop of a turbulent time in the
nation's history. In this collection, the two friends write about their lives, loves, and
careers, their problems as they attempt to negotiate the publishing and film worlds,
and their often tense negotiation of society in the United States and abroad.

With this intriguing collection of letters, we see Himes and Williams, who between them have more than two dozen novels and countless articles and nonfiction
books to their credit, as literary adventurers, testing in fact and fiction the tenor of
life, history, and politics in the twentieth century. Reading the letters, we sense that
Himes, born in 1909 and the older of the two men, believes that his life has been
absurd, as the title of the second volume of his autobiography—*My Life of Absurdity*—confirms. ("I feel that I am living in a madhouse," Himes writes in an early
letter to Williams.) It is this sense of the absurd that makes Himes's cycle of Harlem
crime fiction—nine novels written while he was living in France, Spain, and elsewhere, as well as his autobiography—so distinctive and compelling.

Williams, born in 1925 and at the start of his career when he first came into
contact with Himes, also is capable of capturing the elements of absurdity in con-

temporary life, but he is more interested, in major novels like *The Man Who Cried I Am* and *Captain Blackman,* in erecting experimental fictive structures that reveal the deepest historical and political impulses governing contemporary global existence. More completely and systematically than his older counterpart, Williams chronicles in his fiction, from his earlier works like *Sissie* (which Himes praises in several letters) to his most recent novel, *Clifford's Blues,* the quality of black life—and indeed of all human life—within national and global settings. Though Himes spent decades in Europe, he never wrote successful fiction about the European experience; and his autobiography, while offering useful insights into black expatriates in Paris and elsewhere, is far too generalized and biased in its comments on European culture to be of great value. Williams, on the other hand, traveling widely, residing for a time in Spain and the Netherlands but always returning to his home base in metropolitan New York, is a deeper reader of history than Himes, exploring the complexities of the human condition, critical events, and historical cataclysms across several continents, including Europe, Africa, and Asia. In their letters and their fiction, both men treat race as the third rail in their lives and their literary production, offering special insights into the subject without reducing existence to one obsessive element. But as we see in many of these letters, race is integral to their personal and literary adventures; it is, as James Baldwin (who appears in the letters) observed, the price of the ticket.

Himes and Williams first met in 1961 at the New York apartment of Carl Van Vechten, the novelist, photographer, man-about-the-city, and supporter of African American writers and artists. (He was known to some black writers as the "Great White Father," but Himes and Williams always valued their friendship with him.) Himes already was a good friend of Van Vechten's, while Williams was a new acquaintance of this helpful patron of writers, having come to Van Vechten's attention with the publication of his second novel, *Night Song.* Himes was already famous in certain literary circles, a former convict who had started writing in prison in the 1930s and 1940s, had published several promising naturalistic novels in the forties, knew Richard Wright and James Baldwin, and, like these two writers, had chosen exile in Europe to life in the United States—in Himes's case in 1953. At the time of his initial meeting with Williams, Himes was on the cusp of transcontinental celebrity with the success of his crime thrillers featuring the Harlem detectives Grave Digger Jones and Coffin Ed Johnson that he had written for the French publisher Gallimard's popular Série noire. Himes would achieve a degree of fame and, for the first time in his life, modest financial security with the publication of *Cotton Comes to Harlem* in 1964 and its subsequent adaptation to film.

A controversial and difficult personality, prone to suspicion and anger, especially in his later years as he suffered a series of strokes and other infirmities, Himes might have sensed in Williams, who was sixteen years younger, an admirer who would look after his affairs in the United States. Indeed, Himes enjoyed being a sage or mentor to younger writers like Williams, Melvin Van Peebles, and Ishmael Reed, although he often fell out with them (including Williams, as a break in the correspondence reveals) after succumbing to irrational suspicions or suffering imaginary slights. However, in the early years of their relationship, and indeed for more than a decade, Himes genuinely liked Williams and admired his work, and this affection was reciprocated. During these years—until an unfortunate rupture caused by Himes—the two friends were mutually supportive. In the first letter in this collection, Van Vechten, known to friends as Carlo, alludes to a letter Williams had written to him expressing pleasure at having met Himes. Replying to Williams, Van Vechten writes, "Chester likes you too. People say bad things about him because he doesn't like most people and shows it."

Himes at the time was shuttling between Europe and New York, trying to advance various projects that included a documentary film on Harlem for French television and a screenplay, *Baby Sister,* both with disappointing results. This early correspondence is especially valuable for its insights into Himes's confrontational personality and the efforts of individuals at the NAACP to prevent *Baby Sister* from finding a major film producer. In fact, Himes refers to a 1962 memorandum composed on NAACP stationery in which Herbert Hill wrote to a Swiss producer castigating the film script for *Baby Sister* as a "travesty on Negro life in Harlem." Himes already had fallen out with a member of the NAACP executive board—his cousin Henry Moon, who was at one time director of the Urban League, as well as Moon's wife, Mollie. (Mollie serves as a model for the Harlem hostess in the satire *Pinktoes,* published in Paris as *Mamie Mason,* a novel in which Himes parodies his distinguished relatives along with other luminaries like Richard Wright.) That Himes reinvents episodes from the time in the mid-forties when the Moons had graciously invited him to stay with them in their luxurious New York apartment on St. Nicholas Avenue and were upset by his penchant for amorous behavior is confirmed in a letter Himes wrote to Williams following his return to Paris. "I wrote a satire on the Negro middle class in the frame of a story lampooning Mollie Moon. . . . Hill, in his enthusiasm, showed the story to his colleagues at the NAACP, and most of them recognized themselves. He was told the story was about Mollie Moon—then Mollie got hold of it."

In the same letter, Himes tells Williams about his problems with New York agents and publishers, insinuating into his complaint a request that Williams handle his affairs, retrieve manuscripts, and find a new agent for him—in effect, that he protect and advance Himes's interests in the United States. This plea for help would become a motif in their relationship and the correspondence. In a long reply, Williams willingly accepts his new friend's multiple requests for assistance. He later acknowledged that he was "handy and willing to be used," confirming a tendency that Himes had with many of his friends and even more so with the women in his life. Williams adds, "I did talk to the people at Farrar, Straus and Cudahy, who were about to publish *Sissie* and who were to be very supportive during the Prix de Rome fiasco, about Chester and his work, but as I recall, his persona, that of being difficult to deal with, made him a creature to be avoided."[1]

The Prix de Rome controversy referred to by Williams reflects the difficult passage that African American writers encountered in the publishing world of the 1960s. Williams at that time was coming into his own as a novelist. He had been recommended for the prestigious Prix de Rome, offered by the American Academy of Arts and Letters, by a distinguished panel of jurists that included John Hersey, Louise Bogan, S. J. Perelman, and John Cheever. However, the director of the American Academy in Rome, Richard Kimball, obviously concluded after interviewing Williams that this was one writer who did not fit the profile of earlier novelists like Ralph Ellison and William Styron, who had been residents in Rome. Williams's second novel, *Night Song*, vividly capturing some of the excesses of New York's jazz demimonde, might have led Kimball to confuse the writer with some of his creations. In any case, both Williams and Himes were scarred by skirmishes with a literary world that tolerated only a few writers of color at any one time.

Undaunted by the Prix de Rome scandal, Williams persisted in what would become a highly productive and significant career. At that time, he conceived a project in which he would write a nonfiction study of several black writers, which he details in a letter to Himes. Although this particular project never was realized, it did provide Williams with the incentive to write in the future books on notable African Americans, leading to studies of Richard Wright, Martin Luther King Jr., and Richard Pryor. He planned to include Himes in this study and asked him for autobiographical information, which Himes provided in a twelve-page letter dated October 31, 1962; this letter is so significant that future Himes biographers will have to treat it as a primary document. And Williams subsequently did conduct an extensive interview with Himes (again mentioned in several letters) that led to its publication in a new journal for black writers, *Amistad 1,* which Williams and Charles Harris, an editor at Random House, published in 1970. This interview remains one of the most important sources of information on Himes; it did much to bring Himes to the attention of both the literary establishment and a new generation of African American writers.

During the 1960s, Williams came into his own as a novelist with the publication of *The Man Who Cried I Am* in the fall of 1967. This novel, which deals with the global consequences of American imperialism as history is filtered through the

---

1. John A. Williams, e-mail to Gilbert H. Muller.

consciousness of the central character, a writer named Max Reddick, on the last day of his life, is arguably the most important political novel to grow out of that volatile decade. (Williams in the novel re-creates, in thinly disguised form, a famous encounter between Wright and Baldwin that Himes had witnessed while in Paris.) During this period, as he notes in a commentary on these letters, Williams traveled extensively for *Holiday, Newsweek,* and other publications, finding himself in Africa, Spain, the Netherlands, Israel, Cyprus, and elsewhere without ever catching up with the equally peripatetic Himes.

Even as Williams's literary production was prolific during this decade, Himes's writing was starting to decline, precipitated perhaps by his first minor stroke suffered in Sisal, a village in the Yucatan, in 1963. Several letters from Himes, along with letters from Lesley Packard, an Englishwoman who became Himes's companion and later his wife, discuss the first of these gradually debilitating strokes. Relatively happy in his "primitive little fishing village," Himes worked feverishly on his latest Coffin Ed/Grave Digger novel. In March, just as he was finishing his novel, Himes suffered what he referred to in a letter to Williams as a "brain spasm" that left him slightly paralyzed. After he recovered, Himes returned to Europe, moving restlessly from country to country, especially France and Spain, "passing time," as he states in one haunting letter, "on the outskirts of life." Williams, meanwhile, continued to look after Himes's affairs, especially in connection with a divorce Himes was seeking from his first wife, while becoming mildly perplexed by Himes's celebrated talent for ignoring friends. "We can't figure out whether you're trying to avoid us," Williams wrote during a trip to Paris in 1966 with his wife, Lori, "or if the brothers [are] keeping you all for themselves." The first signs of strain in the friendship appear during this period, with Williams expressing perplexity at Himes's neglect and, in turn, the older writer apologizing for his "seeming indifference."

By the end of the decade, however, the mild breach in the friendship had been repaired, and between 1969 and 1972 Himes and Williams exchanged letters frequently. Himes, now living in Alicante, Spain, with Lesley, initiated the correspondence with a New Year's greeting to Williams, Lori, and their new son, Adam, and from there the correspondence ranged over personal and professional events and issues. Replying to Chester's first letter of the year, Williams tells of an episode in which he was invited to a party for Gwendolyn Brooks, who never bothered to show up. They share candid assessments of the Spanish mentality, of politics and racial matters in the United States and Europe, of discrimination and other vagaries in the publishing and book reviewing worlds, and of daily rhythms of their lives. Several letters deal in seriocomic fashion with yet another request Himes makes to Williams: to locate a special food for Chester's adored cat, Griot. Williams also commiserates with Himes over a biased review of *Blind Man with a Pistol* in the *New York Times*: "You shouldn't be upset by anything American reviewers write. They are stupid, establishment-partisan, and totally untruthful about themselves, so they have to be untruthful about us. When was the last time you saw a book written by a black author reviewed by a black critic?" In May 1969, Williams and Lori traveled to Alicante to interview Himes for the *Amistad* article. ("My Man Himes" can also be found in Williams's *Flashbacks: A Twenty-Year Diary of Article Writing.*)

Himes, when not fretting over the haphazard construction of his new house in Alicante, praises Ishmael Reed's *Yellow Back Radio Broke-Down* in a letter to a Doubleday editor, and in a letter to Williams calls *Sons of Darkness, Sons of Light,* which Williams published in 1969, a "good" book. (Williams in a subsequent letter admits that *Sons* was something of a throwaway novel, a sensational narrative of race war written after *The Man Who Cried I Am,* composed "to keep eating, to keep in practice, and to test reaction.") But for Himes *The Man Who Cried I Am* is in a special class: it is "a blockbuster, a hydrogen bomb; it is by far the greatest book, the most compelling book, ever written about THE SCENE. . . . It is a milestone in American literature, the only milestone . . . produced since *Native Son."* Williams was grateful for the praise, admitting that he too thought of *The Man Who Cried I Am* as his favorite novel. Williams worked assiduously to find a publisher for the first volume of Himes's autobiography, *The Quality of Hurt,* until Himes asked him to give up and turned the matter over to an agent. Himes ultimately was able to obtain a contract for the autobiography with Doubleday, although he was not happy either with the advance of ten thousand dollars or the firm's notorious reputation for discrimination within the publishing industry—a subject that both writers discuss in their letters.

By 1971 Himes was prepared to settle with Lesley into a house they had built in Alicante, and he provided Williams with a detailed account of the tribulations that had beset them during and after construction. Reading almost like a treatment for a decidedly grotesque film on home building, this letter, written in 1971 in the form of a quasilegal brief, offers insight into the state of Himes's precarious mind. His letters to Williams remain lucid, and Williams in turn commiserates with his exiled friend while discussing the pleasures that he and Lori take in their country house in the Catskills. But it is clear that Himes feels isolated and decidedly dissatisfied with Spain and the Spanish people. "All I want to do is get the hell out of here," he confesses to Williams at the end of his summation of events.

With the release of the film version of *Cotton Comes to Harlem* in 1970, Himes found that the media in both Europe and the United States were ready to give him what he terms in one letter "the treatment—TV in France, TV in Germany, *Life* magazine butter-up, and all that crap—they seem to think they've found themselves another 'good nigger.' But I've got news for them." In the same June 23, 1970, letter, Himes praises a book on Martin Luther King Jr. that Williams had just published. With the book's provocative title, *The King God Didn't Save,* and its critique of King's espousal of nonviolence, Williams soon discovered that he had created a firestorm of protest and resentment. Himes, however, congratulated Williams for his courage in deflating King's mystique. "I think this is the most timely book ever written. Because we twenty-five or thirty million blacks aren't going to fall on our knees in nonviolent prayer, like the backers of King have hoped." By the autumn of 1970, as Williams laments in letters to Himes, his book on King, savaged in a review by *Time* and abandoned by the publisher, was all but "dead."

What was not dead was Williams's productivity, which progressed with the completion of a biography on Richard Wright, *The Most Native of Sons,* written for young adults. In the Wright biography, Williams discusses the friendship between Himes and Wright: "Richard and Chester Himes would come together and talk about their work, the problems in America, and their future. . . . Himes was far, far more bitter than Richard about the racial situation, not only in America, but around the world, but Himes, when most of Richard's friends began to slip away for one reason or another, remained his chief ally and confidant, his friend and brother." During this period, Williams also completed *Captain Blackman*—what he calls in a letter to Himes his "soldier book." *Captain Blackman,* a highly experimental novel tracing the participation of black soldiers in the U.S. Army from the Revolutionary War to the Vietnam War, is one of Williams's major novels but largely neglected by critics. Growing out of the Vietnam era, and tempered by Williams's own harrowing military experience as a young navy recruit in World War II, this novel in its conclusion picks up the apocalyptic overtones seen in the King biography, *Sons of Darkness, Sons of Light,* and *The Man Who Cried I Am.* Williams's soldier book was published in 1972, the same year as *The Quality of Hurt.* The two friends read each other's books and formed a mutual admiration society. Williams writes, "Your inscribed book came today. Chester! Chester! Bravo!!" Himes writes in return, "I salute you, John A. Williams, for this novel alone makes you one of the greatest, most unbiased, bravest historical novelists of this time, or any time." Williams, in one of several warm letters that the two friends exchanged during this period (letters in which Williams's son, Adam, figures prominently, for the young boy and Himes had taken an instant liking to each other) indicates he looks forward to reading the second volume of Himes's autobiography.

However, when the second volume was published in 1976, Williams was shocked by the older man's portrayal of him. Accusing Williams of having appropriated copyright on an article and perhaps even withholding money from him, Himes caused a rupture that would not be fully repaired until Himes was near death.[2]

---

2. Williams responds: "Himes was paid, along with sixteen other well-known writers, the agreed-upon fee of $50.00 for his contribution to a book I edited in 1966, *Beyond the Angry Black* [Cooper Square Press, 1966, 1969]. As for the copyright, some writers or their agents provided them, and if others didn't, I did, and with the approval of the publishers, not for my gain, but

Himes and Williams had last met in 1972, during Himes's return to the United States for the publication of *The Quality of Hurt,* and shortly afterward, following his return to Alicante, Himes suffered another stroke. Hearing about it, Williams in correspondence that year wished Himes well, shared information about his own medical problems, and offered chatty details about such mutual friends and acquaintances as Ishmael Reed, John O. Killens (who also had suffered a stroke), Romare Bearden, and Melvin Van Peebles.

Perhaps the multiple strokes had debilitated Himes to the point where his anger and suspicion of even his closest friends, and especially of Lesley, had become uncontrollable. By 1974 Himes's physical and mental condition had declined precipitously. He had prostate and hernia surgery in May 1974 in London, followed by hospitalization in June in a Spanish clinic for hemorrhages. He had been in a coma following the London surgery, and his emotional state, never predictable during his entire life, deteriorated to the point where Lesley was fearful for his erratic behavior and his angry public outbursts. But Lesley remained loyal. She cobbled together the manuscript for *My Life of Absurdity* (which in addition to the attack on Williams contained jaundiced opinions of other friends, the women in his life, Europe and Europeans, and humanity in general) and cared for Himes in the last years of his life. After his divorce was finalized (thanks to the earlier help of Williams), Himes and Lesley married in London in 1978.

Hearing of Himes's worsening condition, Williams decided to repair their friendship with a long letter in November 1983. He refers to the rupture caused by Himes's accusations in *My Life of Absurdity*: "A couple of our mutual friends have been urging me to write, and I have just put off doing it until now. I hope you understand that I was deeply hurt and angered by your comments about me in the second volume of your autobiography. This was particularly true because I never tried to beat you out of any money; the thought never occurred to me. On the other hand, I do recall lending you what money I had when you needed it." Putting aside grievances, Williams offered in this long letter a summation of professional and family life, along with acerbic comments of the Ronald Reagan revolution, the sort of running commentary on America that helps make their correspondence so compelling. Himes died the following year, and Williams wrote to Lesley expressing his and Lori's condolences: "When Chester was Chester I loved him."

Williams continues to live and write in the metropolitan New York area. Retired now from Rutgers University, where he held an endowed chair in English at the Newark campus, he has cemented his reputation as a versatile artist—a person

---

for the protection of the authors. The work of all authors included in *Beyond the Angry Black* always did, and still does, belong to them. Himes was alone in mistakenly thinking he had been treated unfairly."

working in fiction, nonfiction, poetry, opera, film, and more. By remaining in America, he has achieved the lasting fame that might have eluded Himes in his self-imposed exile. And he has stayed closer to the American grain, offering in his fiction a panorama of national life that Himes also had explored deeply in his early fiction but had abandoned for concentration on his crime fiction. In any case, John A. Williams has an important tale of his life and times to tell (hopefully in his own future autobiography); and his friendship with Chester Himes, which he enjoyed, lost, and tried to reclaim, will be part of the story.

GILBERT H. MULLER

Acknowledgments

Acknowledgments

Lori and I wish to express our gratitude to the University of Rochester Libraries and the staff of the Department of Rare Books and Special Collections, with special thanks to Melissa Mead and Leah Hamilton; the Syracuse University Libraries and its Department of Special Collections, and to former director David Stamm; the Amistad Research Center of Tulane University; the Yale University Library and the Carl Van Vechten James Weldon Johnson Memorial Collection of Negro Arts and Letters; and a very special thank-you to our friend Lesley Himes in Alicante, Spain.

The Williams to Himes correspondence is housed with the Chester Himes Papers at the Amistad Research Center, Tulane University, New Orleans, Louisiana. All other materials are housed with the John A. Williams Papers at the Rare Books and Special Collections Library, University of Rochester, Rochester, New York.

Dear Chester, Dear John

August 2, 1962

Dear John,

I was happy to get your letter. Chester likes you too. People say bad things about him because he doesn't like most people and shows it. I have known him a long time, and we have never had an argument. I admire his books. *Yesterday Will Make You Cry,* his jail experience, is probably the best, but it was so cut for publication that in that form it was worthless. Besides, the name was changed. I can't remember what it *was* called. He said yesterday that he was flying to Paris today, but he has announced his departure several times already, and it has not taken place. Marianne remains.[1] She is actually a famous photographer, but like all talented women she wants to do everything. She is enchanting and completely unselfconscious in her passion for Chester.

I hope to see you again soon, and let me know how your new books progress. My warm regards.

O yes, the mss of *Yesterday Will Make You Cry* is in my Negro collection at Yale, and you can read it when you go there sometime.

Carlo[2]

---

1. Marianne Greenwood, photographer and, at the time, Himes's companion.
2. Chester and I first met at the home of Carl (Carlo) Van Vechten, whom I'd met two years earlier on the publication of my second novel, *Night Song.* It was obvious that Himes and Van Vechten were very good friends. I never knew how they had met, but I believe it had been in that fabulous apartment overlooking part of the west side of Central Park. Carl was married to the actress Marina Marinoff and had established at Yale University the James Weldon Johnson Collection of Negro Arts and Letters. In addition to being well known as a portrait photographer, he was also a gifted novelist whose work includes *Nigger Heaven,* published in 1926.

39, rue de la Harpe
Paris 5

October 11, 1962

Dear John,

I am back in Paris, and where I go from here I don't know. Antibes got too hot for me, and I rushed back here where it is safer. I wrote a short, angry piece about the Mississippi racists for the weekly journal *Candide* (I'm enclosing part of the front page) in which I compared the U.S. racists to the French OAS; I said basically the only difference was that the U.S. racists were going to win and the French racists lose. Antibes is one of the hot beds of the OAS. It is essentially a village of poor, gangsterlike Italians and very rich French and foreigners who support them. It is the only city on the Cote d'Azur that makes no concessions to tourists; Catholic and fascist. So when *Candide* hit the newsstands I got two threats from the OAS, and some people warned me it was dangerous in Antibes for me. I was living alone there in the old quarter without friends (in fact, I have no acquaintances in Antibes), so I got the hell out and came back to Paris. That really does not worry me; I simply did not feel inclined to get involved with the OAS on top of all the trouble I am having with publishers, etc.

If I didn't tell you before, let me give you a little of the background. I wrote a satire on the Negro middle class in the frame of a story lampooning Mollie Moon. Mollie's husband, Henry Lee Moon, publicity director of the NAACP, is my cousin, and I lived with them for a while in their Harlem apartment back in the 1940s. This book has been published here in two versions: in French as *Mamie Mason,* with great success, and in English by the Olympia Press (*Lolita,* etc.) as *Pinktoes.* The publisher of Olympia Press, Maurice Girodias, was requested by Herbert Hill, labor secretary of the NAACP, to submit a chapter for the anthology he is editing for Knopf. Girodias sent him a chapter about a typical middle-class orgy in Harlem, titled "Mamie Mason Gives a Party." Hill and the editors at Knopf were enthusiastic about it, and Hill wrote a letter to Girodias accepting it for publication with thanks and offering to pay what was requested.

But Hill, in his enthusiasm, showed the story to his colleagues at the

NAACP, and most of them recognized themselves. He was told the story was about Mollie Moon—then Mollie got hold of it.

The next chapter concerns my motion picture project. A producer with a firm in Switzerland commissioned me to write a screenplay with a Harlem locale (and incidentally paid me $2,500, and I was the only one). I wrote a screenplay, *Baby Sister*. Arthur Cohn, the Swiss producer, and Rene Lafuite, his French partner, were enthusiastic about the story. Cohn promised to go into production by April 1, and he swore it would be a complete private production of his own. To cut a long story short, Cohn tried the nine major motion picture studios to get the film underwritten. Naturally none would do it. So Cohn went back to New York and showed my screenplay to Herbert Hill, supposedly to get NAACP support. That was when Hill had his chance for revenge. He wrote to Cohn on NAACP stationery that he and his colleagues in the association objected to the story and they would do everything in their power to keep it from being produced (incidentally, I am sending a Photostat of the letter to Connie Pearlstein, as she requested a long time ago, and she will let you see it), so Cohn dropped his option.[3] And that is why the French director [Pierre-Dominique] Gaisseau and myself went to New York on the television gig. Gaisseau got the head of the firm that is releasing his documentary film, Joe Levin of Embassy Films, to promise to produce *Baby Sister*. But Gaisseau gave all this story to a reporter from the *NY Times* and also to the *Post*. When Hill read that Embassy Films was going to produce *Baby Sister,* he telephoned Joe Levin in the name of the NAACP and protested. I don't know whether that is the exact reason Embassy Films dropped the business because Levin has never admitted it. Gaisseau had waited so long before getting a contract out of Levin that when this NAACP protest came along we had no formal agreement with Embassy. So that got finished.

The next chapter concerns my agent. Perhaps you remember how I was running about during my last days in New York to get a copy of *The Primitive* to submit to Berkley Books along with my book *Cast the First*

---

3. Connie Pearlstein, a mutual friend, was later to publish (in 1968) a biography of Richard Wright under her maiden name, Constance Webb.

Stone for reprint. Well, I did not get a decision out of Berkley Books before I left, but Tom Dardis, editor at Berkley, said he would give my agent his decision in a few days. I telephoned my agent before leaving. That was the last I have heard from him.

My agent is a man named James Reach, director of the literary department of Samuel French, Inc., 25 W. 45th Street. He was recommended to me three or four years ago by MWA (mystery writers) for my detective stories. The secretary of my French editor runs an office for Série Noire in New York. She had sold two titles to Avon Books, but I wanted to make contact for other types of books, so I decided to get an agent. I took on James Reach and gave him the account with Avon. Avon contracted for four other detective stories and also for the reprint rights to *Cast the First Stone*—all by the same editor whom Série Noire first contacted. Reach collected his 10 percent, and that is all he has ever done for me. When Hearst Corporation took over Avon, they decided to drop publication of all of my books. Two detective stories and *Cast the First Stone* were unpublished. Avon dropped the books in print as soon as they broke even and returned the rights; and he also returned the rights and unpublished manuscripts of the two detective stories and *Cast the First Stone.* I only learned the full story when I talked to my agent in New York. At this time my agent should have two original detective story manuscripts, a paperback copy of *The Primitive,* a clothbound copy of *Cast the First Stone,* and some other manuscripts.

I would like to get you to help me contact another agent if you have the time. Also there is a risk of reprisals from these people and the NAACP. I would like very much to find an agent who would accept my work on comparative value and try to sell it if possible and get me some money. I cannot use an agent whose personal attitudes are going to affect my agent's behavior toward my work; then I would be better off without an agent.

If you feel you can help me, let me know as soon as possible. Then I will ask you to collect my manuscripts and books from Reach's office and deliver them to my new agent. Also I will wait to write Reach until I have heard from you.

Excuse this long and slightly hysterical letter. But I am having interruptions and want to get this off in today's mail. I feel that I am living in a madhouse. If I find a copy in English of the *Candide* piece, I will send it along. And anyway I think I will just send this Photostat of Hill's letter along to you and ask you to send it to Connie. And ask Connie to have a Photostat made and send it back to me—39, rue de la Harpe, Paris 5. And tell her I will write soon.

I hear a lot about *Night Song* over here, and soon there will be a European edition in English (I hear) along with translations. Let me know if there is anything I can do for you.

All best wishes & thanks,
Chester

-§-

Monday, October 15 [1962]

My dear Chester,
Your letter, clipping, and Photostat of the Herbert Hill memo came Saturday, and I've been working ever since. Nothing surprises me anymore; therefore, I wasn't surprised that the OAS decided to look you up. Some of us never acquire the enviable knack of stirring up hornets' nests. To your business at hand, right off the bat. My publisher has suggested to me Carl Brandt, 101 Park Avenue, as an agent, since I'm about to change too, as soon as I can pay this man back a little money.[4] Fortunately, what I owe my present agent is very little, and I hope to effect the change by the first of the year. Of all the agents I've talked to in this business, with this joker I got a real human feeling, and for me that's more important than all the other. That he's a businessman, cold and hard as well, was apparent too. I told him I'd have to think over my own deal but that I wanted him to

---

4. Carl Brandt, Jr., was a good friend as well as my agent.

think about you. I let him read the part of your letter that was applicable to the situation, and he came off well. He suggests that you send to him, as soon as possible, your very best thing or two with a rundown on all the others. I strongly advise this move because of Roger Straus, who's the best businessman in the business as well as president of F, S & C [Farrar, Straus and Cudahy]. Brandt's office has a nice little hum to it. I didn't like it when I first went in, but I dig now that it's low-key on purpose. It's worth a try. *Second.* Saw Connie tonight and gave her the memo. Tomorrow she'll make a copy, and I'll have it in the mail Wednesday morning, which is the day I want to get this off to you. If things work out well, agentwise, I'm sure Brandt will be on Reach's ass with all four feet . . . and he's got the weight. I enclose a clipping relating some of the American OAS activity in Mississippi. This item was picked up by no other paper that I know of. I think you'll find it not to your liking but as confirmation of your suspicions and mine. I suppose every once in a while the generals, Alexander, Napoleon, Eisenhower, etc., must have their day.

The next is for me. I am beginning a critique of five or six Negro writers: yourself, Ellison, Baldwin, L. Hughes, Wright, and perhaps Claude McKay.[5] I need meat. As much as you're willing to give on all these people that I'm sure you must know. I'm sick and tired of Negro writers being lumped together just because they are. There are differences—experiences, outlook, exposures to certain currents—shit, you know the bit. Whether my publisher wants this or not, I want to do it. I'd appreciate any information you can give me—politically, historically, psychologically. I don't consider myself an expert in this field. I am kind of a half-assed scholar. But I do want to combat a lot of shit that's going around. When I think of you with I don't know how many goddamn novels under your belt, I get furious for the shit that Jimmy B is trying to skate through on. My count shows you far out of sight on the number of novels my group has written. Without being maudlin, you deserve better; anyone who can stand for so long the kind of loneliness writing a novel makes necessary deserves more and deserves

---

5. This project never got off the ground.

most of all a place he can call home. Sometimes I feel like the whole fucking world is coming down around my ears, and I can't strike back; the few times I have cost me dearly, more dearly than I like to imagine, but I was lucky; everything could have been lots worse. In any case, let me hear from you soon about Brandt. If you write him, why don't you stick a carbon in the writer and just send that to me? I'm still waiting for a couple of books from you.

Warmest regards,
[John A. Williams]

-§-

Saturday [October 1962]

Dear John,

Thanks very much for your letter of Monday suggesting Carl Brandt for me—an old and reliable agency as I remember—Brandt & Brandt. I shall surely make the change. But this is just a note as I am taking a train to Frankfurt to see if I can get some money out of my krauthead publishers, and if so I will come to New York in person to try to get out of this mess. Also you may depend I will do the biography bit, and it will be straight and rough. I am still trying to get a copy of *The Primitive* for you—but it seems to be impossible, and the only one I know of is fouled up with my agent.

All the best on your new project, and I'll send you all the material on my return from Frankfurt—which should be Friday or Monday.

All best,
Chester

Monday [October 1962]

Dear John,

I'm back from Frankfurt, where nothing happened but that I got to see my two publishers, the Buchergilde Gutenberg and Ullstein Verlag, without any benefit as far as I know. But finally I have got this letter off to my agent, a copy of which I am enclosing, and now I will write Carl Brandt and then I will get off this autobiographical stuff to you by tomorrow afternoon. Thanks for everything.

All best,
Chester

-§-

Chester Himes
39, rue de la Harpe
Paris 5
France

October 29, 1962
Mr. James Reach
Director, Literary Department
Samuel French, Inc.
25 West 45th Street
New York 36, N.Y.

Dear Mr. Reach,

Upon receipt of this letter, our relationship of author and agent is terminated, and I shall no longer recognize you as my literary agent in any capacity.

This decision has been reached on my part because of the following reasons:

Miss Hackett, U.S. representative of Série Noire, sold my first detective story to Gold Medal Books. The contract was authorized by Don Preston, who was then editor of Gold Medal Books.

Subsequently, Don Preston moved to Avon Books. Miss Hackett submitted to Don Preston, at Avon Books, manuscripts of *The Crazy Kill* and *The Real Cool Killers.* Don Preston accepted the two manuscripts for publication by Avon Books.

I then engaged you as my agent and turned over to you all of my contracts and accounts with publishers, future and present, and ordered Avon Books to make out the contracts for the two books accepted by Don Preston to you.

You took 10 percent of the advance given on the two books for which Miss Hackett made the sale. As a consequence, out of the $2,000 advance— $1,000 for each book—I paid you $200 and Miss Hackett $200.

You took 10 percent out of the $500 royalties paid me by Berkley Books on the reprint of *If He Hollers Let Him Go,* for which I negotiated the contract personally in 1955.

Subsequently, you took 10 percent of royalties from all books accepted by Don Preston for Avon Books, in spite of the fact the original contract was made by Miss Hackett.

Up until the present time you have not made one contact that has resulted in the sale of any of my works.

I have repeatedly requested you to demand the return of my rights on *For Love of Imabelle* from Gold Medal Books. The book has been out of print for years.

You advised me in June 1959 to accept $250 advance royalties on my book *Run, Man, Run.* Subsequently, Avon Books has returned the manuscript in (according to you) damaged condition.

As far as I have been informed, you have made no effort to have the manuscript retyped at the publisher's expense; nor have you made any effort to submit it to other publishers.

When the Hearst Corporation took over Avon Books and Don Preston was replaced, you informed me that my detective story series would be dropped. One by one, publication of the titles *The Crazy Kill, The Real Cool*

Killers, The Big Gold Dream, and *All Shot Up* was terminated. As far as I have been informed, you have not demanded the return of the rights.

When I was in New York in July 1962, you informed me that Avon Books had decided not to publish *Be Calm* and *Cast the First Stone* and that the manuscript and book had been returned to you. You had not taken the trouble to inform me previously.

As far as I have been informed, you have shown no interest in the sale of the books and manuscript of mine that you now have.

During the latter part of July 1962, on my own initiative, I submitted two books, *The Primitive* and *Cast the First Stone,* to Tom Dardis, editor for Berkley Books, to be considered for reprint. I had to leave New York before Mr. Dardis made a decision. I turned the negotiation over to you. Now three months have passed, and you have not written a single line concerning the outcome.

All of the work I have so far written during my entire career has been in your command for more than four years with the result that the only sales have been made through a contact made by Miss Hackett.

In view of these and many other complaints on my part too numerous to mention, our relationship can no longer be of any benefit to either of us.

As a consequence I request that you give Mr. John A. Williams, 434 Lafayette Street, New York 3 (Telephone: Gramercy 7-5748), the entire lot of my work, books and manuscripts of books and manuscripts of short stories, notes, etc., and all correspondence relating to it. Mr. Williams will call for it or send a messenger to your office for it, as soon as it is convenient.

All sums of money now owed to you will be paid out of future royalties.

Sincerely yours,
Chester Himes
Witness: Lesley Packard

Chester Himes
39, rue de la Harpe
Paris 5

October 29, 1962

Mr. Carl Brandt
101 Park Avenue
New York, N.Y.

Dear Mr. Brandt,

My friend John A. Williams informs me that he has talked to you of my great need of an agent in the U.S. and suggests that I write to you about it.

I am enclosing a copy of a letter to Mr. James Reach, which will define my situation. So now I will tell you a little about myself.

My parents were bourgeoisie school teachers, and that finishes that. After two years at Ohio State University, I served a prison term of seven years for armed robbery, and while in prison I began writing short stories for *Esquire* magazine (1934).

I learned, more or less, what it meant to be a Negro in the U.S. after I was released from prison, in 1936. Subsequently I lived in Cleveland, Ohio, worked for the WPA, did a stint at Malabar Farm for Louis Bromfield, and went with him to Hollywood in 1940. I was not in the armed services because of spinal injuries suffered in an accident in Cleveland (I fell down an elevator shaft), but I worked in war industries in Los Angeles and San Francisco.

In 1944, I received a Rosenwald Fellowship to complete my first novel, *If He Hollers Let Him Go* (which has a Los Angeles shipyard locale), which was published by Doubleday & Co. in 1945 with moderate success. In 1950 it was reprinted by NAL [New American Library] and again in 1955 by Berkley Books.

My second novel, *Lonely Crusade,* was published by Knopf, Inc., in 1947, with great optimism. It was a dismal failure and has never been reprinted in the U.S., although the French translation in 1952 won the Paris critics award.

My third novel, *Cast the First Stone,* was published in 1952 by Coward-McCann. The story is culled from my prison experiences and should have been successful, but it was not.

NAL bought the reprint rights to *Cast the First Stone* for $2,500 but after three years decided against publishing it and voided the contract. Avon Books paid an advance of $1,500 for the reprint rights in 1959 or 1960 but decided against publication. I now have all the rights, and the book is for sale.

My fourth novel, *The Third Generation,* was published in 1954 by World Publishing Company, and the reprint rights were sold to NAL for $10,000. It was reprinted as a Signet book about 1956 or 1955.

My fifth novel, *The Primitive,* was published as a Signet Original in 1956 with a very limited distribution. Victor Weybright wrote once to say they could not sell it in the stores, and Walter Freeman, associate editor of NAL, wrote: "We had a little trouble with *The Primitive* when it was put on the NAL list. But that is meaningless. . . ."

I was then living in Europe (since 1953), and all my novels with the exception of *Cast the First Stone* had been published in France with critical success but, of course, it being France, no financial success.

In late 1957 I began writing detective stories with a Harlem locale for the collection La Série Noire, chez Gallimard. The first, *La reine des pommes,* which I rushed out in a couple of months, won the grand prix for detective stories in 1958 and was an astounding critical success and a true bestseller in France. It has now become a detective story classic over here, but even so I earned only $3,000 from it. It was published in the U.S. in a cut version by Gold Medal Books as *For Love of Imabelle.*

During the next three years I wrote six additional books in the series (all but one concern the escapades of two Negro detectives in Harlem—Grave Digger Jones and Coffin Ed Johnson); but finally I became discouraged and quit when I found it impossible to collect all of my royalties from Gallimard and after the Hearst Corporation dropped the series in Avon Books.

In the spring of this year Librairie Plon published my latest novel, *Mamie Mason,* all about the doings of a Harlem hostess and the interracial set in Harlem, with considerable success both in sales and in the press. A slightly different version in English was brought out by the Olympia Press in Paris under the title *Pinktoes* but has not been published in the U.S.—and perhaps will never be.

I have been dabbling in the movie business, and I have written a rather long and loose screenplay titled *Baby Sister,* which has attracted considerable attention (mention has appeared in the *New York Times,* the *Post,* and *Variety*, in addition to the French, Italian, and German press), but nothing definite has come of it.

I shall begin work soon on the story of a strange love affair between an American Negro and an American white woman in Europe (France, England, and Mallorca) wherein from beginning to end he is trying to get her to go home.

That brings me up to date.

My immediate problem at the moment is to get sufficient money to sit down and write my book. This might happen at any moment, but more than likely it won't. So before anything else I wish to sell *The Primitive* and *Cast the First Stone* to a paperback house. Beyond all doubt, these are my best-written books, and, frankly, I fail to see why they should not be of great public interest—as entertainment.

As I wrote in my letter to Mr. Reach, I submitted the books personally to Tom Dardis of Berkley Books, who showed great interest at the time, but I have not heard from him in three months.

I have all rights to both books. *Cast the First Stone* had fair reviews in 1952 but a small sale and has never been reprinted. *The Primitive* had a sale of a little over 100,000 as a Signet book but has not scratched the surface of the market.

I would like to have John Williams send you these two books first, and then, if you wish to accept me as a client, I will send you a synopsis of my first European book, tentatively titled *It Rained Five Days.*

Thank you for your time and interest.

Yours sincerely,
Chester Himes

Chester Himes
39, rue de la Harpe
Paris 5

October 31, 1962

Dear John,

I am finally getting around to write the material about me, etc., for your project. I have been plagued so much lately with one fucking thing and another I am beginning to feel like Job. First it was a cyst on my left eyelid, which I had to have cut out; then it was a front cap on a tooth that broke off and became infected; then Monday morning I woke up with a jaw that looked as though Sonny Liston had been here, and even now it hasn't gone down. But I got off the letter to Brandt, which I had to make more personal than I wanted or else he would find himself handicapped by various rumors (am enclosing a copy). Now to get on with the autobio:

Most about me is well known but not all fitted together. I was born in Jefferson City, Missouri, in 1909, where my father taught blacksmithing and wheelwrighting (known as a professor) at Lincoln Institute (now University). I have two brothers, one a year older, the other seven years older. My mother also taught music and stuff.

When I was five my father left Lincoln and moved to Cleveland, Ohio, where we lived for part of a year until he got a job teaching at Alcorn College, Alcorn, Mississippi. We were there seven years. My mother wouldn't let us attend school in Mississippi, so she taught us (my brother and me) for six years; then we did our first year in school at Haines Institute, Augusta, Georgia, where she taught that year (most of this is contained in my autobiographical novel, *The Third Generation*). Next year we moved to Pine Bluff, Arkansas, where the old man taught at Branch Normal Institute—all state schools for Negroes, as you know. While there my brother lost his sight in an accident, and we moved to St. Louis so he could be treated at Barnes Hospital. I went to Sumner High School in St. Loo for about a year and a half; then we moved to Cleveland. That was 1925, and I was sixteen. I did one half year at East High School in Cleveland and graduated in January 1926. The following month I took a job as a busboy for room service in the Wade Park Manor Hotel there, and during my second or third week I fell two floors down the elevator shaft and got banged up considerably—broke my left arm off at the wrist, fractured three vertebrae, broke my jaw and spat out teeth like gravel, and internal injuries. I was in a cast in the hospital for four months and came out wearing a back brace. (I mention this mainly because it had a great deal to do with influencing my life.) The accident was due to a fault in the elevator closing, and the hotel was responsible; and had my parents had more savvy they could have won a suit for considerable damages. As it was we settled for a $75 monthly pension from the Ohio State Industrial Commission and $50 monthly from the hotel. My parents had put all their money in a house outside of the Negro ghetto (the same as we are still doing), and my father was eking out a living with small construction jobs. My brother's schooling was sponsored by the Ohio State Care for the Blind, and he was attending school at East High. My older brother left home some years previous and was working as a dining car waiter, living in Detroit.

I was a good boy. I saved my money, took care of my health, and entered Ohio State University in Columbus that fall. Somehow, even in the South, up until then I had been sheltered from the impact of race prejudice. Looking back I wonder how it was possible, but I had always felt superior to the southern crackers and rednecks whom I had seen, and I felt no sense of oppression. Ohio State University changed that. At that time Columbus was as Jim-Crowed as the Deep South, and even on the campus Negro students could not live, were excluded from the surrounding cafés, movie houses, recreation centers, etc., and could not even use all the facilities of the student union. So I began spending more and more time in the Negro ghetto, which was miles away from the campus, going with whores, drinking homebrew (this was during Prohibition) and white mule, and getting a dose and all that. I lost interest in my studies, had some rows with cracker instructors, and was only permitted to stay after the first quarter because of my physical condition—I was considered an invalid. One night I went to a formal dance given by the Sphinxes (Alpha—Negro fraternity) of which I was a member and got bored and took a group of couples to my favorite whorehouse to play the Victrola, drink beer, and dance. One of the whores who sort of liked me came downstairs and pitched a boogey-woogey, cursing and breaking records, etc., and my guests broke and ran. One of the girls reported it to the dean, and I was called into his office and permitted to withdraw from the university. I was relieved. I was getting fed up with the Jim Crow setup.

Back in Cleveland I wandered about the ghetto, in and out of the pool rooms, whorehouses, etc., and one day I went to a gambling club where they were playing blackjack. I never left—spiritually, that is. I began running a blackjack game, bought a car that I didn't dare take home, hung around gamblers, pimps, and landprops.

My mother and father were having violent quarrels and disagreements at that time and were planning to become divorced. I was fed up with it. Mostly it was about the manner each of them thought I should be disciplined. When the case was scheduled for court, I stole a car, drove to Columbus, cashed some bogus checks, and got arrested for the first time. After a month or so in jail (my parents were tangled up in their divorce case), I was released on a bench parole and five-year suspended sentence. When I got back to Cleveland my parents were divorced, the house was up for sale, and they had moved to separate quarters. I went to live with the old man, my brother with my mother.

I went back to the gambling club. But it had lost its fascination. So one day I decided to get some money and go to Mexico—Tijuana to be exact. One night I got a big pistol and went out in an exclusive suburb and robbed a rich Jew and his wife in their house (I had some particulars from their Negro chauffeur), took some money and jewelry from a wall safe, and miraculously escaped the police and got away and took the morning train to Chicago. I was captured in Chicago trying to sell the jewelry to a fence. It was one of those fatal coincidences. A white woman in the Blackstone Hotel charged she had been robbed by a Negro prowler—and they thought, naturally, it was me.

However, an agent from the Cleveland insurance company came and identified the jewelry, and I was extradited and taken back to Cleveland. My father got a shyster lawyer who advised me to cop a plea, assuring us that I would get off with probation. Sure enough, for two months my case was being determined in the probation department. But one cold morning, December 27, 1928, I was summoned to court and sentenced to twenty to twenty-five years in the Ohio State Penitentiary. It so happened that neither my parents nor attorney were in court that morning. And two days later I was taken to Ohio State Prison in Columbus.

I was in prison for seven and one half years. I went in when I was nineteen years old and came out when I was twenty-seven. I was five years in the main prison (where the famous prison fire of 1930 occurred, which I wrote about for *Esquire,* by the way) and two and a half years on the farm.

I began writing my third or fourth year in prison (just to pass away the time) and during the years 1931–33 I wrote a number of short stories for such Negro publications as *Abbot's Monthly, Bronzeman, Pittsburgh Courier, Atlanta World,* and others. *Esquire* magazine, which had just begun publishing as a monthly, accepted my first story, "Crazy in the Stir," which was published in August 1934. *Esquire* always used my prison number below my name and identified the prison. My second story, "To What Red Hell," October 1934, was about the 1930 Easter Monday prison fire, and according to Meyer Levin, who was first assistant to fiction editor Arnold Gingrich, "received the greatest curtain call of any story ever published by *Esquire.*"

Through correspondence, I came to know Arnold Gingrich well. When I was released in May 1936, the Great Depression was on. I went back to Cleveland. My mother was living with relatives in South Carolina. My father was working for the WPA. My brother was studying in Columbus. (In the meantime, my blind brother, with the aid of the Ohio State Care for the Blind and my $75 monthly pension, which had been paid to me in prison until just before I was released, had graduated from East High with honors, taken his BA and MA at Oberlin College, magna cum laude, Phi Beta Kappa, etc., and was doing his doctorate in sociology at Ohio State University.)

I lived with my father at first, but he had very little money, and what is more he was involved with a woman who was taking that, and I had it hard. (Since I've just got through having it hard in the last sentence, I've been out to the dentist and had a tooth pulled, and it wasn't a bit hard—in fact, the old snag came out like it was sent for in three parts.)

To get back to this account, in 1936 I married a former sweetheart, and we began slowly starving together. I was desperately trying to sell short stories to the popular magazines. I had not begun writing protest stories, and most of my stories were about crime and criminals, as for instance "The Night's for Crying" in the *Negro Caravan*. *Esquire* had upped the pay from $75 to $100, but I did not sell to any other magazine and very rarely to *Esquire*. During this time I wrote the first version of my prison novel, which is over twice as long as *Cast the First Stone*.

I met Langston Hughes during this time; he was living in Cleveland with his aunt and writing plays for the old Karamu settlement house on Central Avenue run by those formidable people the Jellifes. But Langston was of no help and offered very little encouragement.

I also came to know my cousin Henry Lee Moon (now publicity director for the NAACP), whose family lived in Cleveland and were rather well off. His father, "Uncle" Roddy, was a retired meat inspector, and aside from giving my wife and me a free meal every now and then, they were of no help.

I met Grant Reynolds (the great politician), who was then minister of the Congregational Church, and Sidney Williams, who was the Cleveland director of the Urban League. My brother Joseph got his doctorate from OSU and began working for the Urban League in Columbus, Ohio.

I think it was around the winter of 1937–38 that I went on the WPA as a laborer, digging sewers and dredging drainage about 10 miles from where I lived. After writing many letters of protest to the local and state headquarters of the WPA, I was promoted to research assistant (at $95 monthly—$65 for labor) and assigned to write vocational bulletins for the main Cleveland Public Library. I became interested in the CIO and did voluntary work for their paper, the *Cleveland Union Leader*. Then I was promoted to professional status (writer) and assigned to write little stories about interesting factors of Cleveland's history. A short time later I wrote a story culled from the old papers about two religious sects (the Shaking Quakers and the Mennonites) expecting Jesus Christ to visit their respective camps at the same time on the same day and the ensuing acrimony. It was a funny story, but my superiors didn't think so, and I was immediately demoted to research assistant again. I blew my top. I wrote long, intense, emotional, and extremely angry letters to the state director of the WPA, to the national director in Washington, and finally to President F. D. Roosevelt personally. I think that was the beginning of my protest writing—at least those letters were long enough to make a book. At any rate an investigator (a Negro) was sent from Washington, and I was reinstated as a writer. It was during that time I wrote most of the articles about the history of the CIO for a yearbook the Cleveland Industrial Union Council published.

I was transferred from the public library to the Cleveland branch of the Ohio State Writers Project and assigned to writing the first third of the "history" of Cleveland. Later my supervisor, a big fat mannish woman who wrote detective stories, told me that they had sent me to her for her to fire me. Instead, she just worked the hell out of me. I wound up writing the entire history of Cleveland by myself, but later the manuscript was either lost or destroyed—the Western Reserve University Historical Society made a great effort trying to find it but never did.

Naturally, I was still trying to write short stories for the slick magazines and also trying to get a job with one of Cleveland's three newspapers. Finally, the editor of the *Cleveland Daily News,* one N. R. Howard, gave me an assignment writing vignettes about various places in Cleveland, street scenes, etc., of the various ethnic groups of which Cleveland was chiefly composed at that time. These ran in a box on the editorial page, under the heading "This Cleveland" and signed "C.H." Not even the staff of the paper knew who I was, and if they had learned I was a Negro they would have protested—at least so the editor said. So I wrote these vignettes (prose poems really), which became extremely popular, and the editor kept my identity a secret and paid me $1 for each one published—$5 a week—out of his pocket. I did this for about two and a half months; I think I had about fifty published; and then I quit. It required my visiting different places about the city every night, standing on cold street corners in sections where no one spoke English, to get the atmosphere; and obviously I had no time for any other writing. Howard wanted me to write a full-length column for $15 weekly, but I declined.

It was about that time that Richard Wright published *Uncle Tom's Children.* One of the girls who had worked with me in the library wrote a book called *Wasteland* (or was it *Waste Land*?), which won the $10,000 Harper Award, and Dick wrote the preface, and Jo Sinclair (Ruth Seid) went to New York and met him. Strangely enough, that was the first I had ever heard of Dick.

The year before, my cousin Henry Lee Moon crossed up everyone and married Mollie Lewis (the great Mollie Moon), and in 1940 my wife and I went to New York to visit them and put up at the Theresa Hotel—my first time in New York.

(I suppose you know the story of how the thirty-odd Negro writers and intellectuals went to Russia in 1930 to make a film of the *Freeing of the Slaves.* Henry and Mollie were among the group, along with Langston Hughes, Loren Miller, Arabelle Thompson [probably Louise Thompson], Ted Posten, and others. Naturally these brothers could never do anything together, so the Soviets got disgusted and sent them home—or least sent them out of Russia. But instead of coming home, Mollie went to Berlin and stayed four years and has always since been an authority on the rise to power of Hitler and the Third Reich.)

Anyway, in 1940 Mollie and Henry lived in that fabulous apartment on West 66th Street (beside the stables) along with such characters as Ted Posten, Arabelle Thompson, Katherine Dunham, Eddie "Yale" Morrow, etc. Mollie tried to get Richard Wright to come to a party she was giving for me, but Dick declined. He was living in Brooklyn at the time. As far as I remember, Langston was the only writer whom I saw. I never met Countee Cullen, Claude McKay, Bud Fisher, or any of the others.

I returned to Cleveland, quit the WPA, and through the instigation of the Jellifes, went to work for Louis Bromfield at Malabar Farm. I was the butler, and my wife was the cook (she was an excellent cook too, but most of what she had ever done before then was live the life of a courtesan more or less).

I worked for Bromfield a summer, during which time he read my prison manuscript (*Black Sheep*) and promised to help me get it published or made into a film. He didn't get it published, but that fall he took my wife and me out to Los Angeles, where he went to write the screen adaptation of Hemingway's *For Whom the Bell Tolls* (at $5,000 weekly). He talked my book up and sent me to see some people. A few of the Hollywood people knew me as a name from my stories in *Esquire*—which used to be the Hollywood Bible—but no one suspected I was black. When they saw my face I was finished—period.

Langston had given me a list of people to see—Loren Miller, of course, and a chap named Welford Wilson, who had a great influence on my life (inadvertently). Willy Wilson wanted to be a writer, but Willy was a hard-working, conscientious, obedient communist. Willy was working then with the U.S. employment agency by day and with the communists by night. Willy introduced me to all of the important communists (both black and white) in L.A., and I suppose he was assigned to recruit me. Anyway, I was given the works—taken to cell meetings all over town, to parties, to lectures, and all that crap. I met all the local heroes of the Spanish Civil War and all the communist script writers—Dalton Trumbo and John Howard Lawson, etc. They housed me and fed me and interviewed me. From lack of work I used to go around with a Negro chap who used to collect salvage from the Hollywood sympathizers to sell for money to be sent to a Spanish refugee camp in Mexico. Most of the brothers in the party used to clothe themselves from the salvage from the Hollywood bigshots—I had more expensive clothes than I've ever had since. But the communists had a use for me. I was used to prove a point. So they would send me out practically every day to apply for work in various firms that did not employ Negroes. I must say here in Los Angeles at that time was as Jim-Crowed as Atlanta, Georgia. The only employment for Negroes was in the kitchen, and all white restaurants, bars, and many white film theatres refused to serve Negroes. This is when and where I got all my material for *Lonely Crusade.* In fact, all of the characters in *Lonely Crusade* existed and were the same in real life as they were in the book; and a great deal of the narrative and many of the scenes were taken from real life. That is the real reason the Communist Party hated the book—every character was identifiable, and, of course, I was Lee Gordon.

In the end I got pretty well shattered going around to these white firms to get refused, and one day I went up to San Francisco to get a job in the Richmond Shipyards [Henry J. Kaiser Yards]. From working there and later in the Los Angeles Shipyard in San Pedro Harbor, I got material for *If He Hollers Let Him Go.* I worked at Richmond as a ship fitter, living in SF and commuting, and I watched the growth of prejudice in San Francisco and Oakland as the tremendous influx of southern white and Negro workers poured into the area.

I returned to Los Angeles at the request of Hall Johnson to work as a press agent for the filming of *Cabin in the Sky.* But MGM wouldn't hire me; instead, they hired a local Negro reporter and isolated him in a dressing room (for an office) at the extreme far end of the abandoned dressing rooms, known as "Old Dressing Room Row." In the beginning of the making of that film members of the all-Negro cast were not permitted to eat in the big barnlike MGM cafeteria and had to bring their own lunch and eat on the set—such stars as Ethel Waters, "Bojangles" Bill Robinson, and Lena Horne. Lena finally protested to Louis Mayer, and he let the "niggers" in to eat.

I was getting madder and madder. My wife had got a good toadying job (through Juanita Miller) as codirector of women's activities for the eighteen USOs of the Los Angeles area; and naturally she had become a bigshot. We had a very pleasant little house too, out on top of a hill in City Terrace. It was an isolated house next to a reservoir with only a Mexican couple for neighbors, and I used to keep my Winchester rifle within reach at all times. Incidentally, we got the house from a Japanese family who were sent to the stockades right after Pearl Harbor.

(This is getting awfully detailed.)

It was there I wrote the first draft of *If He Hollers Let Him Go.* It was my original intention to write a mystery story wherein white people were getting killed all over town and no one could conceive of the motive. The motive was simply the compulsion making a Negro kill white people, most of whom he didn't know and had never seen, because they were white. But it turned out differently and became *If He Hollers,* and I was given a Rosenwald Fellowship in 1944 to finish it.

I went to New York to live with Henry and Mollie Moon in their fabulous apartment at 940 St. Nicholas. It was during the time Roosevelt was running for his last term. The communists, the liberals, the Negroes, and the Negrophiles and friends were getting together to elect Roosevelt. Henry Lee was working for the CIO Political Action Committee, and Mollie was giving parties sponsored and paid for by various groups, including the Democratic National Committee. It was then and there I met everybody and came to know them well. There is hardly a prominent middle-class Negro of today I did not meet at that time—Walter White and company, Lester Granger, Ralph Bunche—oh hell, all of them. It was from this time and from these people I have taken the scenes and characters for my book *Mamie Mason* (*Pinktoes* in English).

I met Ralph Ellison then, although he was never invited to Mollie's parties. But I had a private party one day when Mollie was absent and had Ralph and [his wife] Fanny, Constance Curtis, and some others whom I've forgotten. Ralph was a nice joker then, congenial, attentive—he used to give some nice dinners in his basement apartment on St. Nicholas—that was before he had learned it all. He had written the first version of his book, which was a great deal different from the final version, and he was very greatly influenced by Richard Wright. In fact, Dick once accused Ralph of imitating his work in detail, and Ralph replied indignantly, "Who am I going to imitate, if not you?"

I never saw much of Langston in New York. However, the first time I met Dick in person was at a reception Langston was giving for W. E. B. Du Bois in the apartment at 143rd and St. Nicholas he shared with his aunt. Du Bois was reigning in the place of honor in the middle of the settee, surrounded by admirers, when Dick arrived with an African writer. By then Dick had published both *Native Son* and *Black Boy*. But he was practically ignored by that gathering of intellectuals and middle-class matrons, and he was antagonistic and resentful.

The next time I saw Dick was shortly after *If He Hollers* was published. The Book of the Month Club had *If He Hollers* listed as one of the alternates, and Dick took me up to the offices to meet some of the people. The people I met were not important people—the only one I remember was Vivien Wolfert, sister of Ira Wolfert, who was working in publicity for BOM. In fact, during all the years I knew Dick, he never introduced me to anyone of importance. That was one of Dick's failings—to keep the important people to himself. I remember once attending a reception Dick gave for Simone de Beauvoir, and he didn't even introduce me to the guest of honor. As a matter of fact, I didn't find out who she was until talking to some of the other guests days later—not that I give a damn one way or another.

Anyway, I came to know Dick very well, and none of his faults or failings ever bothered me at all. I met Ellen Wright at a party given by the editor of Black Metropolis for Cayton and Drake before a radio broadcast. Dick, by the way, wrote the first big review for *If He Hollers* (a joint review with Arthur Miller's *Focus*) for the old *PM*. I met Arthur Miller then, and we were on several radio programs together.

In fact, I met everybody connected with writing and publishing who was in New York the year after the publication of *If He Hollers*. Bucklin Moon was my editor, and *If He Hollers* was promised the George Washington Carver Memorial Award by Doubleday & Co. But there had been trouble. When the manuscript was ready for the printers, Buck went to Florida to work on his book *Without Magnolias*. Some woman editor (I never found out who) cut the manuscript to pieces (in fact, she deleted the entire first scene between Bob and Madge in the hotel room) before it went to the printers. Then the editors did not want to show me the galleys. I blew my top when I saw the galleys and restored all the parts (more than thirty pages) that had been deleted. Then *If He Hollers* had an advance sale of 10,000 and hit the bestseller list on the second week of publication. Then someone at Doubleday (I never found out who) ordered the printing to be stopped at Garden City, and orders were not being filled. I had many letters to this effect from all over the country. Ken McCormick had become editor at Doubleday, and I told this to Ken. They beat me down that it was not true, that I was hysterical, etc. (even Buck joined in). Why would they stop the sale of their own book? they asked. Seven years later, in the flat of Vandi Haygood, Buck admitted I was right but that they were trying to get him out of the company and he had to go along with them. So when the book came up to be considered for the George Washington Carver Memorial Award, one of the top women editors threatened to resign if it was given the award. Buck admitted this but wouldn't tell me her name. So the award was given to a book by a white woman out of St. Louis—*Mrs. Palmer's Honey* (Honey being the name of Mrs. Palmer's maid).

Because of this I had Blanche Knopf buy my contract from Doubleday. Then I went to northern California (in the Ku Klux Klan area) and wrote *Lonely Crusade.* As you probably know, everybody (and I mean *everybody*) jumped on *Lonely Crusade.* The communists crucified it. *New Masses* led off with a three-page review (while advertising Arthur Miller's *Focus* on a facing page) written by a Negro named Brown, titled "Himes Carries the White Flag," and I was compared with Senator Bilbo and the traitors who squealed on the slave revolts. Also the communists started a campaign against the stores selling it; members would buy a book, damage it, and take it back to the stores, demanding their money back and making scenes. Willard Motley wrote a dirty, incredibly vicious review for the *Sun-Times* (in Chicago), taking statements indiscriminately from the dialogue and saying, "Himes states . . ." James Baldwin wrote a review (it was the first I had ever heard of Baldwin) for the Socialist Party's *Union Leader,* headed "History As Nightmare." Dick had no offers to review it, although he wrote a fair preface for the French edition. *Commentary* ran a long diatribe, stating once, "in between sweaty sex scenes reads like a graffiti in a public urinal." *Atlantic Monthly* stated, "Hate runs through it like a stream of yellow bile." I could go on for pages. I was canceled off the radio program of Mary Margaret McBride, off *Author Meets Critic;* Macy's and Bloomingdale's canceled lectures and took the book out of stock. Critics even complained of the manufacture of the book, stating publishers had given it too dignified a format. The Knopfs refused to support it. Carl Van Vechten knows some of this story.

Anyway, I got hurt. My father had come to New York to see some of the broadcasts—all of which got canceled. He said by way of consolation, "New York is not the only city with skyscrapers."

It was a long time before I could write again. As you know, *Lonely Crusade* disappeared after selling about 1,400 copies and has never been considered for reprint.

I went to Yaddo a year or so later and started another book, but I gave up after eighty or ninety pages. I came as near to having a nervous breakdown while at Yaddo as I will ever come. While there I went to Chicago and gave a lecture at Mandel Hall at Chicago University, titled "The Negro Writer in America." When I finished not one single person, white or black, applauded. I went back to Yaddo and stayed drunk for six weeks.

During that time I was working as doorman, bellman, etc., around the "Borscht Circuit" (Sullivan County, the Catskills, Copake, etc.). I learned something about the Jews, at any rate.

Then I got Margaret Johnson as an agent and began working on my autobiographical novel, *The Third Generation*. I like *The Third Generation* the *least* of all my novels (even including the detective stories). It is a subtly dishonest book, made dishonest deliberately for the purpose of making money. Strangely enough, it didn't live up to expectations. The World Publishing Company sold the reprint rights before publication to NAL for $10,000 and spent their half, or more, in advertisement—such as full-page ads in the *Times Book Review,* the *Tribune, L.A. Times, Chicago Tribune.* Even so, the book didn't sell.

Before then, however, Coward-McCann had published a cut-in-two version of *Cast the First Stone,* which didn't sell either. The business with *Lonely Crusade* had made bookstores leery about my books.

So in 1953, even before publication of *The Third Generation,* I took my $5,000 and came to Europe. On board ship (*Isle de France*) I met one of our typical hurt white women—this one was a Boston socialite, daughter of the *Mayflower,* DAR, direct descendant of John Hancock, and all that crap, middle-aged, married to a Luxembourg dentist, four daughters, separated—and *sick.* I took her to London for seven months, to Mallorca for nine months. During the first seven months in London we wrote a 560-page book based on her life and a recent love affair and nervous breakdown. I always think it was a beautiful book of its kind, and I still believe it should have made a fortune—it was like the Caldwell women's books, only better.

We called it *The Silver Altar* after the Jungfrau mountain in Switzerland (where the ski accident takes place). My publisher, Victor Weybright (my Jewish publishers at World could not stomach the fact I had written this book with this woman and refused it), was in London, and when he found out (I don't know how) that I was living with this woman, he didn't speak to me or answer my letters until I saw him this summer in New York. I tried to submit the book only in her name [Willa Thompson], but word got out in the industry that I had worked on it, and no one would touch it. I got broke with that book.

Then I sat down in Mallorca with a kind of don't-give-a-goddamn attitude and wrote *The End of a Primitive* (*The Primitive*), which I like as much as any book I've ever written. Somehow I got back to Paris with 800 old francs left (about $2), borrowed enough money to last a few weeks, and sent out five copies of *The End of a Primitive*. A copy went to NAL. The editor, Walter Freeman, sent a cable of acceptance, offering a $1,000 advance—which I had to take—and NAL kept all world rights. Gallimard took the book here for Du Monde Entier but too late, and NAL got the advance. As you know, the book has disappeared.

I took the $1,000 and sent Willa back to Boston to try to sell the book in her name. But Houghton Mifflin knew about me. Then I came back to New York to try to get Kenneth Littauer to sell the book. In fact, everybody was enthusiastic about the damn book, but they all wished I hadn't written it. When I went with Willa to see Littauer (I had known Littauer since 1940, when he was fiction editor for Collier's), he suggested that I sit in a chair out in the reception room because there was not enough space in his office, so I talked to him through the door. Then he told me what a shame it was that Octavius Roy Cohen was no longer writing his blackface stories for the *Post*.

Anyway, we didn't sell the book. I got the rights from *If He Hollers* from NAL and sold them to Berkley Books and went back to Paris as fast as I could. Willa had already returned. I made a contract with her, giving her the right to sell and submit the book in her name as her book. I forget now how it came about, but we cut the book down to 250 pages (for Alexander Korda's brother to make into a film; I remember now).

Korda didn't take it for a film, but Willa sold the cut version personally to Beacon Press in Boston and we fell out and the book went into the hands of a lawyer, who now controls it. We got $1,000 for the cut version of the book, which was published under the title *Garden without Flowers* ($450 each), but it has also disappeared. Willa has disappeared also.

During 1956 and 1957 I was here in Paris and stone broke. Looking back it seems impossible that I existed. *The Primitive* didn't earn a cent, but my good friend and editor Walter Freeman was sticking one or two dollar bills into letters in which he would elaborate how hard it was for him to keep up the payment on the new Olds and the new house and the deep freeze, etc.

During the end of 1957, Marcel Duhamel, editor of the detective story collection La Série Noire, offered me a thousand bucks advance to write some detective stories for him. Naturally, I jumped at the chance. I knocked out the first one in about nine or ten weeks—then I could live again. After that it took only four or five weeks to write one.

The first one, in French *La reine des pommes,* won the detective story prize for 1958 and besides being a bestseller got the unanimous acclaim of the intellectuals over here. It was a real true bestseller and has by now become a French classic and is universally known in France; and I personally have become famous over here. But I would have to write six of these books each year to live even moderately well. French publishers have to be taken to court to pay any royalties over the first advance, no matter how many copies have been sold. At least 500,000 copies of *La reine des pommes* have been sold, but I have only been paid for 100,000 copies (not even that, for the accountants have made a mistake in my accounts and I have wound up owing Gallimard $2,600—which can only be straightened out in court).

That's all for now.

Here is a list of my books in the U.S. and France; a few have been published here and there, England, Scandinavian countries, etc., but of no great importance.

If He Hollers Let Him Go, Doubleday & Co., 1945

S'il braille lâche-le, Albin Michel, 1948

Lonely Crusade, Alfred A. Knopf, 1947

La croisade de Lee Gordon, Correa, 1952

Cast the First Stone, Coward-McCann, 1952

The Third Generation, World, 1954

La troisième génération, Plon, 1957

The Primitive, NAL, 1955

Le fin d'un primitie, Gallimard, 1956

Detective Stories: *For Love of Imabelle* (Fawcett); *The Real Cool Killers,*
   The Crazy Kill, The Big Gold Dream, All Shot Up (Avon)

In French: *La reine des pommes, Il pleut des coups durs, Dare-dare, Tout*
   pour plaire, Couché dans le pain, Imbroglio negro, Nous envervons pas
   (Gallimard)

Mamie Mason, Plon, 1962

Pinktoes, Olympia Press (Paris) 1961

John, if you need any elaborations let me know, and anyway, I'll send
you a few accounts of my experiences with Dick, Baldwin, Bill Smith, and
others sometime soon. At the moment I am beat with writing (and no
wonder), and tomorrow and Sunday I won't have a chance, so I'll go out to
the post now and get this off without even reading it over—which is not
necessary I know.

And thanks for everything. Hope to see you soon.

Chester

-§-

November 2, 1962

Dear John,

Since I started this autobiographical account I have been interrupted
constantly until this afternoon, and now I hope to get at it and get it
finished. I live in a ground floor studio with my Paris girlfriend [Lesley
Packard], an English girl who works for Time-Life, and my front (and only)
window is right on the street. This street is right off Place St. Michel and
easily accessible. By now all the brothers have found my address. I have to
get out of here if I'm ever going to write anything—that's for sure. In the
meantime I got a letter from James Reach stating that I owe him $504.88,

which I must pay before he will release my material. So until this is paid off there is no need to contact Reach; but I will airmail a copy of *Cast the First Stone* to Carl Brandt, and in a week or so I'll have the synopsis of a new book ready. Now to get on with my bio. Thanks very much for all your help.

Chester

-§-

November 1962

Dear John,

I have got my copy of *Sissie* and have read it, and I am sending a letter to the publishers and enclosing a copy for you.[6] It is a great book; in fact, it might very well be a greater book than I alone could say. I must write you at greater length when I have got some distance from the story; now it holds me in a vise. And I am bone tired from reading it. It shook the very hell out of me. There is no doubt about it being the best book written about an American Negro family; and there is no doubt about the characterization of Sissie being one of the best ever made of a woman in any literature. You come pretty damn close to answering the eternal question, What is a woman? I like the very hell out of the book. And I will write you more about it in the next few days. Anyway, I can say now that your last two books, *Night Song* and *Sissie,* put you at the very top of all the American Negro writers who have lived.

I hope to see you soon.

As ever,
Chester

---

6. *Sissie* was my third novel, just about to be published in the new year, 1963.

Chester Himes
39, rue de la Harpe
Paris 5

November 6, 1962

Editors
Farrar, Straus & Cudahy, Inc.
19 Union Square West
New York 3, N.Y.

Dear Sirs,

I have just finished reading an advance copy of *Sissie* by John A. Williams.

In my estimation this is, without comparison, the *greatest* novel written about an American Negro family, and certainly one of the very best books written about any family (of whatever race) anywhere.

It is a work of extraordinary virtuosity (comparable to the best of Charlie Parker in scope and melodic phrasing) and depicts the truth of American Negro life on all essential levels. More important, of course, than its virtuosity is its truth; it blasts in the mind like one big explosion of all our sacred myths and washes the brain of all our patterned subterfuge and rationalization (thank God).

But it is the characterization of Sissie that makes this book great in the literature of the world. Sissie the matriarch is memorable. Sissie the wife is totally human. Sissie the mother is a martyr to Negro male oppression in a predominantly male society. But it is Sissie the woman who is incomparable. As a woman, Sissie is magnificent. As a woman, Sissie will be remembered as long as there are women.

Mr. Williams is one of the very few writers (male or female) who can write about that most wonderful being on earth—a woman.

Sincerely yours,
Chester Himes

Carl Van Vechten
146 Central Park West
New York 23

November 15, 1962

Dear John,

Thank you *so much* for *Sissie,* and I promise to read it as soon as I get a couple hours free, which *will not* be this weekend. I will write you as soon as I have read it, of course.

As for Chester, he is always in trouble, as you who have read his letters will understand. What I can't fathom is that he is much too intelligent and sensible to permit this to happen, but it never fails.

My very warm regard,
Carlo

Chester Himes
39, rue de la Harpe
Paris 5

November 20, 1962

Dear John,

I have sent out several short stories and pieces to various New York magazines, and I have taken the liberty to ask that they be returned in your care. I hope you won't mind too much, but I didn't want to have them returned here, as I intend to come to New York as soon as possible to try to get my affairs straightened out; and I am in the hopes that I might score with some magazine or other before my arrival—in fact, I could use the money for transportation. If you will just put them aside someplace; and if there are any letters, will you please just open them and drop me a line if they need answering. I know you are quite busy yourself, and I wouldn't ask this favor if it wasn't an emergency. And I hope things are going all right on your various projects.

As ever,

Chester

-§-

Chester Himes

39, rue de la Harpe

Paris 5

December 3, 1962

Dear John,

Thanks for your letter of November 29. Carlo wrote me a letter raving about your new book, *Sissie.* If I like it better than *Night Song* I'm your fan forever. My copy of *Night Song,* which you gave me, is making its rounds—at the moment Nicole Barclay of Barclay Records has it. By the way, do you have a French publisher? Also my publishers in Germany are Ullstein Verlag, GMBH (Frankfurt-Berlin-Vien), and the socialist bookclub, Buchergilde Gutenberg (Frankfurt), who I'm sure would like very much to see it— they've published Richard Wright and me of the brothers. Would you mind if I sent my copy over to Germany? And let me know how you dig the French publishers. I know these bastards well, but I can't say anything very good about them. And about your friend Phil Lomax, I hear he is living in Copenhagen, but I have not seen him in months.

Being broke on Christmas is a way of life for me, but this Christmas I want very much to get back to the States and try to do a little business—at least see Carl Brandt if nothing else. I have so much to write about I don't know where to start—and I'm not even sure I can do it. I still have the old "try," but I badly need some advice. So I'm hoping Krim or someone else (*Esquire* maybe) will come through with a little dough to get me back; or perhaps my Germans—Ulstein, etc.[7] Part of my reportage on Harlem will be published in *Die Welt* in January and all of it by *Présence Africaine* same month (but no money). The French think I have betrayed them, saying I'm a human tool, but that is of no great consequence.

I have not seen my friend Jimmy Baldwin either. In fact, I never see him. Years ago when Dick was alive I saw him two or three times here, and that is all. We do not know the same people. I heard he was in Paris from a friend of his, a photographer for the magazine *Afrique.* But chances are I will not see him; we do not go to the same places either. Good old Jimmy; I hope he has a fine time.

I'm glad you like Vermont. I spent quite some time in Vermont around Burlington, Westford, and then in the country with my friend and family the writer-brother Will Thomas (Bill Smith), and I met the editor of *New Horizons* (I think). I like the people, and strangely they liked me. (Even though they do celebrate the cake walk.) As a matter of fact, I like Vermont as much as I like anywhere I've ever been.

I hope to see you soon. And keep 'em rolling. I'll be the first one to be in Stockholm when you get the Nobel (and help you spend it).

As ever,
Chester

December 21, 1962

Dear John,

Merry Xmas and all best wishes. I am hoping to get to NY on the *Queen Mary* about January 3–4. I'm sure you'll have a great year coming with *Sissie;* it's a great book. There are good chances Book of the Month Club will take it. Anyway, all best for you.

Chester

---

7. Seymour Krim was a close friend, a writer and book and magazine editor.

January 6, 1963

Re: Hack #11804
Driver #5786
New York City Police Department
Hack License Bureau
54 Worth Street
New York, New York

Dear Sirs,

On January 3rd, 1963, at about 7 P.M. I hailed a cab at Fifth Avenue and 47th Street. I was in the company of Mrs. Lynn Caine, 20 Park Avenue, and Mr. Chester Himes, 39, rue de la Harpe, Paris, and the Albert Hotel, 10th Street and University Place, Manhattan.[8]

The cab was going south on Fifth Avenue. The roof light was on. As it approached 47th Street the traffic light changed to red. I approached the cab door. The driver was making motions to wave me away; he may have tried to lock the door against me, but I had opened it already.

We sat down in the cab. Before we could give the driver our destinations he said he was going to eat. We remarked that his light had been on. He had not had an "Off Duty" sign in his windshield. The driver reached over and turned his light off. "There, my light is out," he said.

The traffic light had changed to green. I gave him our stops: 20 Park Avenue and 10th Street and University Place and said if he didn't want to take us to carry us to the nearest precinct house. He said, "I'm not taking you any farther than this corner." He drove across 47th Street and pulled to a stop, waiting for us to get out. We sat for some moments in the silence. I repeated our destinations once again and demanded as an alternative that he take us to a police station.

Finally he put his meter down, turned his light on, and carried us to Mrs. Caine's home at 20 Park Avenue. Mr. Himes and I bid her goodbye and continued on to the Albert Hotel. Mr. Himes had taken the cab number—11804—and the driver's identification number—5786.

---

8. Lynn Caine was my publicity director at Farrar, Straus and Cudahy.

The driver was reckless throughout the trip, driving at excessive speeds and, after we left Mrs. Caine, narrowly missing at least one pedestrian. Please consider this a most vigorous complaint against this driver.

Sincerely,
John A. Williams
434 Lafayette Street
New York 3, N.Y.

Sisal (Yucatan)
Mexico

Monday, January 31, 1963

Dear John,

I arrived Saturday night without trouble, although we were an hour late getting away from Idlewild [Kennedy] and had another hour behind schedule in Miami, which threw us in Merida long after dark and after arguing a little to take me to Sisal for $6. I had no idea it was 55 kilometers (34 miles) from Merida to Sisal or else I would have paid the driver the tip he asked for without comment. I burst in on Marianne taking a shower, and everything is all right. This is a very primitive little fishing village, though there is a shower and a toilet in the house, running water. It is a rather large palm-thatched house with six rooms, faintly reminiscent of a cottage, with two rooms completely empty—the big dining room containing four chairs and a table. The main entrance hall with a latticed front is Marianne's workroom. The palm-thatched roof is tremendously high, and only the bedroom, off to one side, has a ceiling. There is a terrace surrounded by a low stone wall fronting on the sandy beach, and thirty yards down the beach is the sea. We are directly across the end of Cuba, but it is beyond the horizon. This beach runs infinitely in both directions, and all about the house is cluttered with fishing boats. This house is the only one directly on the beach with a terrace, and I have discovered that this low stone wall is the sitting place of the neighborhood. At one time yesterday we had about twenty little Mexican children and many adults running through the house in their little shifts and bare feet. I forgot to tell you, when I arrived at night it was 87 degrees, and they say that this is about how cold it gets. People go about barefooted and half naked and yesterday swam in the sea, and the sun burns down—although a storm came up last night, and today it is cloudy but still hot. Now if I can clear my mind of all sense of guilt, trepidation, anxieties, etc., I will be able to write, because if I can't write here, I can't write anywhere. Give Joyce my love.[9] I'll probably write to her. I'll see you.

—§—

Friday, February 1963

Dear John,

I have finally got your letter and the clipping from *Jet* (1/31/1963), but the mail takes long in these parts; in fact, we only have four mail days per week. I see your point about *The Primitive,* and perhaps it will be too strong for Carl also. But I wrote *The Primitive* sitting in the sun in the backyard in a house in Puerto de Pollansa and Deya, Mallorca, filled with tranquilizer pills, and everything was crystal clear and no more horrible than the life of Jesse from a distance of 5,000 miles and five years (or in fact all life in America), and it amused me in the same grotesque, morbid (if these are the right words) fashion that I would be amused seeing a white man who was chasing a Negro boy suddenly fall and break his neck. And it never occurred to me that Americans would find it objectionable—or any more objectionable than "normal" life in the U.S. taking place every day. In fact,

9. Joyce Cadoo was one of Himes's friends. We three had dinner one evening.

it always strikes me as funny (in a strange way) that white people can take problems of race so seriously, guiltily, when they make these problems themselves and keep on making them. It's like a man taking a rifle and shooting his toes off one by one and crying because it hurts. Anyway, *The Primitive* was also an exercise in writing, and I am rather proud that I wrote it. It wasn't intended anyway as a message; it was intended more as a mirror.

My detective story is going fine; I have done seventy-five pages of the first draft. In fact, this is the first one I have written a first draft for; the others I have just stuck an original and two copies in the typewriter and sent off whatever came out.

Marianne is fine and in good health and working hard on her own story. The Mayan Indian family next door clean the house and bring out hot meals to the house and we have no chores, and it all costs very little. But even so Carl had better get me some money soon, or we'll be broke. I'm finding it isn't easy for two people to write in the same house; but it's a big house and we'll survive.

Thanks for the clipping from *Jet*. Alan [Morrison] did a nice job. He had to put in that boost for Baldwin, I suppose, but I didn't really say any damn such thing.

The weather is holding up, although we have some cloudy days, and it's getting a little chilly toward night.

Give my love to Joyce, and Marianne joins me in sending love to Lorrain. Keep up the good work. All best wishes.

Chester

February 6, 1963

Sisal (Yucatan)
Mexico

Dear John,
This is just a line to say winter is here in Sisal, and I am still alive. This is the season of the "Northers"; it's not so cold, but the fisherman can't fish and

food is scarce, for fish is the main diet—fish, beans, tortillas, chilis, and a few vegetables when available. Actually the food is quite good when there is plenty of fish, for that also means the fishermen have some money; and the woman next door who supplies us with food is married to a fisherman and has a fisherman for a son and a son-in-law. All the people here are of Mayan descent, and the village lives entirely from the sea. Anyway, my exercise with Grave Digger and Coffin Ed is going along, sometimes well, sometimes poorly, sometimes rapidly, sometimes slowly; but it should get finished in the next ten days; then I will have to retype it, and I will just make the deadline. These people have been celebrating the "Virgin" for the past five days, with much dancing, celebrating, and cactus juice, and the village today is not only without food but there is no drinking water, since we depend on rainwater to drink, well water to clean, and sea water to provide food.

And how is everything going with you? I was thinking the other day, why don't you compile an anthology of writing by Negro expatriates on various places in Europe? I can supply you with a list of names, such as Ollie Harrington, Alain Albert, Bill Smith, Herb Gentry, Phil Lomax, Melvin Van Peebles, etc., and you could send them a form letter asking them to contribute articles, experiences, stories, poems, etc., concerning places in Europe. Actually with the interest folks have in the Darker Brother abroad, you might be able to get an advance on the idea, and I'm sure the brothers will participate—although what you will get will certainly not (on the whole) be literature. Anyway, it's an idea.

I haven't had a line from friend Carl, and if he doesn't come through soon I shall be eating fish bones that the dogs are very fond of here. Give Joyce my love, and Marianne joins me in sending love to Lorrain and all the best for you.

Chester

Sisal (Yucatan)

Mexico

February 25, 1963

Dear John,

I expect to be in New York within a week on my way back to Europe, and I will see you then. I've written to my editor at Editions Plon to send me an airmail ticket out of the balance that will be due me on the book, and I'm sure he will.

I got myself broke and in debt to the fishermen here, who are very kind and nice people but don't have any money and can barely support themselves, much less me. So I'm going to Paris, where I can live fine even though it won't help me in the U.S.

Perhaps you can find out for me what gives with Carl Brandt.[10] I haven't heard from him since I've been here, although I've written several times trying to get definite information about my *Garden without Flowers* royalties, for which he has all the papers.

Marianne and I have discovered that we can't possibly live together without our separate careers and our egos and without money, so we have come to a parting of the ways.

I should be through with this fucking book, but I'm right up to the end and am stalled simply for lack of concentration. I must admit Brandt worries the hell out of me too. I can't move now without him, since I've referred everyone to him, even the people dabbling with the idea of making a film from one of my books—and I can't move with him because I have no contract. Anyway, I'll see you soon. Take care.

Chester

---

10. Brandt did not take on Himes as a client.

Sisal, Yucatan, Mexico
March 6, 1963

Dear John,

I am enclosing this letter from Carl. It makes no sense, but it does not
surprise me. But when he speaks of "financial obligations," he frightens me.
I told him I owed my former agent, James Reach, $504, and supposedly
I owe Blanche Knopf $2,000 she advanced me to write a novel titled
"Immortal Warning," which I did not write. However, I offered her the
script of *Cast the First Stone* and *The Third Generation,* which she turned
down. I wonder if the Treasury Department is trying to get me for income
tax evasion. It's the only thing I can think of. I haven't made any income
to amount to a damn, and almost all of that in Europe, but still somebody
seems to have a knife for me. If you could find out what he means, it will
help very much. As it now stands I'm afraid to stop in N.Y.

Excuse this bad writing. I am in the hospital in Merida. Just as I reached
the last few pages of my book I had a brain "spasm" and became slightly
paralyzed.[11] Thinking about the U.S. no doubt. Anyway, after five days in
the hospital I am much better—almost back to normal, and I hope to be
out and back in Sisal by the weekend.

Please write me whatever news you might have for me as soon as
possible because I'm trying like hell to get back to France, where I am safe,
and please send Brandt's letter back before I leave.

I hope everything is going fine for you, and I hope to get to see you
when I pass through New York, but I don't know. Marianne joins me in
sending love to you and Lorrain. Give Joyce my love.

See you,
Chester

---

11. I do not know what he meant by "brain spasm," but given his history of having a series of
them later on, I would guess it to be a slight stroke. From this point on Himes walked with a
barely noticeable limp.

Chester Himes
Sisal (Yucatan)
Mexico

Tuesday, March 12, 1963

Dear John,

I received your letter of the 8th in record time. I am still in hospital La
Iberica in Merida, which is the big town here in the Yucatan (about 55
kilometers from Sisal), but I will be going home in a day or two. Thanks for
everything, but there is no great emergency. I'm preparing to send my draft
of the detective story to Plon, and I will get my transportation back to Paris,
and I will get a few thousand marks from Germany eventually; but anyway
I hope your friend Krim comes through soon if that is possible because it
will facilitate matters. Anyway, I'll be in New York at least by next week.
Chances are Marianne will come with me. There is no need of me bothering
Carl anymore. I will see what I can do on my own. I'll see you soon.
Marianne joins me in sending love to you and Lorrain.

Chester

TIME-LIFE News Service
HOME: 39, RUE DE LA HARPE
Paris 5
TIME-LIFE PRESS AGENCY
17, AVENUE MATIGNON
Paris 8
TELEPHONE ELYSEES 05-39
TELEGRAMS TIME INC. Paris
TELEX 27904

13 March 1963

Dear Mr. Williams,

I received a letter from Chester saying that he was in the hospital with "brain fatigue." Since then—almost nine days ago—I have heard no word at all. I have been hearing from him almost twice a week and find this lack of communication rather bothering.

I am writing to you because I know Chester was in touch with you in the recent past, and I cannot think of anyone else to whom to write. There is no panic whatsoever—I just want to hear that he is well and that everything is going fine for him.

The letter he sent me came from Sociedad Espanola de Beneficencia, Quinta "La Iberica," Merida, Yucatan, Mexico.

I would like to take this opportunity to tell you that I have read *Night Song* and *Sissy,* both of which I enjoyed tremendously. . . . In fact, they are the most popular books in the house (not counting Chester's).

> Yours sincerely,
> Lesley Packard

TIME-LIFE News Service
TIME-LIFE PRESS AGENCY
17, AVENUE MATIGNON
Paris 8
TELEPHONE ELYSEES 05-39
TELEGRAMS TIMEINC. Paris
TELEX 27904

Friday, 22 March 1963

Dear John,

Thank you very much for your kind, prompt letter. I did, in fact, receive a letter from Chester the very same day. He seems to be much better and also seems very cheerful about the future. He asked me to telephone Plon and ask them if they had received the manuscript. They told me they had already arranged for a cheque to be sent to him and that they were very, very pleased with the story and think it will be a great success. I will quickly write to Chester and give him this good news, but he will most probably be in New York when this letter arrives, so you will have the chance of giving him the news, I'm always a little afraid that in order to stand the pace in New York he will turn to a few nips of whiskey, and, after this relapse, I'm not so sure it is a good idea. I can, however, understand very well that he might feel many pressures. We in Europe live at a completely different pace, and, in spite of strikes, etc., we have . . . or seem to have . . . fewer problems to think of.

I do hope that you will pass through Paris next autumn, and we'll all have a chance of having a few nips of whiskey together.

A writer you may know, William Gardner Smith, just telephoned me to ask if he might borrow *Night Song*.[12] My words were not kind; they were true.

I am giving your address to a Swedish silversmith (Chester has almost certainly spoken of her), Torun. She will be coming to New York very shortly and would like to meet you. I'm not sure whether she will arrive while Chester is still there, but if he is not she will be able to introduce herself through me.

I saw Emile Cadoo yesterday, and he is saving me a copy of *Jet* because he says there is a picture of you and Chester in it. I think Chester had already mentioned this to me, but I have not yet seen it.

Do forgive this rather untidy little letter, but today seems to be full of deadlines, and I'm being thrown questions from all directions.

Thank you once more.

Sincerely,
Lesley

---

12. William Gardner Smith was one of several African American authors then living in Paris. Also a journalist, he wrote the highly acclaimed *Last of the Conquerors* (1948). Smith died in 1974.

April 1963–December 1968

In this period, between the spring of 1963 and the winter of 1968, our correspondence became scattered, and it really did not pick up again until December 1968. During this time, both Chester and I were on the move, both literally and professionally. Chester was trying to get his life together and recovering from various illnesses while writing his proverbial butt off.

I got lucky. I published over a dozen magazine articles and two fiction pieces and traveled to Israel, Egypt, Sudan, Cameroon, Ethiopia, Zaire, and Nigeria, where I met Malcolm X and James Meredith in Lagos and Kano, respectively, and coproduced for WNET Omowale: The Child Returns Home. The Man Who Cried I Am, Africa: Her History, Lands, and People *(a young adult book),* The Protectors *(using the psuedonym J. Dennis Gregory), and* This Is My Country Too *(an account of my travels across the United States) were published during this period.*

But the most important event during that period was my second—and lasting—marriage, this time to Lorrain Isaac on October 5, 1965. We planned to live for six months in the small village of Castelldefels (just south of Barcelona), where I had lived briefly in 1958, and then in Amsterdam for six months. But I became ill with a bleeding ulcer and had to be hospitalized for three weeks, so we sailed on the France *six weeks late. After driving from LeHavre to Castelldefels, we were soon settled in a charming little house overlooking the Mediterranean, within walking distance of the beach and a short drive in our Citroen Trois Cheveaux into Barcelona. The writing was going well (I was working on* The Man*), and we enjoyed an active social life with the poet Phil Levine and his family and their friends passing through. We also met many interesting Americans in the arts at the Instituto Americano. Norman Narotzky, a painter who was married to a Spanish woman, still lives in Barcelona, and we are still in touch. Another interesting encounter was with Henry Roth (*Call It Sleep*) and his wife, Muriel, who were living in Seville. I persuaded him to come to Castelldefels to do a television interview for WNET with me called* The Creative Person: Henry Roth.

Meanwhile, Chester had returned to Lesley in Paris. Through her I got back in touch and told him of our plans to travel through France when we left Spain on our way to Amsterdam and expressed the hope of seeing him en route.

132 rue d'Assas

Paris 6

October 8, 1965

Dear John,

I've taken a room with bath for you at Hotel Stanislas, 5 rue Montparnasse, at 45 F. per day, about $9, and I've paid for the night of October 20. I suppose you can stay as long as you want if you find it satisfactory. Rue Montparnasse, as you probably know, runs from Boulevard Raspail to Boulevard Montparnasse beside the church near the Select. I will be in London when you arrive but should be back on the 21st or 22nd.[13]

> All best,
> Chester

[Undated card, probably mid-October 1965]
Congratulations and my very best wishes for a long and happy marriage.
> Chester

139, rue d'Assas

October 22, 1965

Dear Lorrain,

I've returned from London to find your letter about John's sudden illness. I am very sorry that your plans were so suddenly disrupted. Give John my

---

13. I had to cancel this reservation because of my hospitalization and our delayed departure.

very best expressions of get well, etc., and tell him not to worry. It just means he has to stop drinking for a while, and of course that's very hard to do in Spain, but it is possible. Some years ago I went down with an ulcer in Hamburg and was put on some medication and a diet by an internist there. I lived in Paris for three months without drinking or breaking my diet, so anything is possible. But the day it was over I drank one bottle of French gin, and I have never been troubled with ulcers since.

I realize this is a somewhat stupid kind of letter to be writing to a friend who's just been hospitalized with bleeding ulcers, and you must forgive me. It's just my way of saying I look forward to seeing you both well and happy in the near future. I think it will work out all right with Hotel Stanislas, but if not, let me know.

With hopes for the best,
Chester

§

Apartado 63
Castelldefels (Barcelona)
Spain

March 20, 1966

Dear Chester,
We can't figure out if you're trying to avoid us or if the brothers—namely, Sanders at Paris Ebony—wouldn't give us your address, keeping you all for themselves. You know how brothers can be. We have been in touch with Sanders. In fact, we left your vitamins with him when we came through Paris. I don't know what his shtick is, but he is a strange cat, indeed.

In any case, we had to write back to New York to get your address from Putnam, after hearing from all over Europe that you were in Copenhagen, or near there. I couldn't figure out how you could stand that motherfucking cold, man, because I am just getting to stand this goddamn Spanish cold.

Your boy Herbert Hill stole a title from me, *Anger and Beyond* [what he actually stole was *Beyond Anger*], and put it in his new anthology, which I am not in, naturally, having told him in Washington, the day of the march, that I wouldn't shake his motherfucking hand for nothin' in this world. Also, that piece I did on you for the *Trib* mentioning how he fucked over you, must still rankle him. That's good.

Are you coming down this way? We may go to London toward the end of next month for a week or so. Not sure yet, because there are a couple of things in the works. Phil Lomax wanted your address, but I won't give it to him unless you want me to.[14] Meantime, drop us a note. I know you're a prolific letter writer. Best, as ever.

John

P.S. We're only here until the end of May; then we go north to Holland, if we can find a good deal.

-§-

La Ciotat
France

March 25, 1966

Dear John,

I've simply been moving, trying to find a place to live and work. Anyway, I never was a great one of the soul brothers in these parts, and it is perfectly normal for them to say they don't know where I am. I went to Denmark principally to get warm; I have spent the coldest winter of my life in southern France. And Copenhagen was warm inside, and I stayed inside. Otherwise, it's not my cup of tea, as the English say. There are any number of chicks (not all beautiful) around trying to give away some funky pussy, but on the whole I found the Danes egocentric, stupid, and over-sensitive

---

14. Phil Lomax, a writer and friend from Brooklyn, went to Europe about this time when nearly every African American there believed each black newcomer to be an agent of the U.S. government. Lomax died—mysteriously, some claimed—only a few years after arriving in Europe.

about their little country. As you can realize, my sense of humor would not endear me to such people—in fact, they don't even know the slave has been freed and seriously believe that those soul brothers on whom they lavish so much sympathy and white pussy are still in fact slaves. Any one can hardly exonerate the soul brother either; he acts like one.

I'm living on Daniel Guerin's place in this house Rustique Olivette that used to be a French writers' colony—in fact [Andre] Swartz-Bart wrote *The Last of the Just* here. You must have heard of Guerin; he's the rich French leftist authority on the brother—but I get along with him all right, chiefly because I so seldom see him.

If you pass through Marseille on your trip north, please stop by and see us. La Ciotat is about 30 kilometers east of Marseille in the direction of Toulon, and there are trains every hour or so—but I suppose you have your car. We have plenty of room, but there is a central heating (by coal) and it is about as Rustique as it can be.

Lesley joins me in sending you and your wife our best. And you must forgive me for not recalling her name this morning. I'm writing my autobiography, by the way, and thousands of names are filling up my head.

All best,

The address, in case you stop by, is Rustique Olivette, chemin de la Haute-Bertrandiere; Tel. 08.45.77—you can dial from anywhere in France.

Chester

Chester Himes
Poste Restante
13 La Ciotat

May 2, 1966

Dear John,
I got your letter of March 20 and am glad to hear the book is coming along. I thought I'd better drop this note to tell you we will no doubt be up and

leaving here at the same time you will be leaving Barcelona, and doubtless will miss you again. Daniel Guerin gave me use of his house for June, but I don't think I'll take it. I hope all goes well with your several projects, and perhaps we'll see you somewhere before you return to the U.S. Too bad you're not passing this way sooner; we got lots of room. Lesley joins me in sending you and Lori our best.

Chester

Chester Himes
13 Venelles
France

24 April 1967

Dear John,

Thanks for the copies of *Beyond the Angry Black*.[15] It's a good job. I was glad to get news of Lomax; I liked his story "Pollution." And I was happy to get news of John A. Williams. Best of luck with your forthcoming novel.

I'm sorry you couldn't come by La Ciotat on your way to Amsterdam last spring; we had a big house with plenty of space; and we have a big old farmhouse here with orchard and swimming pool, etc., which belongs, as you can guess, to an American white woman, a Mrs. Rubenstein née Curtis from Boston or Philadelphia or such. But I'm getting pissed off with France again, and Mrs. Rubenstein née Curtis in particular, and I think we might go to Amsterdam for the summer. I'll appreciate it if you can give me a little information on the subject, or anyway Phil Lomax's address—if he still lives there. Although I heard from a brother in Copenhagen that he moved there.

Lesley joins me in sending love to you and Lori.

Chester

---

15. I edited this collection of short fiction that was published in 1966 and included Himes, Shirley Jackson, Richard Wright, John Howard Griffin, Langston Hughes, Dennis Lynds, James Baldwin, and others.

Chester Himes
C/ Duque de Zaragoza, 2
Piso 9
Alicante, Espana

3 December 1968

Dear John,

I've mislaid your present address on W. 92nd Street; the last address I
have for you is 365 W. 22nd Street, and that was a long time ago. As a
consequence I'm writing to you in care of your U.S. publisher. Naturally, I
am asking for a favor.

I want to get a divorce from my wife from whom I've been separated
since 1950 and whom I haven't seen since 1955—and then only briefly, five
or ten minutes. I had always expected and hoped Jean would get a divorce
from me, but the last I heard she never has. I seem to remember hearing
from someone five or six years ago that she was living in Chicago and still
using the name of Mrs. Chester Himes. It should be easy to get a divorce;
anyway, she deserted me in 1950.

Things are getting so complicated I must legalize my relationship with
Lesley. We have lived together for so long I suppose it would stand up in
court, but now that we are going to live permanently in Spain it would be
better if we were married. We're building a casa north of Alicante, and it
should be ready for occupancy next October.

I want to ask you if you know of an attorney who could arrange to get
me a divorce without my having to appear in the U.S. I don't want to go
back to the U.S. unless it is absolutely urgent.

How is your wife and your new child? Please give her our best regards.

I suppose you can tell from this letter that I am getting to be an old
man. All these petty affairs make me nervous and absentminded, and I am
beginning to suffer from loss of memory. Anyway, I'm still alive. I should
complain.

Well, Lesley joins me in sending our best regards.

Sincerely,
Chester

P.S. By the way, I saw a review of your last book [*The Man Who Cried I Am*] in the Sunday *Times*—it wasn't a bad review, but it was by a London brother who wanted to carp.

-§-

December 12, 1968

Dear Chester:

To be sure, I was very surprised to hear from you, and at first—I must tell you all this—I was angered. After all this time, while I worried about you, asked about you, and fretted over you. Why? Why me, now, when you seemed to have made it patently clear that it made no difference whatsoever to you that I, we, were concerned and always wished you nothing but the best? I could never understand it; I asked nothing of or from you. I never demeaned you or coveted your status. More than you could ever know I shared your misfortunes and grief; I was elated that finally, at least, you were making the money you should have made years ago. I don't ask you reasons for avoiding me. Knowing the way people are, I can imagine some of the things that would've gone down. No matter. I've had my brief say, for what it's worth.

I was in touch with Roz Targ only last week, and she told me that she'd be seeing you in Barcelona, Christmas.[16] One of the things I told her was that Hoyt Fuller wished to get in touch with you in order to set up a whole theme issue of *Negro Digest* on Chester Himes. She said she'd be in touch with you. Fuller's already done one on Wright, and it came off very well.

About the attorney: We have a young lawyer named Anthony Burton. His father was a cut buddy of A. J. Liebling, and Tony, we think, is very good. I'm thinking of using him on future contracts instead of an agent.

---

16. The Targs (Roslyn and Bill) were old friends as well as agents for Himes.

I left Brandt & Brandt over a year ago. Burton does handle divorces, but yours, of course, involves special circumstances. I'm passing on to you the things he must know before agreeing to taking on the case: (1) where were you married; (2) where were you living when the desertion took place; (3) where is Mrs. Himes living now; (4) how rushed are you; do you want this done in a smashing hurry; (5) a formal arrangement, involving a retainer, would be mandatory in this case.

These are the points he asked me to raise. You might also be a bit more positive if at all possible about her last or present address, simply because the longer it takes to locate her, the more money it's going to cost you. If you send this information to me, I'll pass it on to him, and I assume on that basis he will accept or reject your suit. At this point he isn't sure whether it would be necessary for you to return.

Lori and Adam are well; I'm barely making it.

> Best regards,
> John

Chester Himes
C/ Duque de Zaragoza, 2
Alicante, Espana

18 December 1968

Dear John,

Please believe me, I hadn't realized the effect of my seeming indifference toward you and Lori and your son, who was expected when I last saw you. It is somewhat shattering to realize that most people must think the same of me. However, the truth of it is I haven't felt that way at all, and I sincerely beg your forgiveness. The hell of it is I haven't been doing anything of any importance (or even great interest) during this time. I have just been vegetating, staying alive, trying to keep warm. My seeming "success" hasn't meant a damn thing to me; in fact, news of it never reaches me. I have been passing time on the outskirts of life; I haven't been in communication with anyone in my sphere of interest whatsoever; Lesley and I have been almost entirely occupied with finding someplace to stay (park) for short periods of time before moving on to places equally uninteresting. We spent all last winter running up and down the rocky southern coast of Spain, trying to make up our minds if we wanted to live in Spain and whether we could afford it if we wanted to. Finally we bought two plots in an urbanacion north of Alicante, and then we spent the summer on the outskirts of Paris, spending most of our time keeping away from the rioting students and workers; then we came back to Spain in October to try to have a house built. Anyway, you should know that doing business with the Spanish consumes all of a person's time and tries one's patience. Frankly, I have no idea what is happening to my work; my only contact is Roslyn Targ. I have left Putnam and gone over to Morrow for my next book—*Blind Man with a Pistol.* We have an apartment here until the end of May, when we will go to London for the June publication of *Blind Man* in England and then pass time until we return to Spain around September 1, at which time I hope my house will be built. [Samuel] Goldwyn picked up his option on *Cotton* and intends to go ahead and make a film with Ossie Davis and Godfrey Cambridge from a chickenshit script written by Arnold Perl.[17] Most of my money is supposed to come from a percentage, so I did what I could for the script (for free, of course, as Goldwyn is greatly opposed to paying).

Let me put in a word here about your friend Hoyt Fuller. I have been getting word for more than two years that Hoyt Fuller wants to interview me, and I have been sending back word for two years that he can interview me at any time he wishes. Fuller telephoned me when I was last in New York, at the time we last saw you, saying he would come to New York to interview me. I said he could come anytime. The next time I heard from him was in Paris last summer when Art Simmons said Hoyt Fuller wanted

---

17. *Cotton Comes to Harlem,* a 1965 Himes novel, was eventually made into a film with the same name. Ossie Davis directed, and Godfrey Cambridge had a starring role.

to interview me. I told Art to tell him anytime he wished. I didn't see Hoyt Fuller—in fact I didn't hear of it again. Now Hoyt Fuller may interview me whenever he wishes; and that's all I'm going to say about him.

Thanks for the information about your attorney friend, Anthony Burton. I will now try to answer the questions about my marriage he finds essential:

1. Jean Johnson (she had been married, but I do not remember her married name) and I were married before a justice of the peace in Cleveland, Ohio, on August 13, 1937. This fact is correct as near as I can remember.
2. We were living in New York State when the desertion took place in the spring of 1950. Jean was employed as the director of recreation for the Women's State (New York) Reformatory, Mt. Kisco, New York (or if that is not the name of the city, it is where Billy Rose had his big fabulous estate). I was living in a rented room on Convent Avenue at 142nd Street.
3. The last I heard of Jean she was living in Chicago, employed in some capacity in welfare work, which is her field. She was either using the name of Mrs. Chester Himes or her maiden name of Jean Johnson.
4. I am not rushed for this divorce at all. And if it is necessary I will return to the U.S. The main thing is I do not want it to become more expensive than I can afford.
5. I understand that I will have to pay a retaining fee.

I think any directory of welfare workers in the vicinity of Chicago will list Jean under one of the two names mentioned in (3). But if not, there is a writer living in Chicago named Dan Levin who is certain to have her address.

Lesley is in the front room taking Spanish lessons from a little Spanish girl who is even a great deal smaller than Lori. But she joins me in sending all three of you our best regards. I like the name Adam for your son, irrespective of all the lumps it has taken on Powell. And I'm sure, John, if things seem slow to you now, they will soon pick up. I'm certain you know that the main thing in this game is to keep putting books out. Even if you have to put out a lot of fillers—who knows but what they might become classics with time. Look at Hemingway. Anyway, we hope to have you down for a visit eventually.

> *All best wishes,*
> *Chester*

-§-

Mr. Anthony Burton

December 30, 1968

Burton and Davidowitz
350 Fifth Avenue
New York, NY

Dear Tony,

I've heard from my friend Chester Himes, and he is interested in your services. I enclose page 2 of his letter to me, which answers all the questions you asked me to put to him. If you're willing to handle his divorce, I suggest that you write to him directly at his address:

> Mr. Chester Himes
> C/ Duque de Zaragoza 2
> Alicante, Spain

I'd like to have this page back, if I may, either a Xerox or the original. And don't be less than businesslike with him because we know him. We think he can well afford this divorce.

If we don't see you before the New Year, the best. My two elder sons are here, and we plan to go to the country for the rest of their holiday on Thursday.

> *Best regards,*
> *[John A. Williams]*

Chester Himes
C/ Duque de Zaragoza, 2
Alicante, Spain

7 January 1969

Dear John,

I have received a letter from your friend J. Anthony Burton, giving me all
the information pertinent to applying for a divorce in New York State. It
seems that the first thing for me to do is to locate Jean, and then we can
decide on what steps to take. As I wrote to him, I think that the best thing
I can do is ask Jean to divorce me—assuming, of course, that she will be
willing. I do not see how she could be reasonably unwilling, providing I
paid for the cost; it is going on nineteen years since we separated, and for all
I know she might even have her divorce and be married again. In any event,
I will write to a few people in Chicago whose addresses I still have, and
maybe I can locate her, and then I will write to Attorney Burton again.

Today is actually the afternoon of January 6, which as you no doubt
know is the biggest celebration in this country; and I have got so sick of
it all I'm wondering if I can really live in this country. The celebrating
started on December 6 and has been continuing nonstop.[18] And do you
know something? These Spanish people have money to spend, and they
have been spending it. My agent, Roslyn Targ, and her husband, Bill
Targ, were here (in Barcelona) from the afternoon of December 31 to the
morning of January 3, and Roslyn looked forward to having a shopping
spree on January 2. But the shops were so crowded with Spanish shoppers
she could hardly get inside, and the prices were just as high as on Fifth
Avenue—$1,000 handbags, $30 men's shirts, etc. Even in this little country
town of Alicante, the shops have been crowded for a month, the prices are
the same as in Paris and New York (higher than London), and the people
are insufferable. Maybe I'll feel more tolerant when they all go back to work,

---

18. The Feast of the Three Kings, the Spanish Christmas holiday, begins December 6 and ends
    January 6.

which they have to do soon, and then I hope to be able to get some work done too.

Lesley is fine; we enjoyed our few days in Barcelona (because we didn't try to buy anything), and it was a letdown to get back here and find these people still in a state of frantic panic for still another fiesta.

I hope this finds you and Lori and Adam all well and in good spirits.

Lesley joins me in wishing all three of you a very happy and prosperous New Year.

All best,
Chester

January 14, 1969

Dear Chester:

I got your letter last Friday morning and planned to answer sometime Saturday. Friday night we were invited to a dinner party for Gwen Brooks— except she didn't show up.[19] A captive of the young "militant" blacks here in town to whom she seems partial. Strange for a woman of her gifts. The guy who invited us was a transplanted Chicago cat who mentioned that he'd worked with Jean Himes. Lori and I were both thunderstruck, in view of our correspondence with you. He agreed to dig up her address. He called today. In the meantime, today I called Burton, who told me that he'd been in touch with you and advised that you forget about a New York divorce; also that you'd thanked him. He thinks you'd be better off with a Chicago lawyer and will write you about that if he hasn't already. I think he's right. Illinois divorce laws have always been more liberal than New York's, even

---

19. Gwendolyn Brooks (1917–2000), the much-honored African American poet, poet laureate of Illinois, and author of several volumes of award-winning poetry, including *Annie Allen*, which won the Pulitzer Prize in 1950.

now. Jean is working with the Chicago Model Cities program. Her office number is 955-2210. My man did not have her address after all, just this, but it's a start, if you want to go ahead. She's still using your name. Clarence Cooper fell by today.[20] Haven't seen him for a year. He's quite some cat. Now on his fifteenth book, beat to his socks, but brain razor sharp. What can I say about the Spanish brother? Franco has become more and more to his liking, and this, of course, means more bread.[21] We also found prices quite high in Barcelona and Madrid and the people very often insufferable. Times change. From my first time there about a decade ago and certainly from your first time there longer than that. We're supposed to get together with Roz and Bill whenever they want us—and whenever we're free. Well. Our best to you; stay in good health. We're a real kind of family scene, and it's rather nice, even though Adam is my favorite pain in the ass sometimes. Hasta la vista, hermano.

John

-§-

Chester Himes
C/ Duque de Zaragoza, 2
Alicante, Espana

21 January 1969

Dear John,

Thank you for your letter of January 14, including the information about my wife, Jean. I am indeed pleased to have her working address and phone number; and I am glad to know that she is well and employed. I have not heard as yet from your friend Anthony Burton, but I think I will write and

---

20. Clarence Cooper, Jr., was a very good writer who died too young. He is the author of many novels, among them *The Scene, The Farm,* and *The Dark Messenger.*
21. Francisco Franco was the leader of Spain from 1936 to 1975.

ask him for the name of that attorney in Chicago, although I am hesitant about approaching him again since he will not come in for a fee. Anyway, I shall wait to hear from my old friend Sidney Williams in Chicago before I take any further steps. I was amused by your reference to Gwen Brooks. I've never met Gwen, but from all I've heard of her I fear that she would not like me. And I don't think I know of Clarence Cooper. Is he a brother?

For a time I considered paying a flying visit to New York for the publication of my book *Blind Man* in February, but my editor does not think it will serve any purpose. Me neither. But I was just trying to be cooperative.

Anyway I don't have any great hopes for this book. As of now I just want to write one more in this series and close it. Then if I get my autobiography written, that'll be it.

The less said about the Spanish brother the better. You know, I can't stand any of the white people on this earth whom I have yet met. But I am ashamed to say I can take the Americans best of any of them, despite their challenging hypocrisy and violent idiocy.

Lesley joins me in sending our best to you and Lori and your little "favorite pain in the ass sometimes," Adam.

> Sincerely,
> Chester

January 30, 1969

Dear Chester,

Sorry I can't help you on the Chicago end. I don't know a lawyer there, yet there must be at least half a million of them. I've not been back in touch with Tony regarding this. When I last talked to him he said he would write suggesting that you get an attorney in Chicago.

Clarence Cooper in many ways reminds me of Chester Himes. He's prolific—sixteenth book out soon. He's a brother. Ex-junkie, ex-alkie, time here and there. He's got lots of Himeslike soul. Not many brothers know about him to bother to get to know him. I think Gwen would like you very much, really. We've been reading about the happenings in Spain; how do they fix you? How long is the exception or suspension of some constitutional rights to be? I agree with you completely about the Spanish brother; he is a bitch.

Let me get down to some more business with you. I heard sometime ago that you were working on an autobiography. You mentioned it in your last letter. A friend asked me to write to you on his behalf. The friend is Charles F. Harris, a black editor who was at Doubleday and now is at Random House. I've known him about eight years, coming to it slowly and cautiously. I like him very much; we think alike, and I've promised to do a book for a new series he's starting. I'd like this to be between you and me; Roz Targ doesn't have to enter the picture yet. Harris is extremely interested in your autobiography. He wants to buy it, but he first wants to know if you've contracted for it yet. Next, a general idea of how much you want for it, so he can put the facts on the table at Random. He's also willing to travel to Spain to talk with you about it. Let me fill you in some more. I think I can say Harris and I have worked hard spearheading some kind of cooperation between black writers, particularly the younger guys. If we ever get the chance to review each other, for example, no harsh words. We steer guys to publishers, talk with them about their problems; we steer them to numerous teaching jobs that've proliferated. In short, we're trying to create a new kind of interchange between black artists (it goes among painters too) that hasn't been experienced here before. Another example: I'm putting together a series of black biographies for Roger Straus for teenagers; I match the writers with the subjects. Harris is doing a book for me on William Monroe Trotter. It's a whole great new thing; the jealousy bag is over. So, I'd like to hear from you about your autobiography and pass it on to Harris. We're all fine here, Adam growing every day, etc. Lori sends regards.

John

Chester Himes
C/ Duque de Zaragoza, 2
Alicante, Espana

6 February 1969

Dear John,

Thanks for your last letter and the one before giving Jean's telephone number; I've written your friend Burton asking him for the name of a Chicago attorney, and I think things will work out alright.

I'm glad to see by this envelope that this is "Human Rights Year," but what are all those birds; why are some brown, some red, and some black? No white birds? And where are they all flying in such a hurry? And last, what have all these birds got to do with human rights? Reminds me of the descriptive copy for the Dell paperback for my book *Run, Man, Run,* which I have protested loudly and clearly, by the way. They go on talking about, "She had grown up in the streets of Harlem . . . singing was her racket, but men were her trade. . . . She never discriminated . . . etc." What she? Who are they talking about? I wrote a book about a psychotic white detective killing two brothers and trying to kill a third. And here they go putting down this shit about some black sister of their mind. I find this all very confusing in my old age.

I'm glad to learn of Clarence Cooper. All the best for him. Tell him just watch out for "them," but I'm sure he knows this.

All we know about what is happening in Spain is what we read in foreign newspapers that are allowed into the country. Most foreign newspapers have been banned for the past week; therefore, we don't know a damned thing. But everything looks just the same; the people haven't changed—superficially anyway—the weather is just the same. But I suppose somebody must be getting hurt, and all the hurters must be loose.

That is very exciting news about your friend Charles Harris at Random House and the big plan for interchange between black artists; and good news about your series of biographies for Roger Straus. I've always felt that Roger Straus is a very sympathetic guy but not very strong, but I've never cared much at all for Random House. But that is beside the point; I'm very happy to find our brothers getting into high places.

As far as my autobiography goes, I don't know when I will finish it, if ever. After I work on it a month or two I get extremely bored and also extremely discouraged by the thought no one will believe it anyway if I tell it straight. On the other hand, Roz already has a contract to handle all rights, if and when I ever write it. But anyway, that won't be soon, for I have now commenced on the wildest and most defiant of my Harlem series, which will wind it up and kill off my two detectives. So you can see, I'm not particularly interested in my autobiography at the moment. Anyway, all my autobiography—if I do write it—will do is make white people the world over feel foolish and vindictive. Tell Harris I'm sorry.

Lesley joins me in sending warmest regards to you, Lori, and Adam.

Chester

—§—

Chester Himes
C/ Duque de Zaragoza, 2
Alicante, Espana

10 February 1969

Dear John,

Sometime when you and Lori, or either one of you, are in a supermarket, will you look at the label of a cat food called Treat and take down the name and address of the manufacturing company for me. When we were in New York year before last we found a cat food of a mixture of fish and liver made by Treat that our cat would eat—which is the only cat food I have ever known him to eat. When we are in France we feed him on canned colin that has the trade name of Pom Pom Rouge, which costs about thirty-five cents a can, and usually we take along about fifty cans when we go to other countries. Our cat has always been very difficult about his food; rather than eat anything he doesn't like he will starve himself to death. He will eat most beef liver, and he ate some fresh fish we found in Amsterdam, but he doesn't care for this soft Spanish liver, and he won't eat any of the fish. So if I get the address of the manufacturers of Treat I am going to order him a case or two.

Which makes me think of the other inconveniences in Spain. If it wasn't that I have to live here, literally, because of the prohibitive cost of living everywhere else, I would not be here. But with what little money I earn I have to live here or live the life of a beatnik. Anyway, my health is so delicate I couldn't undergo the rigors of that kind of life anyway.

I have been thinking again of the program you and Harris have cut out for yourselves—that is, creating some kind of organization of black writers. Of course, as you know, the success of this venture depends in great part on the goodwill of whitey, and as I grow older I'm coming more and more to the conclusion that whitey doesn't have any goodwill. That's a pity too, because his hand is the hand that feeds me.

Anyway, if you remember about this Treat sometime, I will appreciate its address. However, there is no hurry. All best wishes for your project with Roger Straus. Which reminds me, do you ever hear anything about William Gardner Smith? I haven't heard a thing about him for at least two, perhaps three, years.

Lesley joins me in sending our warm regards to you and Lori and Adam.

Chester

Chester Himes
C/ Duque de Zaragoza, 2
Alicante, Spain

8 March 1969

Dear John,

I hope this finds you and your family well and in good spirits. I have just received a letter from your friend J. Anthony Burton, giving me the name and address of an attorney in Chicago who might be willing to represent me in my divorce action.

In the meantime my book *Blind Man* has been published, but I have only seen the chickenshit review in the *N.Y. Times Book Review*. I don't mind this joker playing the dozens and talking about my birthplace, which I haven't seen since I was four years old, nor even him calling me "prejudiced," although he doesn't state what he thinks I'm prejudiced against—or whom. I simply object to the fact he can't read.

I wrote him a personal letter when I first saw the review, pointing out that, in my opinion, the operational phrase in the preface was not "vulnerable soul brothers," as he claimed, but "unorganized violence." "Unorganized" is the key word. I had talked about unorganized violence on the Dutch television the week before I wrote this preface, and actually that led to my writing it. As I pointed out in my letter, I don't think there is any point in debating whether "soul brothers" are vulnerable or not. Everyone is vulnerable. The United States is vulnerable; the Soviet Union is vulnerable. It is just a matter of who is the most vulnerable. And in our case at this present time, violence is necessary. But *unorganized* violence is stupid, pointless, and makes us more vulnerable than we are. And if no one understands me, that will be no more than has always been the case.

By the way, I wrote to your friend Hoyt Fuller, stating my willingness to be interviewed at any time, and I received a letter from him asking if I would be willing to have my picture taken. This is where he began to lose me. But I wrote back to him stating that I was perfectly willing to have my picture taken, and I enclosed two glossy prints of me that had been made last summer that he could use if he wished. Then I had William Morrow send him an advance copy of *Blind Man*. (I suppose you received your copy all right.) Since then I haven't had a line from him. I must confess, I don't dig Mr. Fuller. He had written to the publicity director of Putnam's, although he had gotten my address from you. Why all this theater?

Anyway, I hope to soon get my divorce, and I sincerely thank you for your assistance.

Lesley joins me in sending our warmest regards to you, Lori, and Adam.

All best,

Chester

March 19, 1969

Dear Chester:

We held off writing, looking for your cat food company, which neither of us is able to do, unfortunately. Things here are as messy as ever. My mother's back in the hospital with her second coronary in just one and a half years; my oldest boy has his ass on his shoulder because I told him he wasn't shaping up worth a damn, even though he just turned twenty-one, and I'm getting sick and tired of having to work so hard for a living. That's the way I feel today. Tomorrow, we're driving to the country for a few days, so it'll be better. I read the review in the *Times,* and I read the book and agree with your views on unorganized violence. Did I not recognize Torun and her young soldier?[22] I haven't been in touch with Hoyt recently. Anyway, I had not known about all the correspondence you'd already had, and that, of course, makes me wonder just what old fucking bag he's into. Totally unorganized, but then anyone who works for John Johnson has got to be that way. I've been going through a series of luncheon meetings, boring as hell, with movie people about the last novel [*The Man Who Cried I Am*] and also the one coming out in May [*Sons of Darkness, Sons of Light*]. Talk about insincerity. Waste of time. The next one who calls gets the works on the phone; no point in me wasting my fucking time. You shouldn't get upset by anything American reviewers write. They are stupid, establishment-partisan, and totally untruthful about themselves, so they have to be untruthful about us. When was the last time you saw a book written by a black author reviewed by a black critic? See what I mean? Not that that would be any better, but it could be a start. I'm told that Connie and Ed [Pearlstein] have cut out for Mexico. At the end of this year, man, we're going somewhere too. This year has been a bitch, a carryover from last. I'm still in a cotton patch. Lori and Adam are well and send regards. Keep in touch.

John

---

22. Lori and I had met Torun, a silversmith designer, in New York.

Chester Himes
C/ Duque de Zaragoza, 2
Alicante, Spain

24 March 1969

Dear John,

Thanks for your letter. I'm sorry that you are having so much trouble with
your mother and your son, but at least your son has a great chance to
straighten up, if for no more reason than his youth. It becomes difficult to
overcome trouble as one grows older. It's the same with our cat. If he doesn't
learn to eat what he's got he's going to die. Speaking of Torun and Charles,
I had supposed they would be recognized as the prototypes for this scene,
and I had intended to change it, but there was so much to do on the damn
book before I could offer it for publication, I simply overlooked it. But it
doesn't seem that I will ever see Torun again unless by accident. Since she
moved to Wolfsburg (Volkswagen country) in Germany, she hasn't written
to anyone I know of, and seemingly she has broken all contacts with her
past. Anyway, she hasn't written to us nor replied to any of our letters. Have
Connie and Ed really left for Mexico? If not I'd like to ask you to telephone
Connie and have her find out the name and address of the manufacturer of
Treat cat food, which is sold in the supermarket across the street from the
Albert. I would have written her direct, but Connie and I have not been
on the best of terms since the publication of her book. She had made some
comments of me and my personal life that were untrue, and she attributed
some statements to me about James Baldwin, Ralph Ellison, and others that
I did not make, and I asked Putnam to have them deleted from the book
before publication. So we have not been on the best of terms. But I am glad
to know she has made it to Mexico, where she had always wanted to go to
live; and I have always liked Connie and still do. Speaking of Hollywood,
I gather that the producers are frantic about books about blacks, but they
don't like any that have yet been written. Hollywood wants something that
won't offend anyone yet will still offer some blacks for entertainment. And
that, in this world, is practically impossible. Nevertheless, they are serious
in their own way; they *do* want books, or anyway screenplays, about blacks.

I wonder why they don't employ blacks in great number and high pay to write them some screenplays like they do whites, but seemingly they haven't thought about this yet. Anyway, let me wish you the best of success for your book coming out in May, and if you let me know the title and publisher I'll ask the *New York Times Book Review* to review it, if you wish.

Lesley joins me in sending our best to all of you, and she'll write to Lori as soon as she gets time, but what with cooking, housekeeping, going to school, and typing my old manuscripts she hasn't much time.

Chester

March 30, 1969

Dear Chester:

You'll be pleased to know that Lori persevered, even if I didn't, and dug up Tabby Treat, Usen Products Company, Woburn, Massachusetts 01801. And I hope this information saves that cat. I'd be pleased if you did do the review. The novel is *Sons of Darkness, Sons of Light,* Little, Brown (for May). It's not a book that carries much, or at least not too much, of me; just a review of things. Little, Brown carries it as a lame duck book, on option, although I've already signed with Doubleday. I've been raising hell over the jacket and the jacket copy, which is a good indication that they haven't really sweated and don't intend to. Which is all right. I know they're going to sweat enough to get their money back, and that's all right too. Hollywood, Hollywood. Baldwin has been out there trying to do a screenplay of *Malcolm X,* but the word was that they slipped in a white writer and now Baldwin is out altogether. In any case, he had no business with it in the first place, I don't think, but that's Hollywood. I've finished a teenagers' biography of Wright, and I talked to Connie about a meeting of Wright and King, and she was kind enough to fill me in. There is a "critical study" out on Wright now by a guy named [Dan] McCall, whom I've never heard of. We have formed a black academy of arts and letters for the usual high purposes; I hope it comes to something. Connie and Ed left last week for Mexico, I've just learned from Lori. We are looking forward to early May, when we will move to the joint we have in the country until fall, returning now and again to the city for business. But I hope to finish a couple of large things there and get away from the bullshit down here and drink good mountain water and smell clean air and get good sleep. Should be great. Regards to Lesley; Lori understands; she's pretty much in the same bag.

John

Chester Himes
C/ Duque de Zaragoza, 2
Alicante, Spain

5 April 1969

Editor
The New York Times Book Review
Times Square
New York, N.Y. 10036
U.S.A.

Dear Sir,
This is a request to be assigned to write the review of John A. Williams's forthcoming novel, *Sons of Darkness, Sons of Light,* for the *New York Times Book Review.*

Thank you.

Sincerely yours,
Chester Himes

April 9, 1969

Dear John,

Thanks for the name of the manufacturer of Tabby Treat and all the other news in your letter. Re: Jimmy Baldwin, he shouldn't feel bad about his screenplay effort; Hollywood never uses the first screenplay by an inexperienced screen playwright.

Hope you have a quiet, peaceful, and productive summer vacation in the country. We will perhaps go to Paris for the summer.

Lesley joins me in sending you and your family best regards.

Chester

The New York Times
Book Review
Times Square, New York, N.Y. 10036

April 10, 1969

Mr. Chester Himes
Calle Duque de Zaragoza, 2
Alicante
Spain

Dear Mr. Himes:

Thank you for writing me.

I wish I could send you John Williams's novel for review, but alas it had been assigned elsewhere before I heard from you.

Maybe there will be something else that you would like to do.

With best regards,
Francis Brown
Editor

April 11, 1969

Dear Chester:

I do hope the *Times* will get up off its ass and let you review *Sons*.

Things here seem to be popping all over the place, and best of all is that Charles Harris and I—I mentioned him before to you—have planned a pocketbook-sized magazine. It is called *Amistad,* in memory of the famous old slave ship that the slaves took over. It's designed for the forever proliferating black studies courses in the colleges and high schools around the nation. I say pocketbook-sized, when I really mean a softcover book format. Since Harris is at Random House, he felt that we should give them first crack at it—and they gobbled it up, much to the dismay of several other publishers who wanted it. To be short then, Random House is backing us, two issues at a time, which was our idea, and a good one, I think.

For either the first issue, which comes out next February, or the second, and we're aiming for the first, I'd like to come over for four or five days and interview you about your work of the past, for the future, other writers you've known, black and white, your opinions of them, and, finally, Chester Himes's philosophy or view of just about everything.[23] You mentioned that you were thinking of going to Paris for the summer. I'd have to catch you before then or put it off until fall. What's your schedule? Would you let me do it? What would you charge us? By the way, do you have C. L. R. James's address?[24] Do let me know. We're all fine here and hope you are too, both of you.

Regards,
[John A. Williams]

---

23. The five-hour interview was audiotaped over three days and is reprinted in its entirety in the appendix. Besides the Himes interview, the first issue of *Amistad* also included works by Vincent Harding, C. L. R. James, Ishmael Reed, Addison Gayle, Jr., Calvin Hernton, Oliver Jackman, Verta Mae Grosvenor, and George Davis.
24. C. L. R. James was something like an elder statesman—author, patrician, writer, politician. He had once been married to Connie Pearlstein.

71

Chester Himes
C/ Duque de Zaragoza, 2
Alicante, Espana

15 April 1969

Dear John,

I am enclosing my reply from the *Times.*

It is good news about *Amistad;* your friend Charles Harris seems to be doing excellent work at Random House and all over. It is a good time, I think, for a black review to appear on the scene. Johnson could have done something with the *Negro Digest,* but it seems Johnson Publications can't catch up with the times.

I will be very happy to see you at any time. I will be here in Alicante until the end of next month—May. I will be very happy to see you before then if you wish. The trouble is we don't have space to put you up, this apartment is so small, but we have all the time in the world. If you do come and wish to stay in a hotel, I will book reservations for you. Too bad our house is not finished; it will not be finished until the first of October—if then. Anyway, work on it has been going on—off and on—for about a month, and we have been promised the roof will be on before we leave. We will stay the month of June—and maybe longer—with Mrs. Jean MacKellar, 29 Avenue Raymond-Croland, Plessis Robinson, 92 France, which is a suburb of Paris; and at the end of June we will go to London for the English publication of *Blind Man.*

If you come next month I will let you read a carbon copy of the first volume of my autobiography, if you wish, titled *The Quality of Hurt.* Roslyn will have the original. I have also been working on the most violent story I have ever attempted, about an *organized* black rebellion that is extremely bloody and violent, as any such rebellion must be, but unfortunately came unstuck. Anyway, I'm not near finished with it—and then on the other hand it might never be published.

I don't know C. L. R. James's address offhand. Too bad you didn't get it from Connie before she left for Mexico; she still keeps up a correspondence with him. Anyway, you might write the editor of the *Sunday Times Weekly*

Review, Thomson House, 200 Gray's Inn Road, London WC1; I feel sure they have it. And the *Sunday Times* always replies promptly.

It is good to hear from you and learn that things are going well, and I hope *Amistad* will be a great success.

Lesley joins me in sending warmest regards to you, Lori, and Adam.

All best,
Chester

23 April 1969

Dear Chester:

Both Harris and I are delighted that you will do the interview! We both feel that in order to lock up the first issue, I should do the interview as soon as possible. First issue's for October; I might have told you February, but that's the second. I don't know why you didn't set a fee; we would have had to strain for it, anyway. We can talk about it once I'm there.

Since Lori and I have been under much pressure lately, I decided that we'd both come for about five days, from May 10–15 or close to that time. You might reserve a double for us in a quiet hotel, one that's an American Express charge joint. Lori really deserves something special, and I'd like her to have it for this little while. We will not be bringing the baby.

I'd like very much to look at the carbon of the first volume of your autobiography; who knows but what we can help it along, as it should be helped. My plan is to bring a tape recorder, and we can walk and talk at your convenience. I'll also bring a couple of cameras and will try to dig up the prints of the shots we took when you and Lesley were here.

We did manage to get in touch with C. L. R. James, and he's doing a piece for us on the economics of the slave trade. The first issue should be a motherfucker!

As for Francis Brown at the *Times,* I believe he's a liar. The books aren't

73

even ready yet. In a week or so.

I'd better get this off. Will write again when things are tightened down.
Regards to Lesley and the cat.

John

-§-

Chester Himes
C/ Duque de Zaragoza, 2
Alicante, Spain

26 April 1969

Dear John,

Received your letter today, and Lesley and I are delighted that you will
bring Lori. I must tell you that Alicante is a chickenshit little village of great
pretensions, and as far as I can find out it doesn't have any hotels that are
quiet. There are only four class A hotels in town, the quietest of which is the
Residencia Palace, but they don't accept American Express credit cards and
charge accounts. Only the Carleton—the most expensive hotel—and the
Residencia Bernia accept American Express credit cards. I think the noise
around the Carleton would be prohibitive, so I booked you a room at the
Residencia Bernia, but there is a big amateurish night club in the vicinity
called Pigalle, and I suspect it is noisy too. However the manager has given
me a room for you that he swears is not noisy, but I would advise you to
bring ear-stoppers if you have trouble sleeping. Otherwise it is an acceptable
place, owned by a Swiss corporation I think, and it is just around the corner
from us.

Before I forget it let me ask you to bring one of those inexpensive roller
clothes brushes for Lesley, and I will pay you for it. She has so much trouble
with Griot's hair.

I suppose you will make the last lap of your trip either from Madrid or

Barcelona by a small plane to Alicante. If you arrive in the daytime—any time before 8:30 p.m.—I will pick you up at the airport. However I don't drive at night other than in extreme emergencies.

I'm glad you got in touch with C. L. R. James. I think you should talk to him about Richard Wright if you get the chance.

I suspected the editor of the *New York Times Book Review* was lying. Like *Time* magazine, the *NY Times* has a long history of ill will for me. When I write the second volume of my autobiography I'm going to take dead aim for both of them; but I'm just lying in ambush now.

Anyway, we'll be in correspondence again before you come.

Lesley joins me in sending best regards to you, Lori, and your Adam.

Chester

P.S. I didn't set a fee because I have a tendency to exaggerate; you can just pay me the customary fee you will pay everyone.

—§—

May 1, 1969

Dear Chester:

We are ready. The Residencia Bernia sounds fine, and we are looking forward to getting settled in it for a few days. We will bring a roller brush and a few cans of Tabby Treat cat food. I met Francis Brown yesterday at a party, and it was a standoff; he knows what he knows, and I know what I know. It's all one of those New York games.

We're leaving here the 9th of May, to London. From there we'll take a direct flight to Alicante, arriving at 3 p.m. via BEA.

Amistad will send you a check for $125 at the end of May. We've established that interview fee, which is small, we know, because that for now is about all we can make on our budget. We will plan our schedule, or it is already planned for us, to leave Alicante on the 14th or perhaps the 13th, to spend at least a day in Barcelona. We'll be leaving from Barcelona, back to New York, on the 15th. Hoping you can meet us at three.

Regards,
John

May 18, 1969

Dear Chester:

So we're back, and just getting the hours returned to normal. Of course, we arrived back in the middle of a mess with the mail and lugging the baby's things back home and getting ready to leave for the country on Wednesday. Today, Sunday, is the first day we feel nearly normal.

We thank you and Lesley for your wonderful hospitality while we were there, and I thank you even more for your cooperation. Within the week, Lori will start taking the material off the tape, and I'll push things together, write an introduction for the interview, and we'll get a carbon off for your approval. I hope within the week at least to get your check off as well. We are now wrestling over the wording of one sentence in our contract with Random House, but no problem.

I finished reading your autobiography on the plane, that horrible, crowded plane. We almost ran into a truck while landing at the airport and had to make an emergency return to the air on full power. But we made it. I think it is a fine, fine book. Powerful, extremely human, unbelievably frank. It is the kind of book *men* or a *man* would write if he is worthy of the title. The affair with Willa I think is the most moving document I've ever read of a black and white affair; Lesley is quite right; it does move one to tears. It covers so much ground, yet it ends still in the early fifties. Your descriptions of Wright, [Robert] Graves, Bill G. Smith, French and Spanish life seem to me to be without peer; I can think of nothing else I've read or seen or experienced myself that comes close. I am, quite frankly, ecstatic about the book. I've passed it on to Harris for an undercover reading. Offhandedly, he asked what price you were thinking of, and I said, "At least $25,000."

Perhaps I am speaking out of turn, but do let me know. I want you to get lots of money, so we can visit you again!

Hope you had a good visit with Hoyt. He is a pretty savvy man of letters with some minor pretensions, but he remains solid, concerned, and influential. Hope you enjoy the summer, and we look to hear from you.

Lori and Adam send greetings. I've asked Lynn Caine to send you the new novel, *Sons of Darkness, Sons of Light,* and the other, *The Man Who Cried I Am,* which she should have done almost two years ago.

Best regards,
John

Chester Himes

22 May 1969

Mr. John A. Williams
South Hill Road
R.D. No. 1
Worcester, N.Y.
U.S.A.

Dear John,
This is to inform you that, beginning 28 May 1969, my address will be as follows:

Chester Himes
c/o Jean MacKellar
29 Avenue Raymond Croland
92 Plessis Robinson
France

Sincerely,
Chester

We enjoyed seeing you and Lori. Best to Adam.

Chester Himes

c/o Jean MacKellar

29 Avenue Raymond Croland

92 Plessis Robinson

France

May 22, 1969

Dear John,

Thanks for the letter. We're glad that you and Lori got home safe and sound, even though "in the middle of a mess." We enjoyed your visit tremendously; we hadn't seen anyone to talk to since Roslyn was here on New Year's Day.

Needless to say, I am tremendously pleased that you like my autobiography. As you know, I have great esteem for your judgment, and since it is my autobiography written in a casual relaxed manner, I needed very much to have the opinion of someone whom I respect.

Roslyn knows you have a copy; I wrote her and told her you were taking a copy back with you and that you had recommended that I show it to Charles Harris and Roger Straus, which I asked her to do. Anyway, she knows that I am not happy with Morrow. And I also put a $25,000 minimum advance royalty price on the book, mostly because there is no need of talking to editors unless they are serious. I have been played around with by enough editors—and they are still doing it.

I am looking forward to seeing the piece for *Amistad.*

And I would very much like your new novel, *Sons of Darkness, Sons of Light,* and also *The Man Who Cried I Am.*

Hoyt was by and turned out to be a very polite and intelligent young man. He spoke highly of you and said he had stopped over in New York to look for you. I showed him the prospectus for *Amistad,* and he was very interested and impressed and no doubt surprised also.

We're in the midst of packing. I got the radiator cap from Madrid a week later after an interminable comedy of errors. Anyway, it was the right kind—thank heavens.

Lesley joins me in sending our best to you and Lori and a big kiss for

Adam—or is he at the age when he doesn't like kisses from strange people?

Best wishes,
Chester

-§-

Chester Himes
29 Avenue Raymond Croland
92 Plessis Robinson
France

5 June 1969

Dear John,

We have now arrived in this city of exorbitant prices and French
exaggeration, and it is colder than the ass of a polar bear. Your books *The
Man Who Cried I Am* and *Sons of Darkness, Sons of Light* have arrived with
a note from Anita Kerman of the publicity department, and we are reading
them. Thanks for having them sent to me.

Lesley says she hopes Lori received her glasses all right and that they fit
and are what she wanted. I bought a pair of reading glasses in Alicante (not
at the same place Lori got hers), and the oculist got the lenses mixed up and
put the right lens on the left eye and vice versa, and I had to have the lenses
changed when we stopped over in Barcelona. I hope nothing like that has
happened to Lori's glasses. But the frames were all right.

Lesley joins me in sending our best to both of you, and we hope Adam
is well and in fine spirits and enjoying the country.

All best,
Chester

Your letter just arrived a few minutes after I had sealed this up. We're
glad to hear that you are enjoying life in the country and the "intoxicating
mountain air," which is most unlike this cold, wet air here that is good

only for trees and Frenchmen. I'm glad to hear the situation is improving at Doubleday, and everywhere else I presume. In my day if an editor was called a "nigger lover," the editor who uttered those pleasing words would have been given a medal. Don't worry about Roslyn; you can talk to her if you wish. Morrow likes the book, but what kind of offer they'll make I have no idea. Lesley says tell Lori she's glad the glasses arrived in good shape and are satisfactory. And give Adam a kiss from us if he consents.

Anyway, we'll be here all this month and perhaps all summer?

Best,

Chester

P.S. That's a damn good picture on the back of *The Man Who Cried I Am.*

Chester Himes
c/o Jean MacKellar
29 Avenue Raymond Croland
92 Plessis Robinson
France

8 June 1969

Mrs. Lynn Deming
Editor
Doubleday & Company
277 Park Avenue
New York, N.Y. 10017

Dear Mrs. Deming,
Thank you for the copy of *Yellow Back Radio Broke-Down* by Ishmael Reed. I consider it a work of art, and I consider Mr. Ishmael Reed a genius.

Mr. Reed has created a new form of satire to replace the old obsolete forms of the past, and he has created new definitions to replace the old worn-out definitions.

Mr. Reed's narrative ignites a blaze in the intellect, and no doubt his prose has added years to my life. I say more power to Mr. Reed.

Yours sincerely,
Chester Himes

Farrar, Straus & Giroux, Inc.
NOONDAY PRESS BOOK PUBLISHERS
19 Union Square West, New York 3, New York, Oregon 5-3000, CABLE:
FARRARCOMP
OFFICE OF THE PRESIDENT

June 11, 1969

Dear Rozie:

I am afraid you were right, and the Himes autobiography doesn't work—at least for us. Thanks for giving us a look.

Hope to see you soon.

Best,
As ever,
Roger W. Straus, Jr.
RWS: pm
Mrs. Roslyn Targ
Franz Rorch Associated
425 East 57th Street
New York, New York
BC: John Williams

FARRAR, STRAUS & GIROUX, INC. Book Publishers
NOONDAY PAPERBACKS
Office of the President

June 11, 1969

Dear John:

I am sad about this, for there should be a hell of a good book by Himes on Himes, but not the way he has done it. Thanks, nonetheless, for the tip.

I am sending you a couple of new FSG books separately, which I think you will enjoy for summer reading.

Best,
As ever,
  R
Roger W. Straus, Jr.
RWS:pm
Mr. John Williams
South Hill Road
R. D. 1
Worcester, New York
19 Union Square West,
New York 3, New York,
10003
Telephone Oregon 5-3000,
Cable Farrarcomp

Chester Himes
c/o Jean MacKellar
29 Avenue Raymond Croland
92 Plessis Robinson
France

13 June 1969

Dear John,

I liked *Sons of Darkness, Sons of Light;* it is a compact definitive story
of the dilemma of the black middle class in the certain uprising of the
black masses. It is a good book; the portrayals are clear and authentic,
the soul searching is valid, and the delineation of the domestic issues is
compassionate but exact. It is a good book.

But for my money, *The Man Who Cried I Am* is *the* book, like *the* man.
It is a blockbuster, a hydrogen bomb; it is by far the greatest book, the most
compelling book, ever written about THE SCENE—*the* scene, *scene,* man.
You're the only man whom I ever knew, writer or layman, black or white,
who knows the inside of the scene, the other side. This is a book white
people are not ready to read yet; neither are most black people who read.
But it is a milestone in American literature, the only milestone (legitimate
milestone) produced since *Native Son.* All the others have been just so much
shit—chickenshit. I know this reaction of mine can't mean too much to a
black writer who must earn his bread through his writing. But all that is
part of the SCENE, in the SCENE, as you have written. Besides which, and
where I should have begun, it is a damn beautifully written book.

Of course, guys like me will dig some of the characters—Harry Ames
and family, the black faces in the background of the government—Max I
can guess (who else has so much information)—but Roger sounds like our
"Man" in Amsterdam.

You have them all there, individually and collectively, their women
and their hypes, and, most important of all, so authentically. You have all
the places, the atmosphere, the geography, the weather, and the faces more
accurately than an atlas. I wonder how many readers know this, or will ever
know it. All anyone's got to do to know it is to read history and remember

Hiroshima or Dachau (forgive my spelling) or Sharpesville (forgive my bad memory) or many other current events.

I could keep on and on about this book, but I would just find myself saying what the book has already said—and much better too.

Lesley joins me in sending best regards to you and Lori and Adam.

Chester

June 13, 1969

Dear Lesley,

This is a terribly belated thank-you note, but as you can imagine, we've been running since we got back. Not literally, although the week that we spent in New York before moving up to the country was very hectic. But we've been busy in other ways up here—on the house, the grounds, entertaining weekend guests, etc. And then in every spare moment I had (i.e., when Adam was napping or down for the night) I'd be at the tape recorder and typewriter, transcribing John's interview with Chester. Toward the end I ran into some trouble with one of the cassettes, which apparently got tangled and I couldn't play it back, but with much fiddling we got it working, and I finally finished it yesterday. It ran ninety-five pages triple spaced. John has spent the last two days going over it again, catching whatever I missed, and reorganizing it. I shall type up the finished copy within the next few days. We're going to the city next week for a couple of days, and John will take a copy to Chuck Harris, and after they've had a chance to go over it and decide on a final version, John will send a copy off to Chester, probably in a few weeks.

We had a lovely time in Barcelona with our old friends the Levines and friends of theirs who also came up from Malaga for a few days. Although I hated for the trip to be over, by the end of our stay in Spain I was getting homesick for Adam, so I wasn't too unhappy about returning. He had fared very well in our absence and apparently hadn't missed us one bit. He'd been too busy with his three cousins and their dog. But his face did light up when we drove up to the house, and he dropped everything and ran toward us so excitedly he naturally fell flat on his face. It was a happy reunion.

The glasses, as you know, arrived intact, and the lenses were correct. The only trouble is that they don't fit on my face as they did in the shop. They must have stretched when the glass was being put in. I haven't been able to take them in to be fixed here, but I've put some little rubber bands in at the joints, which tightens them somewhat. I'll have it taken care of next week when we're home. They arrived the day after we got to the country. Perfect timing.

I must tell you that I read Chester's autobiography in three (or was it two) days—a record for me these days. The only chance I get to read is at bedtime usually, but then I'm usually so tired I quit after an hour. But once I began this, I got so engrossed I couldn't put it down. I read for hours the first night and finally made myself put out the light because it was so late and I knew Adam would wake me bright and early. The next evening I put everything else aside (including the tapes) and began reading as soon as Adam went to bed, and I didn't stop until I'd finished. I find myself terribly impatient for volume 2. I hope Chester is hard at work on it.

My niece, who is twenty-one, is spending two months working in London this summer, from June 19 on, and then spending one month traveling. I don't know what your plans are for London, but if you find you'll be there for several weeks during this time and if you think you might have a free afternoon sometime, I'd like for her to meet you. I don't have her address yet, but I can send it on to you if it's feasible for you.

I've come to the end of this letter, and I almost forgot to say thank you for your warm hospitality. You really made my brief stay in Alicante a memorable one. I hope it won't be too long before I can reciprocate. I think both you and Chester would really like it up here. It's beautiful country, peaceful and secluded (just Chester's cup of tea). I hope your stay in Paris is a good one and that you settle happily in your new home in the fall. All our best to you.

Lori

June 20, 1969

Dear Chester:

Before I forget, could you please send a complete Himes bibliography or copy of same, including articles, etc., and years of publication.

We have your letters, and I thank you for your comments. Lynn Caine, whom you know, should have sent that goddamn book almost two years ago. The publicity people are all the same. Your publicity people at Morrow didn't send *Blind Man* automatically; I had to call. They're all full of shit. Ishmael Reed is beside himself with joy that you liked his *Yellow Back Radio*. *Sons* is a tired book, one done to keep financially afloat when it became apparent that *The Man* wasn't going to bring in any money. And it didn't; far, far less than what I hoped for and what we needed. Fuck it.

Roger Straus sent me a note saying that he was not taking your autobiography; he sent the note on a carbon to Roz Targ in which he said, and I quote, "You were right, Roz." Now what the hell does that mean? I haven't spoken to Roz.

Harris, who has by now sent you the teeny little honorarium for the interview, hasn't yet dealt with Random but will in a couple of weeks. A friend, Ed Doctorow, who headed Dial briefly (and offered me a job there) will be up to spend a couple of days with us. I've told him about the book, and he's anxious to read it. Ed is starting a new publishing firm and, of course, is looking for books. Otherwise, Chester, Lori, and I got ninety-seven pages out of the interview, and I've edited it down and Lori's retyping it. When it's all finished we'll pack it off to you for approval, spelling of names, and just to see how you like it. Tomorrow night we're trying out the paella pan for the first time. By the way: you know the Supreme Court ruled in favor of Powell.[25] Isn't it ironic that a black man is the one to bring the branches of government into conflict and rip this mother apart? But then all

---

25. The Reverend Adam Clayton Powell ("Keep the faith, baby"), U.S. representative from New York, had been barred from his seat in the House because he was being sued for a libel he had paid off years earlier and for misuse of funds. He regained and then lost his seat to Charles Rangel. Powell died in 1972.

of us have known this for some time. Whites try not to know it. Lori and Adam and I send the best of cheer and regards.

John

P.S. For the magazine we're very interested in seeing [Frantz] Fanon's "My Treatment of Violence," which you said his widow has. Could you put her in touch with me? Appreciate it.

Chez Jean Mackellar
29, Ave Raymond Croland
Plessis Robinson 92
FRANCE

June 20, 1969

Dear Lori,
Many thanks for your letter. I'm so glad to hear you are enjoying the country and that Adam is in fine spirits.

I'm sorry to hear you are having problems with your glasses, but it probably isn't too serious. In fact, you might be luckier than Chester—they really bombed with his, but it wasn't the same optician. He ordered a pair of reading glasses and they seemed to be fine until he took them off to walk around and then he felt slightly dizzy. So, when we got to Barcelona we went to another optician to have the lenses checked, and the man said that the optician in Alicante had mixed the lenses up—he had, in fact, put the left eye glass in the right eye and vice versa. Can you imagine such incompetence? Another 500 pesetas down the drain. *What* can one do?

Last May when we came to France, there was a revolution. This year we arrived at the above address and nearly lost everything when our friend's beautiful house was flooded by the main sewer in the district. Filthy muddy sewer water came flooding in the washbasins, toilets, baths, showers, etc., covering the expensive wooden floors, soaking everything and smelling foul.

With the help of her Spanish maid and gardener, her son, Chester, and myself, the house is more or less back to normal, but it was a frightening ordeal and could have been a total disaster for us all if the house had not been empty at the time. Other people in the district have lost cars, bedding, clothing, cookers, washing machines, and what have you. Our car was very safe because the garage and the upper part of the house were not touched. Of course, it's a sheer disgrace that the sewer should be so small and so easily blocked . . . typically French. The firemen arrived with an electric machine to pump water out of the basement, but after spending two hours trying to make the machine work they were unsuccessful. We finally got our friend's lodger to get it going—six hours later. I suppose the very fact that it was Sunday didn't help the situation. I'm having a hell of a time typing because all the tips of my fingers are sore from mopping and cleaning the wood, so excuse the worse than usual typing.

It's good to hear that you have not had too much trouble hearing Chester's voice—it can be difficult to understand sometimes. We are looking forward to seeing it.

Chester has been enjoying John's books enormously, but, unfortunately, I have no time to read anything. I will settle down to it when we come back from London.

We are staying at the Durrants Hotel, George Street, London, W.1. I know that both Hodder & Staughton and Panther Books will be demanding a great deal of Chester's time for the newspapers, etc., but if you can get in touch with your niece in time (we will be there from the 24th–1st July) do have her call me. It's better to just use Himes when calling—I've almost forgotten that I had another name, I so seldom have occasion to use it.

We will be seeing Melvin on Saturday morning when we go along to pick up our pictures, etc., which are still hanging on our old apartment walls.[26] Apparently he is in town for a week or so to see his old friends, etc. His girlfriend told me on the phone that he had been working recently for

---

26. Melvin Van Peebles, the filmmaker.

TV in the U.S.A. I really don't know what he has been doing, but perhaps we'll find out soon.

Please give a big kiss to Adam from us both and all the very best to you and John.

> *Love,*
> *Hasta la vista et*
> *Abientot,*
> *Lesley*

June 30, 1969

Dear Chester:

First off, we received the glasses, and they were in very good shape. Lori sends her heartfelt thanks to Lesley for her kindness. We're situated here in the country, looking at the mountains and breathing this intoxicating mountain air. This week I'll settle back into the work routine at the typewriter. I've spent the past few days taking care of details around the house; now I can spend the bulk of the time where it should and ought to be spent. An editor at Doubleday called my editor a "nigger lover," and I insisted that he be fired or I would leave Doubleday. They fired him. Effective this month. It appears, on the surface at least, that some things have changed since 1945 and *If He Hollers*. I've been in touch with Roger Straus and Harris about your autobiography. I don't mean or intend to usurp Roz Targ's function, and I hope she doesn't feel that way. In any case, I hope to have dinner with Roger in about three weeks when we are back in the city for a couple of days. Lori is working diligently on the tapes. I've already written an introduction, but I'm holding off sending it until I can send you the interview as well. Sometimes Adam will consent to be kissed by strangers; hell, sometimes he will even take kisses from parents! Listen. We really had a great time in Alicante; you and Lesley were most gracious.

Coming out of New York in such a rush, you set just the right kind of pace for us. I had hoped that by now your check would be ready from Random House, but we are still ironing out some minor contract details. Hopefully, this month. They've managed to slow up many of our planned moves. I haven't been paid my expenses for the trip yet. But once we get going, it's going to be great. We all send fondest regards.

John

Chester Himes
c/o Jean MacKellar
29 Avenue Raymond-Croland
92 Plessis Robinson
France

8 July 1969

Dear John,

I've got the copies of the interview, and I am going through your version strictly to correct my statements as to fact, but I am not attempting any editing as such, first because it would be too much of a job for me to undertake at this time and then you might wish to let some of the original "Himes" phrasing stay to lend atmosphere. Also, I am somewhat beat, first by the American white woman hysteria of this cracker bitch whom we were staying with (and where we still have to receive our mail) until we went to London and were vivisected by the English press and also by Roslyn's disappointment over the rejections she has got on my autobiography. Anyway, I have decided that if Harris wants to publish it as it stands and makes a reasonable offer, he may have it, and I will write to Roslyn to the effect. Otherwise, I will just sit on it.

Aside from the special phrasings of my sentences, the interview reads very well, and I think it is wonderfully partitioned.

Lesley joins me in sending you and Lori best regards, and keep the chin up—crackers are crackers everywhere, north, south, east, west, at home and abroad.

All best,
Chester

-§-

Chester Himes
c/o Jean MacKellar
29 Avenue Raymond Croland
92 Plessis Robinson
France

9 July 1969

Well, John,
This is some rough stuff and very revealing, and it makes me sad, I must confess. But I too think it has great historical value. But many of my sentences are incomprehensible and incoherent, and it will require much editing. I find that I am unable to help you much there, but I suppose that if one slashes it down to shape ruthlessly, it can be done. As I said in my previous letter, I have just corrected some of my statements as to fact, and I have tried to make some of my more incomprehensible statements more comprehensible. But that is all I am able to do. That and wish you all the best of luck on the job of editing.

Reading my thoughts over like this leaves me sort of staggered; but they are my own true thoughts and opinions for better or worse; they express the end product of my thinking on the "scene" at sixty years, and they won't change now.

In the P.S. of your covering letter you say, "Some may wish to know why you moved to Europe."

Well, the main reason I moved to Europe was the discrimination in the American publishing business. All I could do was write. I was an ex-convict; I didn't have a trade or profession. I could not get a job on any newspaper or magazine, black or white, in the U.S. All I could do to earn enough for food and shelter was work at some menial job, like porter, dishwasher, chauffeur, etc. I was getting old—forty-four. My age was also against me in getting any kind of employment. I made thousands of applications to publishers of newspapers, books, and magazines. I could not earn a living from my writing. The books that I had published would not support me. And most of my ideas for new books were unacceptable in the U.S.—as they are even now. Obviously, I could not get a job on the faculty of any college, white or black. I left the U.S. because I felt I would have a better chance to survive in some other country. As I told many people in Paris during my first years, all I wanted to do was live—*to keep alive.* I suppose I could say that was my main reason for leaving America—just to keep alive.

Anyway, you have all my best wishes for the success of this interview and the success of the magazine *Amistad.*

Lesley joins me in sending best regards to you and Lori, and she says give Adam a big kiss from me.

Chester

-§-

July 14, 1969

Dear Chester:

First off, thanks for the speedy return of the interview material. We'll take care of the editing, and it will make history. We've been having some problems with Random House and *Amistad,* but they are finally ironed out, and so we'll go, as planned, with your interview, or part of it, in the first issue. We may have to run it in two issues.

I don't know if Ishmael Reed has told you or not, but he is as much a

fan of yours as I am, and it is extremely gratifying to me to discover that
so many of the younger writers know of and have read Chester Himes.
They want to know where he is, what he's up to. This "black revolution," or
whatever it is, has shocked them into life. They missed Wright and Hughes,
and Ellison gives them nothing but platitudes from what I hear, and they
are reaching desperately for roots—which means you. I don't think they're
reaching for the wrong reasons, either.

I thank you for the kind words on *The Man,* which remains my favorite
book; the new one, *Sons,* was one of those books you do to keep eating,
to keep in practice, and to test reaction. So far, according to Lori (I've
decided to stop reading reviews) the notices are coming in better than *The
Man,* which I thought would be the case, anyway. I'm sorry they tried to
take you apart in London; it becomes increasingly obvious that, although
we are writing in the same language, when we write or speak, there is
something white folks don't seem to understand. I believe that's why Roz
is having difficulty with your book. Harris is tied up in some Random
House hierarchy but has finished most of the book and likes it. He said
the white folks won't know what Chester's talking about; they want a black
autobiography, not one by a human being. Because he is being held up,
although I expect to hear from him next week—I'll see him in fact because
we have to go into the city for a few days—I've today mailed your carbon
to Ed Doctorow, who is a friend, former editor-in-chief and then publisher
of Dial, now forming his own company. He is extremely interested; if that
doesn't go through, I think the psychological next gambit would be for
me to approach my *female* editor at Coward-McCann. Females have great
sensitivities for *men.* In any case, don't count Random out; I'm just creating
a little storm here.

Adam was ill last week and we had to rush him to a hospital 50 miles
away, the best one in the area. He turned out to have roseola, a baby's
measles, high temperature and all. This week, though, he seems well on
the road back. His two brothers drove down yesterday from Syracuse, or
rather, Saturday, and it was great to have all three here. Lori sends greetings;
she is well, although, like me, exhausted from Adam's illness. Your letter of
the 9th was very moving and much as I thought the case was; I am deeply

appreciative of your sending it. You will allow me, just this once, to close my letter with love to you both.

John

Chester Himes
c/o Jean MacKellar
29 Avenue Raymond Croland
92 Plessis Robinson
France

19 July 1969

Dear John,

Thanks for your letter. It has cheered me up tremendously, and I'm getting to the place where I'm more and more subject to slip into spells of depression. I find these whites whom I have to deal with so motherfucking hypocritical that at times I just feel like taking a gun and going out shooting them all.

I got a nice note from Ishmael Reed, which was also encouraging.

I just recently read the review of *Sons* in *Time* magazine, and I understand what you mean by "black" autobiographies. The whites want to give us the field of black autobiographies for our share of the American literature. Nevertheless, for *Time,* the review of *Sons* was very good; and it had a few words in passing for your other books, which they shied away from reviewing. As I said before, *Sons* is a great book that introduces a new and very valid approach to the appraisal of black-white relations. If I hadn't read *The Man* just previously, I would say it was a very great book. But *The Man* is *the* book, and it can never be cast aside. Each year it will take on greater stature, because it is the story of our time, as much, if not more, than the space program, the nuclear bomb, the missiles. Because it is so devastatingly true. And in time, all people will realize this truth, and most intelligent people in the world will be startled to find that you stated it before it became common knowledge.

I agree with you about my autobiography; I think in the end only a white female editor will be willing to publish it, because in the editorial circles she will be the only one to understand what I'm saying.

I'm glad you have all your problems with Random House ironed out; and I can imagine that most of them stem from Random House regarding Ralph Ellison as the oracle of black writing and all black thought, and anything that doesn't follow the path of his platitudes is regarded as unmentionable. But they—like all the others—will soon find out what it's all about.

I'm glad to learn that Adam is over his crisis and that both Lori and you are recuperating from the exhaustion and the strain. We shall see all of you soon someplace; perhaps we will come to the States in the fall when they've finished making *Cotton.* And then the next year you will have to visit us on our "ranch" in Spain.

Lesley joins me in sending love to you both and kisses to Adam, who should be all over his roseola by the time this letter reaches you, because children recuperate quickly.

Chester

Chester Himes

22 July 1969

Dear John,

I have been thinking about a line from your letter: "He (Harris) said the white folks won't know what Chester's talking about. . . ." You can tell him I'm simply talking about the quality of hurt. Whites in America have hurt everyone they've touched. The white American male has hurt all nonwhites with whom he has come into contact, the strong have hurt the weak, the weak have hurt the weaker; he has hurt the black man seriously, but he has hurt his own white woman mate equally. And that is what I am talking about: the *peculiar and essential character* (Webster) of this hurt. Not only my hurt, but the hurt of this highly placed, highly educated, highly classed (a direct descendant of John Hancock, one of the signers of the Declaration of Independence) white woman who is the end product of his civilization. In her hurt, she comes to me, knowing I have been hurt by the same white man, for succor, for me to absorb her hurt, for sanctuary, for grace. The most important field of human activity is the love relation between male and female, because it is the only creative force given by a divine power to the human race, without which—regardless of all else the human race conceives—it cannot exist. And this alone is the criterion by which the importance of a man is judged. And in this judgment the American black man stands out superior to the American white man, because he holds the female—the mother of the human race—in greater reverence than the American white man; he is more tender, considerate, arduous, and infinitely more aware of the purpose of the woman on this earth. The white man has the wealth, the glory, the power, the acclaim, but the black man has the love and the capacity for love of the female of the species. And that, to my mind, is more important.

Chuck can tell the white folks that is what I'm talking about. See how that goes down.

All best,
Chester

Chester Himes
c/o Toutain
12, rue Abel Ferry
Paris 16.
France

30 July 1969

John A. Williams
South Hill Road
RD 1, Worcester
New York, 12197

Dear John,

This is to inform you that upon receipt of this letter my address will be as follows:

    c/o Toutain
    12, rue Abel Ferry
    Paris 16
    France

All best,
Chester

August 8, 1969

Dear Chester,

Been planning to write to you for a few days now. Just finished talking to Charles Harris, and he says that is some good and powerful stuff you have in your interview. But we knew that; that was the whole point. Ed Doctorow hasn't finished your book yet but is most impressed so far. Asked me what you'd think of some changes, etc., and I said he'd have to write to you when he's finished. The book hasn't finished with the Random House hierarchy yet. And I still have hole cards.

Yesterday I went to Cazenovia College for a talk, and there, one of the instructors for this special six-week session on "Black Excellence" had got from the local library, believe it or not, a copy of *Cast the First Stone.* You're one of the authors they're studying.

I see that you've changed addresses. Have you any word on how your house is coming in Javea? Y'know, it would be nice if you and Lesley came this fall. When you get tired of the city, you could hole up here in the country. There's the furnace and fireplace, lots of working room. (My study is the most complete room in the house.) The kitchen is in good shape, with a stove (bottled gas) that has an oven, a refrigerator and freezer, a washing machine and dryer, and complete peace.

I'm negotiating a movie deal on the last book, which is, as you said, an adequate book. It is distressing to me that the reviews have been so good on it, when I know that from the jump, it wasn't all that good. *The Man* was better. *Sons* was a tired book, done to stay in the money somehow. Ah, shit. You know all this.

Earlier I asked if you could put me in touch with Fanon's widow so I could pursue the possibility of using her late husband's piece "My Treatment of Violence." Any luck on that?

You know, for a couple of years I was worried about my middle son, who is a very good student and athlete and musician and all that—four scholarships, etc. He just didn't seem to be interested in girls. Then I read his journal a few weeks ago—he's a fantastic writer—and began to understand. Then last night he appeared at my talk. Casenovia is only 20 miles from Syracuse. He was with his advisor to the high school paper Dennis used to edit; a tall, handsome redhead gal; and his friend Spero, a Greek kid they call Zorba. The redhead was Dennis's girl, and all this time his friend Spero has been playing this game that Cathy was *his* girl so that Dennis's mother who, like any self-respecting Negro woman, demanded that her sons not bring into *her* family any white women. So Dennis, Spero, and this great teacher and Cathy (whose parents don't know) have been involved in this scene. God, what the fuck we do to ourselves and our children! The dates had been arranged through Spero, with Spero picking the girl up and all. Man, these kids are just too splendid. Well. It was refreshing, very refreshing. Everything here is cool, and we hope all goes well with you both.

Best regards,
[John]

Chester Himes
c/o Toutain
12, rue Abel Ferry
Paris 16

14 August 1969

Dear John,

Thanks for the long, chatty letter. There's no doubt that *Sons* will be a real financial success along with a critical success. You know those sons of bitches have to sooth their guilt about all the other books, even beginning way back with *Night Song*. Accumulated guilt. So they got to atone. Think that's going to let them off. But it ain't going to help them any when their sins catch up with them. When that old wagon comes loaded down with retribution, there is nothing going to help them. But it's good that it works for your benefit at the present. So don't be distressed. It's all normal behavior for the old racist establishment.

I talked to Julia Wright yesterday after I received your letter, and she told me that the piece Fanon did on violence (in my books and another's) was in reality a lecture, but it was mimeographed and distributed to some extent. But Fanon's widow has not been able to find any copies. But Julia said she would put me into direct contact with Mme. Fanon (whom she saw last month at the conference in Algiers), and I will put her into direct contact with you—or at least *Amistad* at Random House. Another angle is that Ellen is going to New York shortly, and I told her to contact either you or Charles Harris at Random House, and she can give you more information about Mme. Fanon.

It's strange that one can still find copies of *Cast the First Stone,* of which only a few copies were printed, and Roslyn has been looking all over for copies of *The Third Generation,* of which five thousand remainders were sold off—at least according to the publisher—in addition to two editions and certainly a great number of paperbacks.

Anyway, I'm glad to hear your son Dennis has come through. You shouldn't worry about things like that. As you say, most kids are splendid, and a hell of a lot of them shake their parents a little bit before taking shape. But that's only because parents are nervous. "Let's don't be nervous"—the French title of *The Heat's On.*

By the way, I met Bill Hutson recently, and he tells me he knew you well in Amsterdam.[27] It seems things are difficult for him at present in Paris, but I hope he'll pull through; he's a nice guy. Also I just received a letter from Phil Lomax, who writes: "Thanks for your best wishes on that story I didn't sell to Hollywood. I don't know where whosis got that bogus bit of scuttlebutt, but I'm as broke and as unsuccessful as I've ever been." Which isn't quite true, because I know his *Amsterdam after Dark* is selling well.

Thanks for the invitation to your farm in New York State, but we have to go back to Javea. The house is supposed to be finished at the end of September, and we must be there to watch how they do the finishing touches.

Good luck on your lectures. You must be in great demand now. Lesley joins me in sending love to you, Lori, and all the family.

Chester

---

27. Bill Hutson, an artist who lived in Europe for many years, returned to the States some time ago and is teaching at Franklin and Marshall College.

August 31, 1969

Dear Chester:

I've held off writing so I could give you word of the goings-on with *The Quality of Hurt.* Forget Random House; forget Ed Doctorow of Sidereal Press. They don't want it. Following our discussion of placing it in the hands of a female editor, I've done just that, sending it to Patricia B. Soliman, a senior editor at Coward-McCann. I don't know just how closely they're connected to Putnam, but it won't hurt for her to read it. I've also suggested that she reissue *Cast the First Stone,* which I've noticed was published by Coward-McCann.

Yes, we know Bill Hutson and thought he might be coming to New York this summer. We suggested that he wait until fall before doing any gallery hustling. Haven't heard from him since then. I like him fine, but like so many of our brothers over there, everything's tight while you're useful, then the hell with you. However, I plan to look him up if I get to Paris for some research later this year. Will let you know. You and Lesley must be getting very excited about the house. And here, we've got only another three weeks to go before moving back to the city. Life. We'll be at 35 W. 92nd Street *after September 26.* Everything else is cool, and we hope you two will be getting settled before long. Do not be put off on volume 2 of *Hurt* because these jerks don't know what's going on. Go on and do it, as I hope you are now. Phil Lomax has always been tight with a dollar and secretive about what he's up to. Looking forward to hearing from Julia Wright.

Regards as always,
[John]

P.S. Syracuse University has a manuscript collection and is interested in your papers. Are you interested in *them*? Please let me know.

Chester Himes
c/o Toutain
12, rue Abel Ferry
Paris 16

6 September 1969

Dear John,

It is always a joy to hear from you, even though the news is not always good.

As to *Quality of Hurt,* I don't think I would like for it to be submitted any more after Patricia Soliman at Coward-McCann. Most people in the trade know by now that you have a copy, and if they want to see it or talk about it let them come to you voluntarily. Anyway, I am in a discussion with my English publisher, Hodder & Stoughton, and they want to know if I'm willing to make some changes. As we haven't arrived as yet as to what changes they might want, I cannot answer them. But the fact is I do not mind making certain changes, and in fact I will make some on my own accord. I have wanted the American editors to be explicit—which so far none has. Because I see no point in changing the story of me and Willa; it is explicitly true, other than I omitted the fact that she is the direct descendant of John Hancock, one of the signers of the Declaration of Independence—which I shall insert before publication. If it is this part the editors want changed, then fuck them. Anyway, I would just not like for it to be submitted anymore. I will survive whether it is published or not.

Speaking of *Cast the First Stone,* I wonder if you can possibly get a copy for me at any cost and I will repay you. It is one of the books Hodder & Stoughton wish to consider of the deal to publish *Hurt* (the other is *The Third Generation*), and I haven't been able to locate a copy anywhere. If you do find a copy, will you send it to Roslyn (Franz J. Horch Associates, Inc., 325 E. 57th Street).

From what I have read of the weather in New York, despite the influence of the hurricanes, it has been a damn sight better than the weather here. Since 15 August it has been like winter in Paris—I've wished to hell I had my sheepskin coat—but today it is beginning to warm up a little. Anyway, you and Lori must have had a long pleasant summer in the country. I gather that Adam is fit as a fiddle again.

I know what you mean about Bill Hutson, but like most of the brothers over here he let himself get too broke to be able to maneuver, and that leaves them desperate and biting any hand that comes in sight. I know because I've been through it. Anyway, I hear from him every now and then, and I can report he's still alive.

As for Phil, he's something else again. He's a great one to cry hungry, but he's doing all right. I just read his guidebook on the nightlife in Amsterdam called *Amsterdam after Dark,* and he has some shit in there that boggles the mind. It was published by an American firm, Macfadden-Bartell, in English, and I have no doubt but it is doing well. If he follows along this vein he'll become rich. Nevertheless, I like Phil (for some reason or other), and I wish him well.

I'll check again with Julia Wright and see what gives with Mme. Fanon.

All my manuscripts are in the James Weldon Johnson Memorial Collection at the Yale University Library—I have been sending them there ever since I met Carl Van Vechten through Richard Wright some time during the late 1940s, and I don't think I would like to change. I am completely satisfied with them.

Well, to tell you the truth Lesley is far more excited about the house than I am. I don't believe in it as yet. I won't believe in it until it is finished and I open the door and go inside of it and begin living in it and pay the taxes and get it furnished and have enough left over to pay for food—then I will believe in it. But we are going ahead with all the preparations we can think of—we are getting together things we will need that we can transport in the car (I've had a rack put on the top)—sheets from London, black art from the black artists of Paris, a secondhand AM and FM Telefunken radio from a sympathetic Swede, etc. Now all that remains is for those Spanish cats to build the house. Well, "In God We Trust."

Lesley joins me in sending warmest regards to you and Lori and kisses for Adam.

Chester

Chester Himes
c/o Toutain
12, rue Abel Ferry
Paris 16

16 September 1969

Dear John,

Reading over your letter of 8 August, I see where you mention that the local library near Cazenovia where you went to give a lecture has a copy of *Cast the First Stone* on its list. Roslyn and I have been looking desperately for a copy for the London publisher of *Blind Man,* Robin Denniston, to read when he goes to New York at the end of this month. I wonder if you could give me the name and address of this library, and I will have Denniston go up there and read it there if he is that much interested, which he seems to be. Anyway, he's an adventurous man; he's just been to Moscow to get a manuscript of [Donald Duart] Maclean's—the British state department guy who defected to the Russians some years ago.

Julia says that Fanon's widow can't find the mimeographed copy of Fanon's lecture on violence with reference to my books. But Ellen says she will be in New York soon and has promised to see you and Charles Harris, and perhaps she will have more information.

I also notice in this letter that you say you are distressed that *Sons* is getting such excellent reviews whereas *The Man* was a better book. Man, that's the way "these people" are; they refuse to recognize our excellence anywhere, so they have to make up for it by giving a lavish prize for the not-so-excellent. I've been noticing that about "the motherfucker" for years. In the end I've come to the conclusion that all a black man can do is take their money and buy bullets.

I also read again the great encouragement you received from contact with your son and other youngsters. The younger generation is *the* generation—but then it always has been, even when I was the younger generation. I read recently where Arthur Miller is complaining that all the members of the PEN Club gathered in Menton are his age. Damn right, I thought.

S. Goldwyn, Jr., finally loosened the top secret restrictions on the movie of *Cotton* and sent me some stills and the cast list. I see Godfrey Cambridge is Grave Digger, Raymond St. Jacques is Coffin Ed, Calvin Lockhart is Deke, Judy Pace is Iris, Emily Yancy is Mabel, Redd Foxx is Uncle Bud, Cleavon Little is Lo Boy, Mabel Robinson is Billie, and about forty-five others, including the white characters whom I haven't mentioned. Judging from the stills, it looks as though half of Harlem is involved and guns are flying all about every which way. Anyway, it'll be something new however it turns out artistically or authentically.

Things here are getting like they were a year ago last May. Tension is building up, strikes are growing, people are getting nervous—and I am getting out. We'll leave about the 27th—you'll already be back in New York. Our address in Spain will be:

Casa Griot, 123[28]

Pla de Mar

Moraira-Teulada (Alicante)

(Over)

Lesley joins me in best regards to you and Lori, and we look forward to you visiting us in our new house as soon as you can.

> *All best,*
> *Chester*

Chester Himes

25 September 1969

Dear John,

Thanks for you letter of the 20th. Sorry we won't be here to greet you, but we'll be looking forward to seeing you and Lori *and* Adam in Spain.

---

28. The new home, Casa Griot, was named after Griot the cat.

He won't be any trouble. We're having a "concentration camp" type fence 2 meters high built all around the 2,000 meters, and he won't be able to come to any harm. Of course, the fence is for keeping Griot out of harm; he thinks he's a big bad cat and is always jumping on every cat he sees, and because I always come to his rescue and chase the other cat away, he thinks they're running from him. But he is twelve years old, which is old for a cat, and he's been indoors, pampered and spoiled, for all of his life, and if he is allowed to go around jumping on younger, tougher cats who've been living in alleys and fighting all their lives, he'll get himself killed. And we wouldn't like that to happen.

I hope you do get to see Ellen. She keeps saying she is going to New York (I'll enclose my last note from her)—but she hasn't gone. But she can give you the address of most of the black writers over here—African and otherwise—and jive blacks like Alain Albert (which is the way I think he spells his name).

Thanks for the information about the book *Cast the First Stone.* I hope the joker who told you about it is successful in stealing it. I used to always steal all the books I wanted from the libraries.

I'll give you my "big friend" Lomax's address in case you might want to see him when you go to Amsterdam, even though he does get on your ass. It's de Costasraat, 49, Amsterdam-W (Tel. 16 52 93).

At last we're all keyed up about getting back to Spain and seeing what the hell those Spanish builders have done about our house. Lesley joins me in sending best wishes to all the Williamses, big and little.

Chester

October 28, 1969

Dear Chester:
This is a note of no consequence, just to wish you happiness in the new crib, and to hope your health is fine.

I'm off next week to Paris, Amsterdam, and London for ten days, for research in Paris and hustling the magazine along the way. The first issue is all closed except for the piece by C. L. R. James, who is holding us up somewhat. But he's been very ill at Northwestern. Saw him there a couple of weeks ago.

Sorry I won't get a chance to see you this trip, but hopefully you'll be coming this way before long. In case you happen to be in Paris, however, I'll be at the Hotel Raphael, 17 Av Kleber from the 5th to the 8th; at the American in Amsterdam from the 8th to the 12th; and from the 12th to the 15th at the Cumberland in London.

We're all well here, and Lori and Adam join me in sending love.

John

Chester Himes
Casa Griot
Pla del Mar, 123
Moraira-Teulada (Alicante)
Spain

2 November 1969

Dear John,

I thought I had written to you since we arrived. But I suppose I haven't. I might say we're living in a sort of state of shock. We put a rack atop the car in Paris and arrived here after having gone through one of the severest rainstorms in Europe's history to find that nothing in the house had been finished and what had already been done looked like an imbecile child playing with mud.

Anyway all we've been doing this last month is trying to make the contractors correct mistakes, which entails knocking out some walls, changing the plumbing, installing ventilation for the toilets and kitchen, and putting blinds on my studio, which meant knocking out the front wall and putting it back.

And even now, not even the studio, 5 meters square, is sufficiently completed to hold the furnishings we brought atop the car for it.

I could go on like this for hours, days, weeks, but I am struggling to hold on to my sanity confronted with the Spanish personality. It is not that they don't admit their mistakes; they admit them readily and set about to correct them making other and even more stupid mistakes, all in good humor and with goodwill—for I have taken pains not to antagonize them. But still nothing gets done. It's not that they're not working; they are working all right, they're just not doing anything. I am trying desperately to stick with it, but I do not have the personality for it, and I find it most trying.

We are camping in a new, jerrybuilt apartment nearby, with a ninth-floor apartment from which we can see our house and watch the workers piddling around and try to keep from going crazy. Aside from the concierge, we are the only residents of this new eleven-story building. It is all a Spanish nightmare, but we are hoping to survive. Others have, and so will we, I suppose.

Best luck on your European trip. I'll write you at greater length when I'm up to it.

Lesley joins me in sending you and Lori our best. Hope Adam is well and happy. And as my friend Lewis Michaux says, "Keep the faith."

Chester

12 November 1969

Dear John,

By the time this letter reaches you I suppose you'll be back home. If I had anything of importance to say, I'd write to the Cumberland in London. But I'm just passing the time on some pleasant pastime. I'm sitting up here in this glass-fronted room on the ninth floor of this jerrybuilt apartment house looking out in the near distance and watching these dim-witted Spanish workers fucking around with my house, and I need to do something to keep from blowing my lid. I don't know how to describe these workers—they try hard enough, but they're so stupid it boggles the mind. If the architect—who is stupid enough himself—orders a crew of workers to put the window panes in the window on the west wall by mistake, because the window is on the *south* wall, the workers will come over here and happily knock a hole in the *west* wall to make a place for the window panes. It goes on and on like that, walls being knocked down, windows being put in the wrong places, light fixtures being covered by wooden blinds. It would be hysterically funny if it were somebody else's money. Maybe I shouldn't complain; at least I've got the beginning of a house. Now if only I can keep my mind.

Hope you found some interesting talent on this trip. By the way, do you know Cecil Brown?[29] Roger Straus sent me the galley proofs of his book, at your suggestion, he said; and I was wondering if you really know Cecil Brown. The name seems to ring a bell in my memory from when we were in Copenhagen the winter of 1965–66. I thought it was a good book, especially about the Copenhagen scene. I found the early days a little fuzzy and not near explicit enough to explain the character's erudition in his years abroad. But from my point of view, not enough to spoil the impact of the book, which was terrific. Hope we feel the same.

What's the news on *The Man,* which I still feel is the last word? Have you found anyone brave enough to attempt the film?

Thanks for letting me blow off like this about the house; I needed it.

Lesley joins me in sending love to you and Lori and Adam—the other *man.*

Chester

---

29. Cecil Brown, screenwriter and author of *The Life and Loves of Mr. Jiveass Nigger* (1969), *Days of Weather* (1986), and other novels.

November 23, 1969

Dear Chester:

Got both your letters and suspected that something was amiss with the house. Those workers sound just like my uncle who tried to help us remodel our place in the country. We were just up there for the weekend—it's still in one piece. We now have a private pond that we can stock fish in and swim in. Saw LeRoy Haynes in Paris and tried to encourage him to get to work on his book. I don't know Cecil Brown, but I know people who know him. I like the book too, and I thought you might. No word on *The Man.* I saw it on Ellen Wright's shelf, but she didn't mention it, and neither did I. I heard in Paris that I was back in the States dying of cancer of the rectum. How's that for hot and shitty gossip? I keep hearing that brave people are interested in doing it for the film, but they've not got in touch with me. How's the first (and second) volume of your autobiography going? When's *Cotton* being released? It's awfully quiet hereabouts. I got Lomax to do a piece for *Amistad.* He's returning to the States, and his stepfather's still alive. Still acting poor but now has found all the right (for him) reasons for returning to the States. Listen. Just cool it on the house; it'll be all right, finally, if I know you and Lesley. Come summer you'll be in excellent shape. Can you imagine, Adam is two! Damn.

Love to you both,
John

Chester Himes
Casa Griot
Pla del Mar, 123
Moraira-Teulada (Alicante)
Spain

5 December 1969

Dear John,

Sounds like you had an interesting trip to Europe despite the gossip. I knew people reading *The Man* would think you the protagonist and logically conclude that you were dying of cancer of the rectum. Such is a hazard of this occupation. Glad to hear that you saw LeRoy and Ellen. I knew you liked Cecil Brown's book, and that was why Roger Straus sent me a copy of the galleys—because I don't know Roger that well. Anyway, he has sent me other books to read, and Cecil Brown's is far and above any of the others. Interesting comments about your uncle's help, but at least he meant well, which is more than I can say about our architect, who is a complete *minus,* if you know what I mean. I forgive him for not having any imagination, but he thinks like a moron. But, as you say, someday the house will be finished, but whether it will be all right I cannot say. Anyway, I hope it will be in shape for you and Lori to visit us this coming summer—or whenever—and bring Adam with you.

And I'll say the same to you about *The Man;* it will all be fine finally; it's too good a book for the moviemakers to ignore forever.

As usual I have no news about the film of *Cotton.* You know more about it than I do, if you have heard anything at all.

I am not doing any work of any kind for the moment. Someday I'll get to work on the second volume of my autobiography and doubtless put the two volumes together—someday.

Glad you saw Lomax. Did he give you copies of his two "After Dark" books?

Am looking forward to a copy of *Amistad.*

Yes, it seems just yesterday when we were visiting you on 92nd Street and Lori was pregnant. And now Adam is two. Time flies.

Spain is the same as always in the winter. At least we are cold.

Lesley joins me in sending love to all three of you.

Chester

December 22, 1969

Dear Chester,

The holidays will be over when you get this, but the Spanish champagne, the brut, is very cheap and quite good for ushering in the new year. We hope you both are well. It had been awfully quiet around here concerning your movie, *Cotton,* although I did hear that it's supposed to open up a film festival in Newark next spring. Everyone working on the committee to have an international writers conference at Fisk next spring was delighted to have your letter in response to the one [John] Killens sent out. No, Lomax did not give me a copy of his book, and after commissioning him to do a piece for *Amistad* and sending out agreements, we've heard nothing. Strange. By the way could you just send me a note of release for your interview, just a few lines, so the attorneys for *Amistad* will be content? Ellen sold us a piece Wright had reworked after publishing it first in *New Challenge,* called "Blueprint for Negro Literature." It's a real gas. Great. The salesmen at Random have gone apeshit over the magazine; we look forward to some degree of success with the first issue, and we are deeply indebted to you for your contribution. Both Adam and Lori are down with colds they can't seem to shake, and so we trundle on toward the holidays, weary and ill. I've just finished the critical study (I like to call it) of Martin Luther King. I feel very uneasy about it, yet I know it is as complete as I can make it. Ever had that feeling? Listen, would you be interested in writing a piece on black writers from the Harlem Renaissance up to now for the *New York Times* magazine? Let me know. Cecil Brown is in town; I'll see him on Tuesday. B. [Bill Hutson] is also in town; I've seen him once, but he is all con and hustle and very hard to take once you peel back that smooth façade. I guess I'm getting old, man. Or maybe I'm learning from you. In any case, keep well, and we hope you have the best year ever. Lori and Adam, although choking with snot, send love and holiday greetings.

John

Chester Himes
Casa Griot
Pla del Mar, 123
Moraira-Teulada (Alicante)
Spain

28 December 1969

Dear John,

Excuse the tone of this letter. I am having serious trouble about my house and am getting prepared to take my case to court; and people are around me at the moment knocking out my brains with remarks, and it is very difficult for me to get off this letter.

However, in view of the disaster that confronts me at the moment (I'm in danger of losing all the money I have), and with all the strange emotions besetting me (I don't know whether it's racism or what)—anyway, I cannot afford to incense or hurt the feelings of any friends or well-wishers I still have. As a consequence I do not under any circumstances wish to say anything about William Targ that will displease his wife, Roslyn, who is very important to me. In fact, without Roslyn's help at this time, I don't know how I'd make it.

In the chapter of my interview titled "The Publishing Business," page 3, line 11, delete the words "Targ didn't do that though . . . because he," and let the sentence read as follows: "Minton was buying up Girodias's (Olympia Press) books. . . ."
Page 3, last line: "Corgi Books" for "Corege Books"
Page 8: "*Newsweek*" for "*Times.*"
Page 9, line 10: "Série Noire" for "Gallimard."

Sorry I can't write more at the time. The rest of the interview seems all right. Lesley joins me in sending you, Lori, and Adam love.

Chester

January 14, 1970

Dear Chester,

I'd not meant to torture you by delaying my reply to your last letter. Now, everything is cool. As soon as I got your letter, I went back over the interview and deleted as you wished. I learned a couple of days ago, however, when I got page proofs, that the changes were too late to have been set, but I've now made them in the page proofs. *Now, finally, everything is cool, so don't worry, and I understand.*

Our attorneys suggested a few other deletions, such as Willa's name and George Schuyler's, which we went along with, and their absence doesn't hurt the interview one bit.[30] This interview, I am sure, is one of the highlights of western literature, simply because it's you talking.

We now expect to have books by the 24th of February, and they will be quite handsome. The literary scene in New York will never be the same; you'll see when you get your copies.

Lori and I are sorry that bad luck seems to have found you once again, but we're sure it'll be of short duration. We're hoping to get to Mexico for a couple of weeks next month for rest and work. There is a man there who collects pre-Columbian heads that have Negroid features only. His theory is that several thousand years ago there was much traffic from Africa to the "New World." Should be very interesting. Spoke to LeRoi Jones the other day, and he sends you his best regards, as do Ishmael Reed and Cecil Brown, whose *Mr. Jiveass* was released today.

Man, I have to go back to the first issue of *Amistad*. It's going to knock you out!

I hope everything works out over there, and soon. I know what it's like trying to write with your head all fucked up over some jive matters that jive people make even worse because they don't *try* to make things better.

---

30. George Schuyler was a prominent black journalist whose career spanned more than thirty-five years. He published fiction and nonfiction works, was deeply involved in Harlem's politics, and was New York editor of the *Pittsburgh Courier.*

There are an awful lot of black folks like that, and perhaps that is why Africa begins in Spain. Strange, but I did find that old racist cliché to be true.

We are all over the flu and year-end depression and send some love to help you guys over the hurdles.

John

–§–

January/February 1970

Chester Himes versus Toscamar S.L.
In December 1967, through STOREY SONS & PARKER (Overseas), Costa Blanca, Javea, whose agent was Maria Teresa Gasull Anglada, I purchased plots no. 123 & 129 of URBANIZATION RESIDENCIAL PLA DE MAR from Don Francisco Ballester Molina and Dona Carmen Rios Sabater, the title deed being notarized by D. Francisco Estela Sendra, NOTARIA, Benisa.

At the same time I met Sr. Don Jose Ribes Pons, the Costa Blanca agent for Bradley & Vaughn, the "Director-Gerente" of Agencia "LA NAO" in Javea, whose charm and personality inspired me with sufficient confidence to entrust his firm, TOSCAMAR S.L. Seccion Construccion, to design and build a house, a studio, and a garage on plots 123 & 129 of PLA DEL MAR, which I had bought through STOREY SONS & PARKER.

At the direction of Sr. Ribes, the architect for TOSCAMAR S.L., Sr. VERET, made a design for the house for my approval.

When I went to the office of LA NAO to discuss the plan for my house, Sr. Ribes introduced me to Sr. Juan Soler Rosello, the constructor for TOSCAMAR S.L., with whom I conducted the discussion through a translator employed by LA NAO.

Subsequently, *all* discussions concerning the construction of my house, the studio, the garage, and the fence were conducted through correspondence with Sr. Juan Soler, the translations from English into Spanish and Spanish into English being made by translators employed by

TOSCAMAR S.L.

On November 30, 1968, I signed a contract with TOSCAMAR S.L. for the construction of a house of 178,60 m2 in accordance with the plan designed by Sr. Veret, architect, to be finished September 30, 1969. The contract was signed by Sr. Juan Soler, constructor for TOSCAMAR S.L. Before the contract was signed, I had written Sr. Juan Soler on November 18, 1968, a letter containing fourteen points, suggesting changes and rectifications of the original plan, and on November 24, 1968, I had received a reply from Sr. Juan Soler, stating that all my suggestions had been carefully studied and the original plan rectified as per my requirements and instructions *and that there would be no difficulty in finishing the house by the end of September 1969.*

On December 2nd, 1968, I made the first payment of 30 percent, 236.940 ptas., in accordance with the terms of the contract.

On January 14, 1969, I signed a second contract with TOSCAMAR S.L., Juan Soler, constructor, for the construction of a fence and a garage, and paid 158.500 ptas. on the signing of the contract. The termination date was September 30, 1969—the same as for the house.

On February 22, 1969, I signed a third contract with TOSCAMAR S.L., Juan Soler, constructor, for the construction of an additional Naya (47.000 ptas.), "Barbeque and fixtures" (9.400 ptas.), and "Celosia (10.120 ptas.)—a total of ptas. 66.520—with a termination date of September 30, 1969, the same as for the house.

The ptas. 66.520 was to be added to the final payment of 236.940 ptas. for the house.

On March 27, 1969, I signed a fourth contract with TOSCAMAR S.L., Juan Soler, constructor, for the construction of a separate studio of 5m x 5m, to be finished at the same time as the house, September 30, 1969. I paid the total cost of 95.000 ptas. on the signing of the contract.

All four contracts were signed before work was begun on the house at the end of March 1969.

The first payment of ptas. 236.940 for the house had been made.

Contracts II & IV, ptas. 158.500 and ptas. 95.000 had been paid for in full.

All negotiations, discussions, and decisions pertaining to the terms and the payment of the aforementioned contracts were made between myself, CHESTER HIMES, and JUAN SOLER, constructor for TOSCAMAR S.L.

The second payment of contract I, for the construction of the house, ptas. 315.920, was made on May 20, 1969. At the time, JUAN SOLER, constructor, assured me that the house would be "finished in September, as it had been foreseen."

I left Alicante and went to reside in Paris at the end of May, feeling confident that the house would be finished by September 30, as had been promised.

On July 8, 1969, I wrote JUAN SOLER, constructor, to ask him if it would be possible to have a cupboard installed in the bathroom while the house was being finished; and on July 11, 1969, I received a letter from JUAN SOLER, constructor, stating: "We will construct the bathroom basin cupboard as per your instructions and have duly noted that the cost of ptas. 8.750 is to be added to your last payment due on completion. We are looking forward to seeing you again on 1 October 1969."

On October 1, 1969, I arrived in Javea with my wife and put up in the Miramar Hotel.

None of the four contracts had been complied with.

Contracts I and III

The house had no windows or doors either inside or out. Large concrete shelves had been built on the north wall of the COMEDOR, which had to be removed. The WC in the hallway was inaccessible. There were no railings on the stairs to the TERRAZA. The wrong tiles had been laid in the bathroom. No LAVADERO had been constructed or begun to be constructed. No "CELOSIA," or "BARBEQUE WITH FITTINGS," had been constructed. The CALOR NEGRO radiators had not been installed.

Contract II

"Una alambrada de 2 m de altura con tubo circular y tela de usada en pistas de tennis y un seto con plantas gandules y una antenna de television de dos canales" had not been installed.

The dimensions of the garage, 5m x 6m, which I had requested for interior dimensions, were exterior dimensions.

The back door that I had requested for the garage had not been installed. The front entrance to the garage was not large enough to accommodate my car. No driveway from the street had been constructed, and a streetlight blocked the pathway.

Contract IV

No windows had been installed in the studio, and no glass panes had been fitted to the sliding doors. The *persina* for the sliding doors had not been installed. The *persina veneciana* for the sliding doors and the two windows had not been installed. The CALOR NEGRO radiators had not been installed.

The house was uninhabitable.

The studio was uninhabitable.

The garage was unusable.

The fence had not been begun.

No CALOR NEGRO radiators had been installed in the house or the studio.

Neither the exterior shutters or the interior Venetian blinds had been installed.

There were no windows or window frames.

There was no ventilation in the WC or over the kitchen stove.

There was no ventilation of any kind in the WC in the studio.

By Christmas, December 25, 1969, the house had not been made habitable.

I engaged the assistance of a Spanish-speaking English national, Miss Paulette Hemingway, living in Altea, to translate for me.

Sr. JUAN SOLER, constructor for TOSCAMAR S.L., had been replaced by Sr. GUILLERMO BOLUFER BUIGUES. Sr. Vincente SOLER, who did not speak English and did not employ reliable translators, was in charge of the construction of my house. I felt desperately the need of a translator and someone who could tell me the various officials in Spain to whom I could apply for instruction and relief.

Paula was acquainted with the attorney who held the license for TOSCAMAR, and for a time she got the various heads of the firm off their asses and to work getting the house completed. But she is a very temperamental girl bordering on insanity, and shortly she was insulting everyone to the place where they suddenly quit work again. But that might have been because I demanded compensation. So through Paula I have employed a number of experts to collect evidence on how I have been bilked—shoddy installations, tile rejects, dangerous electrical installations, etc., and on the obvious visual chickenshit work and lack of work—architects, builders, notaries, engineers, etc.—and I have collected an impressive mass of evidence that the firm intended to bilk me from the start. But now this temperamental girl has turned on me and is about to destroy all of the gain we have made. Through her I have contacted a reliable and able lawyer, and with her help I could probably get my house built right and collect compensation. But she just went right off her rocker—God only knows why—and unless a miracle occurs it seems that I will end up the loser.

Of course I won't lose everything, but I'll wind up with a house that I'll probably never live in and will probably never be able to sell—the Spanish laws concerning property rights being such as they are.

I was typing out this concise summation of events from September 30, 1969, until the present date for the use of the lawyer in case he requested it, and since I owe you a letter I thought I might pass on the copy, which should give you a picture of the situation.

I hope you get to Mexico for a few weeks of work and relaxation. How I envy you. And I'm happy to hear that you are all over the flu and year-end depression. I have been so busy since Christmas; I have hardly realized that a year has passed and a new year begun. All I want to do now is get the hell out of here.

Thanks for the good words from LeRoi and Ishmael Reed and Cecil Brown. I see all the brothers are gathering on the home grounds. I'll probably come myself as soon as I get out of this mess.

And I'm glad to hear your enthusiasm for the first issue of *Amistad.*

Lesley joins me in sending love to you and Lori and, of course, Adam.[31]

Chester

—§—

Chester Himes
Casa Griot
Pla del Mar, 123
Moraira-Teulada (Alicante)
Spain

14 March 1970

Dear John,
This is just a line to ask you to send one of my copies of *Amistad* to Roslyn
Targ, Franz J. Horch Associates, Inc., 325 E. 57th Street, New York, 22.

It is cold here, but we are both well and busy as two broken-tailed
beavers (building Hoover Dam).

Lesley joins me in sending love to all of you.

Chester

31. I don't believe any of Himes's several biographers ever mention this document, which is somewhat like a film script. However, this is a good example of Himes on the attack.

March 1970

Casa Griot
Pla del Mar, 123
Moraira-Teulada (Alicante)
Espana

Dear John,

We have at last accepted our house under protest to keep the workmen from destroying what they had already done, and we have moved in and begun the last task of getting it livable and furnishing it. At least we have our fence, ranging in height from 1.75 meters to 2 meters, with locks on all gates, making it something like a fortress, and when I sit up here behind my wire walls and look over the surrounding estates, the Spanish think the Moors have come again. The worst thing about this house and this country is that it takes so much of me there is so little left even to write letters, much less write anything else. Now I'm fighting for time. I don't know what my lawyer will charge; he hasn't sent his bill. In fact, he's not through with his work; there are still things the builders have to do, and I am turning (deeding) the land to Lesley, so she can inherit the place when I die; otherwise the whole damn thing would go to the state.

Needless to say I'm looking forward with great anticipation to a copy of *Amistad*. And great expectations; I am hoping *Amistad* will become the *voice* of the black artist. We've been without voice long enough.

All I know of the film of *Cotton* is the following paragraph taken from Roslyn's letter: "Received the following letter from Sam Gelfman of United Artists concerning *Cotton:* 'Ah, *Cotton Comes to Harlem*. It's now in its final stages of editing and scoring. We anticipate a print for screening the end of April, or beginning of May, and the release date is sometime in June or early July. I'll surely let you know when we have our first screening.'" (That clears up the mystery of *Cotton;* Sam Gelfman has his big fat ass on it.)

Sorry about the international writers' conference scheduled at Fisk.

I read the nominations for the National Book Award in the Paris Herald. It's the publishers who nominate, isn't it? Or who does nominate? Ralph is the only black writer who's ever won it. Which, in my opinion, just goes to show how the white publishers really think about their black writers. Too bad some black millionaire doesn't go into the book publishing business; he'd have captive black contributors and a captive black audience. Too bad I ain't a millionaire; I'd love to be a publisher—in fact that's the only business I'd contemplate.

John Henrik Clarke found a copy of *Cast the First Stone* for me—it cost him $12, which I had Roslyn pay him.[32] But it turned out that the London publisher—Hodder & Stoughton—wasn't interested anyway.

Lesley joins me in sending you, Lori, and Adam love.

Chester

4 April 1970

Dear John,

I don't remember whether I've written to you since we took possession of our house and moved in, what with all the things claiming my attention. Anyway, my lawyer finally got some sense into the construction company (even their lawyer had to admit their errors), and I got a rebate of 131.000 pesetas for things in the contract that had either been left out or built the wrong way; and I took the keys and moved in even though there are many things about this house I do not like.

But we are in it, and soon it will be as completely furnished as we intend to do at the present, and we are open for visitors. We would love to have you and Lori and Adam any time you wish to come. We have a strong tennis-court type fence completely surrounding the property, about 2 meters high, with locks and bolts on all the gates, so Adam could be left to run free with absolute security. We built this fence to keep Griot in, and so far he has not made an attempt to get over it or out in any way except by the gates if

---

32. John Henrik Clarke was editor of *Freedomways,* published in New York.

they are left open. We have one large guest bedroom, about the size of our living room in Alicante, and another small one off the back Naya with its private entrance. And I have a separate studio away from the back of the house at the end of the plot. In the course of time this place could be made very nice, if I can just get to work and earn enough to support it.

I had expected my copy of *Amistad* before now; I suppose it will arrive soon.

I have just written to Sam Goldwyn asking for information about the film of *Cotton.*

You know it is very remote here; it is only inhabited by the grubbing natives and vegetating foreigners. It is dull too. We have our little German-made television (which you saw) and a Telefunken radio we bought second-hand from a Swede last summer in Paris. I suppose we'll take a trip to Paris as soon as all the details are wrapped up and we pay our lawyer, but we'll stay here all summer. So come and visit us.

Lesley joins in sending love to you and family.

Chester

April 15, 1970

Dear Chester:

It seems that I'm always owing you letters. I am behind. With this one I'm mortified. My partner Harris sent off books and a letter to you at your old address in Alicante, and they just came back. He has your new address; I gave it to him. We are still not clicking just as we should, but time will take care of that, I hope. I had a nice long letter from Roz Targ and called her. Your interview seems to have got a lot of things cracking. In fact, as you might imagine, your interview is one of the things most discussed about *Amistad 1.* By the way, Harris yesterday sent off more copies airmail special delivery. The reception all in all has been what I imagined—coolly hostile. They try not to show it, but it can't help but come through.

Then yesterday I saw Bill Targ up at the Putnam-Coward-McCann offices, and he said that you and Lesley might be coming here briefly, although they're looking forward to seeing you there and in Nice. Do let us know if and when you're coming. We plan to go to the country the first week in May to get it together. Then we'll go back for few more days later in the month, and then move up for the summer in June. *If you come to N.Y., you must visit the country.*

Your place sounds great, even with all the troubles, and damned if we aren't sorry we can't come this year. Again, too much work, but next year, it will be different. I promise you that. Thanks so much for the invitation, though. It's good to know that someone out there still likes us. Yes, I was nominated for the Authors Guild council and won and went to my first meeting. I'm trying to form a committee on the problems of minority group writers, and I'm to prepare a memo on them. If you have suggestions, please send them on.

Finally, spring seems to be just around the corner. This has been the longest, deadliest winter I can remember. Up at the farm the snowfall averaged eight feet deep, and the folks up there are still grumbling about it. Things seem grim at the very best.

Roz tells me that there are signs that they are getting ready for screenings of *Cotton Comes to Harlem,* and she will let me know. Melvin Van Peebles's film *Watermelon Man* is still screening after months and months. I don't know when it will be released. It's supposed to be a funny film, but the subject—a white man who wakes one day and discovers that he is black—is not funny at all. As I say, I don't know what they plan to do with it.

There is something life-sustaining about remote places. At least that's the way I feel now. Just relax and enjoy it. I know I promised to send you some books, and before summer comes down upon us and we move, I'll do just that, so you can keep busy reading. It's a good time to cool it, with the world going mad. I enjoy being up there in the country, the nearest village 7 miles away and the nearest neighbor's house a half-mile distant. It's worth all the fuss. Lori and Adam, who's going from bad to rotten, say hurry on over, and in the meantime send love.

John

Chester Himes
Casa Griot
Pla del Mar, 123
Moraira-Teulada (Alicante)
Spain

17 April 1970

Dear John,

My copies of *Amistad* arrived last night after having gone to Alicante and
back to New York. I read your interview before going to bed, and it reads
well and I find you have done everything I requested. Thanks. I'll get to the
rest soon.

The house is now livable, and you and family are welcome whenever
you come.

I like the format of *Amistad;* it looks good and the subject matter is
intriguing, and I look forward to reading it.

By the way, your introduction to the interview was fascinating. I have
forgotten that Spain can smell sweet; it used to smell that way to me too
fifteen years ago in Mallorca, but lately I've only smelled the rotten odor
of cauliflower. But I'm happy to know that it appeals to your senses. We're
planting lots of flowers and are trying to make our garden smell sweet too.

I'll write more later. This was mainly to say that I have received *Amistad.*

Lesley joins me in sending love to you, Lori, and Adam.

Chester

Chester Himes
Casa Griot
Pla del Mar, 123
Moraira-Teulada (Alicante)
Espana

8 May 1970

Dear John,

I've been digging *Amistad* in between this gardening shit of Lesley's and
all this other chickenshit these Spanish keep putting down, and it's been
a joy and a relief to get back into the scene. "The Southern White Writer
and American Letters" was sharp and to the point—these motherfucking
crackers got a tight grip on the whole operation, and we black writers will
be the only ones to ever get them out. That's why I want black writers to
write; write about anything—white cunt, toejam, Governor Lester Maddox,
anything. And we'll overcome them; anyway overwhelm them. I read C. L.
R. James's dissertation on Baldwin and yours and Harris's introduction and
perceived that this issue is dedicated to the memory of Langston Hughes.

I got a letter from Samuel Goldwyn, Jr., finally, saying, "The film is
finished. We have three previews, and the reactions have been very good."
He says that both blacks and whites feel the film is both honest and
funny and that the bag scene cracks everyone up, "draws a great deal of
laughter and cheers at every preview. Supposed to open—after more sneak
previews—at Woods Theater in Chicago on May 27.

Sorry you told me about Melvin's *Watermelon Man.* It's a direct steal of
an old short story of mine he once read called "The Ghost of Rufus Jones,"
but Rufus wakes up and finds himself white and proceeds to enjoy all the
vices whites have always enjoyed—but it's not funny either to tell the truth.

Roslyn tells me she's getting some nibbles on my autobiography, and
I'm undertaking rewriting some of it and getting together some bits and
things I wrote in Paris about the Latin Quarter scene when I was there.

All I need is peace.

I hope you have a nice summer at your house in the country and do a
lot of work—not in the garden, however. I might turn up in New York next

month to get some new dentures. It's cheering good news about Adam; all good little kids are supposed to go from bad to rotten—how else do you know they're good?

Lesley joins me in sending love to you and Lori and kisses to "rotten" little Adam.

Chester

May 13, 1970

Dear Chester, Lesley, and Griot:
We're getting a wire fox terrier for rotten little Adam to have in the country and for a companion around here. So, hopefully, this'll mark a new stage in his development, since, like his father, he's often anti-people. Well, now, I'm sorry to hear that Melvin tapped your literary vault. I admire his guts and all—you got to have 'em for Hollywood, but shit. He's raising money to do another film, which surprises me, because I understood that he was bankrolled to do three films. The response to your interview has been electric, and we're having clips of them sent to you. As you might imagine, the liberal literary establishment has been our harshest critic, plus some bullshit that Random House itself is trying to put down.

We were up in the country last week after I'd spent three exhausting days taping Bill Cosby for *Amistad* out in Nevada at Harrah's, where he was working. I got myself a riding mower and cut within minutes areas that I hadn't touched in two years. Needless to say, Adam was crazy about it and rode in my lap a little ways. But then he's wild about all machinery: the chain saw, the power tools, etc. Also stocked the pond with rainbow trout. All this is to say that, should you come and we're not here, we'll be going up about the 12th of June, and if you want to come up, our area code is 607 and the rest: 397-4153. You can rent a car and drive up in about three and a half hours or fly up on Catskill Airways, which goes to Oneonta, about 30 miles from us. In any case, we'd love to have you.

We are being overwhelmed with scripts. We need readers, more expense money, etc., so I'm having a big meeting with Random House tomorrow on these matters. The heat has come early. Stifling in the 80s and 90s, it's a bitch, and I can't wait until it's time to cut out. Also, everyone's going mad—the administration, the cops, the construction workers, the landlords, the students—and the blacks and Puerto Ricans are supposed to have a plan for tying up the city this summer, perhaps sometime next month. Coward-McCann is bringing out my Martin Luther King book in August or September, and I'm asking them to send you some bound galleys for comment.[33] My oldest boy's getting married next month to his three-year girl, and at last I'm going to have a daughter, can you imagine?

I expect that I'll be working my ass off this summer upstate, but that's better than working it off here in Manhattan. Love to all. We look forward to hearing from you.

John

Chester Himes
Casa Griot
Pla del Mar, 123
Moraira-Teulada (Alicante)
Espana

24 May 1970

Dear John,
I write this in haste as we're packing to go to Nice and meet Roslyn and Bill Targ.

---

33. *The King God Didn't Save* (1970).

I've now read *Amistad* from end to end, and I think it's all great. But, as you know, it won't go down well with whitey. And that, if no other, is one of the finest things about it. Time to quit trying to please whitey. One white son of a bitch or another goes out of his way every day to do something to displease me—all of it intentional and most of it gratuitous.

Your place in the country sounds ideal—real country too, not a desert like this desert here. Hope you write a book up there this summer as good as *The Man*.

I don't know whether I'll make it back this summer. Things at the present don't look very encouraging. But I'll come and see you if I do.

Congratulations!!! How do you know it's going to be a daughter? Has medicine advanced that far while I've been hiding away in these sticks? Maybe that goes with everything. Anyway, I'm getting very, very tired of this life among these lower-middle-class, pretentious, indescribably ignorant whiteys.

Well, here's wishing you a good summer.

Lesley joins me in sending love to you, Lori, and Adam and the best to you all.

Chester

June 9, 1970

Dear Chester:

This hasty note will find you on return from Nice, Paris, or wherever. We go up on Friday to the country. No, you dope, *we* aren't having a daughter; we're *gaining* one through my son's marriage on the 27th.

Cotton Comes to Harlem opened this week, but we won't have a chance to see it here before we go; catch it later. You got credits in the ads. My movie deal is sputtering—out, it looks like. Anyway, there's very little word about what's going on. That's par for the course.

I've had sent to you bound galleys of the Martin Luther King book; hope you find it interesting.

Nothing else new going on; we're just holding on until getaway time on Friday.

Regards to Lesley.

John

23 June 1970

Dear John, old friend,

To be sure my old overworked think piece was still unexploded; I looked up your letter of May 13, and sure enough you wrote, "My oldest boy's getting married next month to his three-year girl, and at last I'm going to have a daughter, can you imagine?" Now to old pappys like me that means what it says—*you're* going to have a daughter; when I grew up I learned that if your son is having a daughter, that would make her your granddaughter. Right? When you talk to me you gotta be explicit, because I don't see anything improbable about you and Lori having a daughter. A sister to Adam. However, enough of that.

I've been reading your book on King whenever I've had a moment during these last two hectic weeks, and I must tell you you've got some mighty deep stuff there. No one, and I mean *no one,* has got down to the nitty-gritty before as you do in this one. This is not a book about what King did (thank God) but about what he didn't do. And about a lot of other things too that needed to be on the agenda. I prophesy that this book is going to shock the living hell out of the establishment. It's not going to titillate whitey and give him a free come like the *The Fire [Next Time],* but it's going to shrivel his balls. And it's about time. Someone had to tell these people the facts of life; and tell them before it's too late for anyone to tell anyone anything. Which might be soon. Also it's time we blacks take a good long, hard, honest look at ourselves. Before it's too late. Forgive me for using this old stale cliché, but time is getting short. And damn good thing too, for whitey is beginning to go haywire, what with Vietnam, the stock market, rising costs, pollution of the environment and the mind, and our bad breath. I think this is the most timely book ever written. Because we twenty-five or thirty million blacks aren't going to fall to our knees in nonviolent prayer, like the backers of King have hoped. All I can say is God speed.

The press is beginning to give me the "treatment"—TV in France, TV in Germany, *Life* magazine butter-up, and all that crap—they seem to think they've found themselves another "good nigger." But I've got news for them.

I'm still having trouble with this Spanish kind of racism; but I'm going to try to sit them out. Anyway, there's not much else I can do now—too old and too tired. I had hoped to get back to the States this summer, but now all the publicity on *Cotton* has made it impossible. I'll just sit here and try to write the rest of my autobiography.

By the way, I haven't had a chance to tell you—Doubleday has contracted to publish *Quality of Hurt*. They offered ten grand advance, and I took it—or at least I think I have.

Lesley and I are exhausted by our trips. We drove to Nice, drove Roslyn and Bill Targ back here for a one-day visit; they flew back to Paris; we followed two days later. We stayed a week in Paris and then went on to Hamburg for three days—fares and all expenses paid—and they think I think they're doing me a favor. Now I'm trying to catch up on my correspondence, but I don't have too much energy.

We hope we have a chance to see you and Lori before another year passes, but it seems that you are going to be exceedingly busy for quite some time—dodging the slings and arrows of the Establishment if nothing else, and it seems as if I'm going to be exceedingly tired.

Anyway, good luck.

Lesley joins me in sending you and Lori our warmest love.

Chester

July 21, 1970

Dear Chester:

Hope you've settled in after all the travel and fanfare. We're doing nicely up here, but the weather's been terrible. Lots of work on the house and more on this goddamn machine. Perhaps by now you've had a visit from some of the brothers who wanted to look you up while in Spain, particularly Addison Gayle and Ishmael Reed, who were due to visit Spain together.[34] Hope you don't mind my giving them your address. One big happy family, for they, you, and I are all published by Doubleday now. That's good news about your autobiography; I'd heard that it was in the house. Seems they're delighted. Publishers are just like any other whore, maybe worse.

The Black Academy of Arts and Letters is having its first annual meeting in September—the 18th through the 20th.[35] You've gotten a form letter already, but I've been asked by several people to ask if you wouldn't try, try like hell to come for the first one. Doubleday is trying to get some promotion off the ground for a new, kind of strange, book by William Melvin Kelley. He's also published by them. They wanted me to do it, but I don't have the time to write my name in shit, and I shit every day. I suggested you, that you might write something, and this, dear friend (Doubleday is paying), could give you that fare to New York and back for the Academy affair. How the hell about it? I am halfway through my soldier book, and we are looking forward to a real vacation next year. God, am I anxious for that. Might take a gig at the University of California, Santa Barbara, for a few weeks; they've asked me several times. Then maybe Mexico. Dunno.

---

34. Ishmael Reed, the author, critic, and publisher, and Addison Gayle, Jr. (1932–91), also a distinguished critic of literature written primarily by African Americans.

35. The Black Academy of Arts and Letters was established to define, promote, and cultivate African American arts and letters. I joined the first board of directors, which also included Dr. C. Eric Lincoln (president), John O. Killens, Alvin F. Poussaint, Doris Saunders, Dr. Charles V. Hamilton, Dr. Vincent Harding, Robert Hooks, and Charles White. At the first meeting, the Academy elected the late W. E. B. Du Bois into the Hall of Fame. Also honored were the painter Henry Ossawa Tanner, historian Carter G. Woodson, Lena Horne, C. L. R. James, Diana Sands, Amiri Baraka [LeRoi Jones], and Paul Robeson, all chosen for their longstanding contributions to arts and letters.

I thank you for the kind words re the King book. I'm told that Coretta's called a strategy meeting to see what can be done about it. It'll be interesting to see what develops. Pub date is August 17, and I sort of wish we were going to be out of the country.

I go out to Macalester College in St. Paul for a four-day writing seminar on the 26th. Very good bread for just four days, so it's the only gig like that I've taken in quite a while. Wish I had some news to pass on to you, but we only get the paper on Sunday, and the news is mostly local.

Lori and Adam send love and look for you in September.

Best regards,
John

P.S. Still haven't seen *Cotton.* I guess when we get back in the fall.

July 27, 1970

Dear John,

Thanks for your long and chatty letter. First I must say that I'm not very happy to be back with Doubleday, but beggars can't be choosers, and they got the most and they know it. Anyway, it's the only publisher who's not afraid of Willa. They don't know it, but I have hundreds of letters from Willa and some personal agreements notarized by the American embassy in Paris, so I think the most foolish thing she could do would be to sue.

Which brings to mind your King book. It's clear and precise and true and well documented, so what the hell does Coretta think she can do except get her white folks to say you're a dirty s.o.b.?

It'll be impossible for me to make the Black Academy of Arts and Letters annual meeting in September.

Hope you have a brief rest from work and aggravation on your trip to Macalester College in St. Paul, and hope you get more of a breather at Santa Barbara and Mexico if your book is finished by then. I envy your industry; I find it hard to keep up my correspondence, much less write books. Anyway, you are getting better and better, and you're going to storm the walls of the Establishment by sheer superiority.

We're well recovered from our trips and are merely trying to get our garden to grow. We don't have the advantage of rain like you have in New York, but we would gladly swap you some sun and heat for a little rain.

Lesley joins me in sending love to all of you.

Chester

Chester Himes
Casa Griot
Pla del Mar
Moraira-Teulada
(Alicante)
Spain

Sunday, 27 September 1970

Dear John,

It was a pleasure to see you and Lori again in New York and to meet Adam for the first time and also your mother. Adam is an adorable little boy; where does he get his blond curls from? I suppose that's "just like a nigger," as we say. Asking all those stupid questions. Anyway, give him a big kiss for both of us. And thanks for taking me to the airport, etc.

Bad luck plagued me all the way home and even afterward—at least trifling little things that got on my nerves. Jaguar factory hadn't done half the things I requested, BBC was unprepared for my arrival, and everything here in the house, except the garden, seemed to have stopped working. But now I've got everything under control again.

Not a word from that stupid juvenile, Samuel G. After my few words on *Black News* he'll probably never want to speak to me again. Helen Jackson wrote me that you will precede me on *Black News,* and by then probably the

Black Academy will take over and I will probably come on in late October.

I read your book on Dick Wright [*The Most Native of Sons*]; think it's a good book for the school room. Poor old Dick. Was he a great writer or not? I think he was in the beginning, but he ruined his image in time.

The weather is nice here and the tourists have gone and it is very peaceful. I suppose it is quite similar upstate in New York, where you might be by this time. Finishing your book on the black soldier. Well, all best wishes.

Lesley joins me in sending love to you all.

Chester

October 17, 1970

Dear Chester:

I don't know where this cat got his blond curls. Lori says she had blond hair as a kid. I saw it in photos, but Jesus Christ, what do you say when people start looking at you cross-eyed?

We enjoyed having you, as brief and hectic as it was. Had lunch with Roz last week, and we talked, or she talked, about many things, including your return engagement with Doubleday. We saw a part of your show on *Black News,* and it came over extremely well. We'd been out shopping for furniture and rushed back for the last five minutes, a situation that pissed me off. We're in a new apartment down the hall, so we figured we'd buy a few new things.

It gave the Academy a lift to have you here; the cats are still talking about it. We had the big blast and a full complement. Honored Paul Robeson, Du Bois, because we finally managed to get Shirley Graham a visa, LeRoi Jones, and others.[36] As one black businessman put it, "That's the kind of black power I believe in."

---

36. Although LeRoi Jones had changed his name to Amiri Baraka in 1963, I had known him for a long time and continued to call him LeRoi.

The King book is all but dead. Black folks aren't reading it still but talking it to death. It has been just this side of disaster, thanks to our old friend *Time* magazine, and the brothers don't seem to realize that that is exactly what *Time* wished—for them not to read it, and to bloody my head, which really is.

The Wright book is, well, a book. I am just about finished with the black soldier [*Captain Blackman*], another twenty-five pages or so, and then I'll go back over it. ABC is interested in *Sons of Darkness* but doesn't like the deal I have with the black producer, so he and I have made a deal. Bill Cosby, who's involved as a principal and who's always talking about doing things for the brother, is quite willing to have someone else do the screenplay or rewrite the one I've done, confident that "the message will get through." Ah well.

Bill Kelley sent this to me, so I'm sending it on to you.[37] Love to Lesley, and take care.

John

-§-

November 21, 1970

Dear Chester,

I think I owe you a couple of letters. I'm not sure how that happened, but this is an attempt to catch up. We are starting to come down with the winter colds again, and we are still getting settled in the new apartment (at the same address). Hunting season opened last week, and as usual, when the darkies poured out on the hills, the good Lord protected the deer.

I've left *Amistad,* finding it too irritating, too unprofessional, and too traditionally nigger to bear. I'm sure Harris will somehow manage, although

---

37. The novelist William Melvin Kelley (*A Different Drummer* [1962], *Dunford's Travels Everywhere* [1969]).

I suspect the thrust of the magazine will be far less exciting than when yours truly was on it. I think publishing is tightening up in terms of money, and brothers, I'm sure, will be the first to feel the pinch, and perhaps some of them should. There's not a week that goes by when I don't receive some new publication or collection of poems from some new talent who feels that all he has to do is cry, "Right on."

The pics that I took of you I have given to the Black Academy so that you will be suitably enshrined. The Academy is still in the process of growth, so we are having some minor pains. I was told yesterday that Phil Lomax, while being interviewed for a job in black studies, was told by some black students that he had deserted the revolution and therefore was not suitable for teaching them. *I'm sure, though, he found another job.*

Have not heard from Roz, but I assume she must be doing okay. And haven't seen Helen Jackson, but I assume she's doing all right too.[38] Everything else is cool. I am on the very last chapter of this soldier book. It'll be a relief to finish.

Lori and Adam send love, and I look to hear from you at your leisure.

John

P.S. *Time* magazine and other publications of that ilk have killed my King book. In fact, I think the publisher, Coward-McCann, worked with them—c'est la vie!

-§-

January 2, 1971

Dear Chester:
New Year greetings. This is the New American Library edition I told you about, due out late this month. Hope all goes well with you and Lesley.

---

38. Helen Jackson was an editor at Doubleday, Himes's publisher then.

We're just starting to find some time for ourselves, which we can always use. Adam remembers you well; he saw the picture in *Life* that came out last summer and recalls everything about you, including, like most black, or part black, kids, the fact that you stayed to eat. Ain't that a bitch. Write when you've time.

John

-§-

January 1971

Dear John,

Thanks for the check and the note. I'm glad to hear that things are getting back to normal and that you have more time for yourselves. Everything is fine with us; I'm putting together a book of short stories, and we're working lazily about the house. The weather has turned warmer again, and it's pleasant.

I remember Adam just as well; I think he looks like his grandmother in everything but his coloring. He must be the apple of her eye. I remember her very well also.[39]

Lesley joins me in sending love and all best wishes for a happy and prosperous New Year to you all.

[Chester]

---

39. My mother, Ola, was then in her late sixties; Adam adored her.

Chester Himes
Casa Griot
Pla del Mar
Moraira-Teulada
(Alicante)
Spain

30 March 1971

Dear John,

Easter greetings. How was your vacation in the West Indies? And has your book, *The Soldier,* been published?[40] Please have Doubleday send me a copy.

I've been very busy since I was in New York last summer, as busy as I've ever been. I've got two books of short stories together, *Black on Black* and *White on White;* now all I need is to find a publisher.[41] Roslyn has them, of course. And I've been in a long hassle with Doubleday's lawyers about Willa. Finally I've given in to their demands to change her name and background. I've been sitting on the copyedited original since the first of this month, but now I need my unedited original to make the changes, and I'm having difficulty in getting a copy.

Anyway, it's so damn cold and miserable here in "sunny Spain"; work offers the only distraction. Anyway, we're beginning to get our garden growing on this landscape of rocks, and we're having a swimming pool built—when and if and ever. It was promised for the end of this month, but I think it might be finished by June. And then there might not be enough water available to fill it.

Please remember, if you and Lori and Adam ever come across the Atlantic again—or rather when—you must come and visit us.

We were in Paris the first of this month, where I'm having a great season for the first time, and I got a new passport direct from the State Department in Washington—so I should be relatively fixed for five more years.

---

40. *Captain Blackman* was published in 1972.
41. *Black on Black* was published in 1973; *White on White* was never published.

We are both well (Griot too), which is surprising in this weather, and all of us are quite busy on one thing or another—Griot in his usual way.

Lesley joins me in sending love to all of you and a big kiss for Adam. Does he still remember me after all these months?

Write when you find time.

All best,
Chester

April 4, 1971

Dear Chester:

Good to get your letter; your last one sounded like you were about to blow your top. You've recovered. Lots of things going on at Doubleday, apparently. I seem to be having a tough time getting together with my editor, either by phone or letter or in person. The secretaries are utterly undependable in passing along messages. The word is that they're not offering any contracts until May, and this has been the case since the first of the year. Don't know how much truth there is in it, since I've not seen my editor, as I've said. How about volume 2 of your autobiography . . . is Doubleday going to get it?

As far as I'm concerned the soldier book is finished. The editor claims to be uneasy about the start of it, but that's her problem. All these fucking young chicks trying to make reputations. You know the bit. As soon as it's scheduled, and it will not be for this year, as far as I can tell, I'll let you know.

The Black Academy of Arts and Letters this year is offering some money awards in letters, about $500 for each category. It's something we have to do to remain a viable organization, and the feeling among the members is very good about it all. The swimming pool sounds good. Dying to get there.

We have friends, a couple named George and Mickey Gregory, recently retired from working in New York City agencies, who've bought an apartment near Malaga and will be in Spain in the fall. Marvelous people. Would you mind if I gave them your address? We have other friends in Malaga whom we'll put the Gregorys in touch with.

We had a marvelous three weeks in Grenada; we all enjoyed it except the last day when we were hit by a cab driver. Lori and Adam were in the backseat of the VW, and it was a good thing. Lori had X-rays taken of her head, but she's all right. Adam was just bounced around. I got a cut knee, a scratched head, and a bruised arm. Another foot to the left, and it would have been murderous. The cars were a complete mess. Even so, we loved it and hope to return. Adam goes to nursery next fall. Time flies. He does remember you and well, or at least claims to. From time to time he does speak of people we haven't seen in the longest time. My mother, whom you met, has come through the earthquake and aftershocks in L.A. with only broken crockery and smashed preserves. I feel much better being out of *Amistad;* you can't imagine. Our dog has become a big pain in the ass, this fox terrier, and if he doesn't improve over the summer, he won't be back in this pad next fall. He loves to chew on other dogs, and you know dog owners in New York. Maybe what he needs is to get his ass kicked real good by a police dog, and then he'll straighten up. All in all, we're in good shape. Best, all best, to the three of you.

John

June 11, 1971

Dear Chester:

Damn, man! First I heard you were sick (another of those rumors), and I called Roz, and she said, no, he's fine. She/we breathed a little easier and thought briefly of visiting your new swimming pool but changed our minds because money's getting tighter than a turtle's asshole. I'm having trouble with NAL and Coward-McCann, who've done a good screwing job on me, and I don't really have any recourse. The lawyer's explained it all to me. That innocuous clause giving writers the chance to request publishers to open their books is bullshit. First there's a court action. If you win, *then* the publishers open their books, but not if you lose. Terrible. I'm told now that your autobiography is to be out next year, the same time as my soldier book, which I hope to get in with final changes next month. The Black Academy of Arts and Letters will be giving out a little bread this coming fall and has also devised a questionnaire for black writers to better ascertain their problems with publishers and editors. You'll get this material.

We're off tomorrow for the country, thank God, because this place is near collapse; the prices and taxes have now become horrendous, and grumbling and growling is being heard throughout the land. Here in New York, editors no longer fill up all the chic restaurants; advances are going down; publishers are looking two or three times at black writers; and it's just getting to be nasty. Give our best to Lesley, and we do hope to see you soon, here or there, depending on our mutual fortunes.

John

Chester Himes
Casa Griot
Pla del Mar
Moraira-Teulada
(Alicante)
Spain

18 June 1971

Dear John,

It's good to hear from you. No I haven't been sick, but these Spaniards are enough to make a man sick. Being Spanish is a way of life; it doesn't make any sense; you either accept it or fight it—I fight it. The swimming pool is at last supposed to be finished—but it leaks. I've had my lawyer raising hell, and it's scared the shit out of everyone—but it still leaks. Anyway, we're going to use it this summer, leaking or not. But it does look fine—tiled border, shaded patio, surrounded by pines, and ragged hedge high enough to give it privacy. Come on over and jump in. Helen Jackson popped by here for two days, but the pool wasn't filled when she was here—besides it was too cold.

All this shit takes up my time and I resent it, but it's got to stop sometime.

Publishers screwing me all over. These European bastards never pay any royalties—I'm a celebrity over here and practically unknown in the States, but if I didn't get any bread from the States I'd starve, even though the publishers keep insisting that my books don't sell. Putnam's claims that the hardcover issue of *Cotton* didn't sell one copy last year, regardless of the film; and Dell contends that the film didn't help sales, which continued to be bad. It's taken for granted that none of the other titles are selling.

I got all the data from BAAL—it's depressing.

But at least we're both well and Griot is bearing up. Lesley keeps working like a mule in the garden (there's little else to do really), and I keep my bad temper going (I've got quite a reputation for it), but at least I keep these Spaniards stirred up.

I'm sorry about your difficulties with C-M and NAL; they're about the same as mine.

But I'm happy to know you're in there fighting and if we all keep on fighting we might at least get these s.o.b.s' attention even if we don't win.

Hope you and your family have a good summer in the country.

Lesley joins me in love to you, Lori, Adam, et al. And how's the little dog?

We'll be very happy to see all of you if you're ever over this way.

I don't expect to be in the States anytime soon.

All best,
Chester

August 27, 1971

Dear Chester:

Nothing much happening. Just finishing up the summer and planning to
return to the city next week. Much work done on the machine and a lot
around the house. I'm becoming a rather proficient worker in concrete. I
did the front steps and a back patio, and I like it; the finished work gives
me a sense of permanence. The soldier book is scheduled for next spring, as
is yours, I'm told. Did I mention that friends of ours have bought a co-op
near Malaga and will be in Spain in October, looking at it before they move?
They are George and Mickey Gregory, both in their sixties; lovely people.
He was one of the first black All-American basketball players and has spent
a lot of time working for the city of New York. Would you say hello to them
if they dropped in? They know and admire your work and would consider
themselves fortunate.

Charles Harris was fired at Random. Since I left last spring, not finding
it possible to work with him any longer, I don't know what's to happen to
Amistad. When I get back, I'll have to check into it.

We're all well here. Adam continues to surprise. He still speaks of you
once in a while, out of a clear blue sky. Amazing. The Black Academy's first
literary prize situation is a mess that'll work out in the last few moments
before the affair. Apparently, few if any people who're to read books have
done so. It'll work out, though; it always does, but why must we always have
these things when they are not necessary? Could it be a racial trait?

I'm trying to get an assignment to cover the Olympics next summer, so
maybe we'll see you somewhere. Certainly hope so. In the meantime, keep
in touch. Our love to both of you.

John

Chester Himes
Casa Griot
Pla del Mar
Moraira-Teulada
(Alicante)
Spain

3 September 1971

Dear John,

Glad to hear from you that you are all well and have enjoyed summer and done some good work also in concreting. You can become a sculptor that way. But it's a tough way to earn a living—the sculptor, not the mason.

We just got back from Italy, where we picked up a Fiat 500—a great little car for these goat trails. Haven't got caught up where we left off entertaining various people. Did Helen Jackson tell you she dropped by for a couple days in May or June—I forget which. We'll be glad to see the Gregorys. Clarence Major decided not to stop by after we had alerted him about the situation in August.[42] However, it's quiet again now since the French lunatic fringe have gone.

Roslyn told me that Charles Harris had been fired: I had sent her an essay written by Angus Calder, a professor of literature from the University of Nairobi ("Chester Himes and the Art of Fiction"), which I asked her to submit to *Amistad*. By the way, Calder quotes liberally from you in *Amistad*'s "My Man Himes."

I'm amazed to hear that Adam still remembers me. He and Lori are well and active, I take it.

Hope you get the assignment to cover the Olympics next summer. By then our books will have been published (eaten rather) by that dinosaur, and I have no doubt but what we both will need a little diversion.

All is well here, but Spain still gives me a pain.

---

42. Clarence Major, poet (*Love Poems of a Black Man* [1965], *Human Juices* [1966]) and novelist (*All-Night Visitors* [1969] and several other works).

Love from me and Lesley to all of you, and hoping we get together soon.

Chester

[*September/October 1971*]

Chester Himes
Casa Griot
Pal del Mar
Moraira-Teulada
(Alicante)
Spain

Dear John,

We regret that we didn't have more time to spend with you, Lori, and Adam, but as you know we were pushed to the extremity. Next time we're in New York, which will perhaps be soon, we'll have more leisure time and will be glad to accept all of your offers of hospitality, if by then you will still have the time.

Lesley joins me in love to all of you.

Chester

P.S. We arrived safely, but the hectic hours still go on, Spanish style.

October 13, 1971

Dear Chester:

I'm happy to report that Doubleday is in a frenzy of activity for *The Quality of Hurt*.[43] They can be very good, when they're good, the saying is. I've reread the galleys, and it is a classic. Really. "Expatriate literature" will never be the same. Our friends the Gregorys are leaving for Malaga and other parts in Spain on the 15th and said they'd look you up. We were thinking about going to the Olympics next year in Munich, but I can't get accreditation from the Olympic Committee, so perhaps we won't be going there. We are, however, thinking about some kind of trip because Adam can't stand being on the farm all summer long. And he drives us nuts too. We had dinner the other night with the Gregorys and Spinky Alston, who sends his regards.[44] At the moment there is nothing more "new" than a kind of sullen furor stemming from an article written this past summer by a black woman, which took the current line that black men who marry or see white women, etc., etc. It appeared in the *New York Times Magazine*, which piece of junk, you understand, loves that kind of "journalism." The end of it is not yet in sight. I'll put forth my own theses in a novel I'm now working on, which for short I call my "Fuck" book.[45] These sisters have absolutely become quite something else. I'm recovering from a bad cold, courtesy of Adam and his nursery school, and Lori's had to carry the brunt of nearly everything for the past two weeks. She's good at it. My other guys do very well; one will be a writer and may publish a short novel next spring. I understand that you may be in around March; hope to see you then, and perhaps again in the summer sometime. Lori and Adam send love. Me, I'm waiting for volume 2 of *Hurt*.

John

---

43. *The Quality of Hurt* was the first volume of Himes's autobiography. *My Life of Absurdity,* the second volume, was published in 1976.
44. Charles "Spinky" Alston (1907–77), a distant relative of Romare Bearden, was an art teacher and established painter; Jacob Lawrence studied under him. Alston and George Gregory were close friends for most of their lives.
45. This was *Mothersill and the Foxes,* not published until 1975.

Chester Himes
Casa Griot
Pla del Mar
Moraira-Teulada
(Alicante)
Spain

28 October 1971

Dear John,

I was glad to hear from you (October 13) after all this time. These people been fucking with me so much in recent months I think I got the handle to book 2 of my autobiography. We haven't seen your friends the Gregorys, but I'm glad to have word from Spinky Alston (I've been thinking all these years he spelled his name "Austin"). Sorry to hear your Olympics trip is not shaping up, but it's a long time before next summer, and there is still time. Anyway, if you don't go to Munich you and the family come and see us. We have a swimming pool now, 4 meters x 8¾ meters, and the greenery has grown up among these rocks and everything looks better. Our house withstood the deluge of a few weeks back (which many houses didn't), and naturally we feel better that it was those other motherfuckers who lost their houses.

Good luck with your Fuck book; as Jesus Christ is reported to have said, "Fuck everybody."

I hope to be in the U.S. in March and part of April next year. See you then.

Give our love to Lori and Adam and you.

Chester

December 8, 1971

Dear Chester and Lesley,

Hope you have a good holiday season. This is to take the place of a card, naturally. Our friends the Gregorys are back from Spain. Couldn't make it to Alicante, but said they dropped you a note. It looks as though we'll be going back to the Caribbean for a couple of weeks in February, and right now it can't come too soon, for New York is sinking in gray again, in depression and recession, cold, rain, and dog shit. The snow is still to come. I let Helen Jackson borrow some pictures of you I'd taken, and when they were returned, Adam insisted on seeing what the package was. He recognized you instantly. None of this, "What's his name?" It was "Chester!" So there you go.

I understand that you'll definitely be in March. Save a couple of days for us. You might like to get away, and we can run up to the country. *Intellectual Digest* has an excerpt from your book in the latest issue. I saw one of the editors yesterday and told him he'd selected the least important section, the robbery. He was flabbergasted. Said he hadn't made the selection himself. Ah well.

Did I tell you Charles Harris has moved down to Howard University Press, having been kicked out of Random House last July? Anyway, *Amistad may* be published down there, but from the way the legal end of it's going, not for a long while. I've just discovered that one of my writing students at City College a few years ago is a cop. He gave me a novel he was working on then, and it's pretty good, so I have to try to get it somewhere. A brother. Real brother. Let us hear from you when you get time. By the way, Tony Burton called me. I suggest that you also write Peter Heggie of the Authors Guild, 234 W. 44th Street, N.Y., N.Y. 10036, because we've finally got a board that looks like it's going to get active in this battle between crooked publishers and authors.[46] I've an accountant now checking the books at Coward-McCann (Putnam's partner), and a long-running battle's ensuing between myself and NAL, which claims *The Man Who Cried I Am* has sold

---

46. Peter Heggie was secretary of the Authors Guild at that time.

only 150,000 copies, but it's in five printings, and no campus I've been on hasn't had it for required reading. I think Burton would be willing to work with the Guild; and the Guild, before long, I hope, will select a number of test cases.

Lori and Adam send love. Stay well.

John

Chester Himes
Casa Griot
Pal del Mar
Moraira-Teulada
(Alicante)
Spain

18 December 1971

Dear John and Lori and Adam,
Thanks for the letter with all the interesting news. It is always a pleasure to learn what is happening in the more enlightened (although infuriating) departments of the world. I'm delighted to learn that Adam still remembers me, which is more than can be said of many other of my former acquaintances I am sure. Yes, I received a letter from the Gregorys, which contained no surprising news. We were in Barcelona a couple of days the first of the week, and it was a relief to get away from these sticks if only for a breather. As you know, the Spanish coast is dreary if not downright sinister in the winter. We hope to take a suite in the Chelsea Hotel for March if we can get insurance for our clothing (which is not much, but we don't want it stolen) and also Griot; we'll be bringing him along despite all the problems he presents.

I saw a piece in *Intellectual Digest* from *The Quality of Hurt,* also from your interview. I hope to go out and see Goldwyn in Los Angeles and also take Lesley to Greensboro, N.C., to visit my brother Joe.

I've forgotten what the weather is like in March in New York—cold and slushy as I remember. Well, I'll be inside most of the time.

I've got to the place I don't expect any royalties from these publisher mothers. I find they're the same all over the world. And I'm getting tired of fighting—ill health and old age, I suspect.

I'm glad to hear that Charles Harris got settled in Howard University Press. I suppose Random House owns the publishing rights to *Amistad.*

I'm not surprised by Coward-McCann; it exists by not paying royalties. But I'm alarmed by NAL, who is bringing out four paperbacks of mine. I wish you best of luck in your fights with them. I corresponded with Peter Heggie when Hollywood used the title *If He Hollers Let Him Go* on that chickenshit film, and I found him sympathetic and very informative but not very effective. But just thinking of Hollywood makes me want to vomit. I must write Tony Burton a letter, and I will send you a copy.

But anyway both of us are as well as can be expected, and if the sun ever shines again we'll feel better.

Lesley joins me in seasons greeting, love, and all best wishes to all of you, and give Adam kisses for us.

Chester

January 12, 1972

Dear Chester:

Your inscribed book came today. Chester! Chester! Bravo!! We are happy, most happy with it and for you. Addison Gayle, whom I ran into yesterday, had a copy of the NAL edition of *Cast the First Stone.* I had mixed feelings about it. I was glad that it's back in print but salty that some sister in LA who runs a black bookstore had charged me $15 for a copy of the first edition. But listen: it is a first edition, right?[47]

---

47. My mixed feelings had to do with the price, not the book.

Your schedule seems to be filling up by leaps and bounds, but I do hope you save us just a little time when you get here in March. This day is a rather special one for my twenty-year-old.[48] He's just got the galleys for his first book, a short novel that he wrote with someone else. His book'll be out about the same time as mine, in May. So he's walking on air and grinning from ear to ear.

Man, I want to talk very seriously with you for the rest of this note. I just finished talking to Ishmael Reed, who's doing a major review of your book for *Black World*. In our conversation he confirmed for me some of the actions surrounding your book that I felt months ago but didn't want to convey them to you for fear that you'd think me stupid or something. During the past couple of years, to give you some background, there's been a hurricane of sentiment from the sisters having to do with how rotten black men are because they marry white women. This attitude is worse today than it's ever been in our history; it's driven several people, black men and their white wives, out of New York; Ishmael Reed for one. When the sisters write for the *Times* or *Black World*, it's the same old shit, even from the most intelligent of them.

I felt a few months ago, and I discussed this with Helen, that the way she was attempting to set up the promotion of your book was like feeding you to the wolves. She had galleys sent to many people who are into this hate-black-man-because-he's-got-a-white-wife thing. Reed tells me she'd tried to set up interviews with black women writers (who're the great rage with the white male literary set, but that's not new) who are proponents of the every-white-chick-is-a-tramp theory.

But, of course, you must have some inkling of all this. I wanted to clarify it for you; it's there, palpable. You may find that when it comes to face-to-face discussion of the matter, however, most people would rather write about it. There is a certain cowardliness involved here, as you can imagine there must be.

We do not run very much in any literary circles, so I suppose we

---

48. Son Dennis A. Williams. His novel, *Them That's Not* (1973), had a coauthor, Spero Pines. Dennis also published *Crossover* (1992) and *Somebody's Child* (1997).

escape a lot of indirect confrontations, but you can't attend a conference on anything black without running into it. We do far better among our neighbors who've kids Adam's age, and we spend a lot of time out of the city, so we've not been bugged that much by all this nonsense. Ron Fair, whom you've heard of by now, seems to be another victim with his second and white wife. Moved to Switzerland. Sam Greenlee's Dutch wife arrived in Chicago, and he was promptly kicked out of a black writing group.[49] So it goes; I've filled you in. Now you and Lesley come on over, and the four of us will kick ass together.

Love,
John

Chester Himes
Casa Griot
Pla del Mar
Moraira-Teulada
(Alicante)
Spain

8 February 1972

Dear John,
Thanks for your letter of January 12.

First, I don't know what the hell NAL is doing with my books. I found so many printing and spelling errors in *The Primitive* I didn't read any more.[50] I read the end pages of *Cast the First Stone,* and I found that NAL is

---

49. Sam Greenlee, the author, best known for his novel *The Spook Who Sat by the Door.*
50. *The Primitive* was first published in 1955. The title became *The End of a Primitive* in 1990, following Himes's death, with his widow holding copyright.

trying to sell it as an autobiographical novel. I've written them about both, but I know that doesn't mean a damn thing.

I know that Helen is trying to throw me to the wolves in more ways than one. But that is not her fault. The only real contact she has is with black writers and writers' groups, especially black women writers. She is too naive to believe that they really hate me. But that is really of no great consequence. The real villain is Doubleday. Those motherfuckers haven't changed in twenty-seven years; they behave just the same as they did when *If He Hollers* was published in 1945—throw the black writers to the black wolves or wolverines. Black literature is not for white consumption. Anyway, I expect to be stoned. I will stay a few days in New York and return to Europe, where at least I don't have the black racists to contend with.

My plan (as of now) is to stay in New York from March 1 until March 8 or 9, then visit my brother at the University of North Carolina at Greensboro for a few days, then come back here.

We will love to see you and Lori and Adam and the family. I have much business with Roslyn. I will only see the people I want since I'm paying for the trip out of my pocket. There are a number of Lesley's friends and several expatriates in the States we might visit. And fuck Doubleday.

Anyway, everything is under control.

Lesley joins me in love to you all.

Chester

April 24 [1972]

Dear Chester:

Just back from Notre Dame, where I ran into the proverbial drunken priest who claimed to have read everything I'd ever written, including *The Primitive.* How about that?

We are moving into summer, hopefully, and looking forward to getting out of here. A trip to California and then back to the farm. Otherwise we approach the usual publication day bullshit.

Haven't really seen anyone since you left, which gives us a chance to catch up on rest. Best to Lesley. Tell her to care well for the slides. If you get back, we'll see you.

John

-§-

Chester Himes
Casa Griot
Pla del Mar
Moraira-Teulada
(Alicante)
Spain

30 May 1972

Dear John,
As I was reading *Captain Blackman* I kept remembering a bit of dialogue from my book *The Primitive*: ". . . if the white man ever suspects you know how he thinks . . . he'll kill you sure as . . ." Which I sincerely hope will never happen to you, because *Captain Blackman* is without doubt the most shattering book that whitey will ever read and will assuredly give him many uneasy nights.

But for that reason I salute you, John A. Williams, for this novel alone makes you one of the greatest, most unbiased, bravest historical novelists of this time, or any time.

Magnificent, stupendous, profound, informative, spellbinding, but what are adjectives in the face of this explosion in the mind? Whether you're black or white, it will turn you on.

Best wishes,
Chester

June 2, 1972

Dear Chester:

Sorry as hell to hear about the stroke and hope it passes harmlessly. An extended rest should be of great help.

We are preparing once again to get the hell out of this fucking city for the summer. We were in the country for Memorial Day and didn't want to come back, but had to because of Adam's school. But we'll go up mid-month and turn this place over to my son Dennis, whom you met, who'll be working at *Newsweek* again this summer. The older boy, Greg, and his wife, Lucia, are due here today for a short visit.

I have no real idea how the book is going and haven't asked or read any of the reviews; I'll do that next year, as always. Melvin has a new show, and it looks pretty good. Haven't spoken to Gentry, but should have him and his crew up for a weekend.[51] Other than this, nothing exciting except that I'm putting together a small book of my photos and really need those slides Lesley has. Do keep in touch—you have our address in the country; if not, mail arriving here will be sent upstate by Dennis. The back problem has gotten worse, and I'm wearing a brace and beginning acupuncture treatments. So, I'm taking it rather easy myself. Lori and Adam send love.

John A. Williams

---

51. Herbert Gentry, African American painter and expatriate, died in 2003 in Sweden. Gentry began his artistic studies at the end of World War II. He returned to Europe after briefly attending New York University but then moved to the Academe de la Grande Chaumiere in Paris, where he opened a restaurant and an art gallery. His work has been displayed throughout Europe and the United States. Gentry taught at Montclair State College and Rutgers University.

July 13, 1972

Dear Chester:

Just a note to check you out and thank you for the quote, which I understand is being used in advertising.

I've read Ishmael Reed's new book, *Mumbo-Jumbo,* and he's gonna have a rough time with it but is resigned to that fact. He's so far out in front. I suppose that's why so few people like him.

We go back to the city for a couple of days and then East Hampton for about four before returning back here to cut grass, kill snakes, and work. We're all fine, although Adam is bored to death, even though we have a ten-foot pool for him and a large rubber boat to row around the pond and a dozen other things. Next summer we'll have to do something else for a part of the time.

As you perhaps know, John Killens had a stroke last month, a minor one, and he's recovering rapidly and will get over it entirely, I'm told.[52] Nothing else new, or we don't know it up here, which is probably all to the good. Give love to all.

John

February 3, 1973

Dear Chester:

Yes, we got the pictures okay, and we've been well except for occasional bouts with colds or flu or some fucking thing or other. Sorry to hear that you've not been up to par. Ish Reed was in town late last fall giving readings

---

52. The author John Oliver Killens (1916–87) wrote *Youngblood* (1954), *The Cotillion; or One Good Bull Is Half the Herd* (1971), and several other novels, screenplays, and essays. He was a Pulitzer Prize nominee in 1971. Killens taught creative writing at Fisk, Columbia, and the City University of New York.

and told me about your new collection, a copy of which is being sent to me. I was writing to you anyway about a collection of my articles due out in April in which is included the interview we did a few years ago for *Amistad*, which has appeared in other places.[53]

Ish is leaving or has left Doubleday for Random House. It seems that there was some objection at Doubleday in publishing more than one black writer on the same list, which means that Doubleday hasn't changed since you were with them last. I plan to put some heavy shit on my editor at lunch this coming week about that racist bullshit. It's tiring. *Captain Blackman* bombed but good, and nobody at Doubleday wants us to talk about why. As they say, as soon's I get together, it's going to be something else.

Oscar's been replaced. That's for the best, I think. Adam doesn't yet have another pet, although he promises he will be entirely responsible for walking, feeding, etc. Shit. He can't even tie his shoe laces; should I believe him?

There is a small possibility that I'll take my middle son, Dennis, whom you met, to Nigeria for a month this summer. We'll have to see before making anything definite. Love to you three.

John

July 23, 1973

Dear Chester:
If you can find an acupuncturist in France, I urge you to use him (or her) for your arthritis and other ailments. I've had extremely good results from just a few treatments for an old spinal disc injury that crops up from time to

---

53. The collection, *Flashbacks: A Twenty-Year Diary of Article Writing*, was published in 1973 by Doubleday.

time, as you may remember from your last visit.

I went four times last year and twice this year with immediate results. These leave me able to work around the farm, although I often wear a brace to prevent myself from overdoing it.

We're all fine. Adam's thirteen-year-old cousin is here from California, so he's having a ball this summer. The work goes on okay. *Flashbacks* has already been consigned to oblivion, a pattern, I suppose. Doubleday continues to make black writers unhappy, including me, but I'm finishing out my contract of two more books, one of which will be finished by the end of the summer.

I'll be teaching too, for the second year in a row, and I hope that I won't have to in 1974 past June. We saw Gentry at an opening for Bearden, but not since then, which was this past spring.[54]

I have the impression that a kind of evil doldrums have set in around New York, and as far as I know other places as well. We all seem to be sitting and waiting for disaster, which, like a parachute, is already descending around us. Love to Lesley. Take care of yourself.

John

November 2, 1983

Dear Chester:

I have been hearing for some time now that you were ill. I also hear that your health has improved. For the latter I feel grateful; I was sad to hear about your illness. A couple of our mutual friends have been urging me to

---

54. The artist Romare Bearden (1912–88) is perhaps best known as a collagist. He was an organizer of the Harlem Artists Guild and, in the 1930s, of the Spiral group. Bearden often chronicled African American life and was the recipient of countless honors for his work. We met in the 1970s one winter when he was a houseguest of the Gregorys in Grenada.

write, and I have just put off doing it until now. I hope you understand that I was deeply hurt and angered by your comments about me in the second volume of your autobiography. This was particularly true because I never tried to beat you out of any money; the thought never occurred to me. On the other hand, I do recall lending you what money I had when you needed it. So, I was hurt and angered and really pissed. I think I am now over that, but that was the reason for my breaking off any contact.

Our family is well. My father in Syracuse is doing all right, and my mother in Los Angeles is still in her house with the collard greens garden, lemon tree, and orange tree. I was able to get out there three times this year, and she came east for a family reunion this summer, so we've had pretty good contact this year.

Lori is well. She's back in publishing with a small firm here in New Jersey, where we have been now for eight years. We still have the house in the Catskill Mountains, but this place is a pleasant change from New York City, which we can reach by car in about fifteen minutes. Adam loves it. Now in high school, he's a great tennis player and has a little rock band; he plays guitar. We are at the point where we've started looking around for colleges. Can you believe that?

My two older sons have been married forever, it seems. Greg, the eldest, and his wife, Lucia, have a three-year-old son, John Gregory. Greg's a teacher in Philadelphia, and Lucia works for the city there. Dennis and his wife, Millicent, have a four-and-a-half-year-old daughter, Margo Carolyn. He's been at *Newsweek* for quite some time now and is the education editor. His wife's a social worker.

I'm at the Newark campus of Rutgers University teaching journalism and creative writing. For the past year, though, I've been on leave, but I will be returning in January. I am, of course, working on three projects, one of which is a nonfiction book on Richard Pryor, the comedian-actor.[55] The other is a novel, and the third project is a literature textbook. And I am

---

55. *If I Stop I'll Die,* published in 1991 and written in collaboration with Dennis.

writing more and more poetry. As you probably know, the literary scene here is very bad, and there are no signs that it's going to get better. There's a new man at the *Times Book Review*. He comes from the news side of the paper, and how he got to be editor is beyond me. They are bringing in, however, a couple of people from the *Times Literary Supplement*. I don't know if that is good or bad. And time I don't think will ever tell.

Reagan seems to be as popular as ever, even after Lebanon and Grenada. Those of us who think we are wise believe that things must certainly get worse than they are now, so it's a relief to hear from time to time that, while Spain might not be heaven, it is certainly different. It has been six years since we visited there, taking Adam with us. We think he had a good time. Someone wanted to buy him when we visited Morocco, but I was feeling kindly toward him then and declined the offer. I have not had cause yet to regret it.

Charles Harris is still at Howard University Press, totally unchanged from what I hear, but some things do tend to become institutions. I don't know many people in the business any more. A whole new breed, it seems, with values and ideas about literature that now seem ten times as shallow as those held by people we used to know.

I hope, Chester, that these lines find you in good shape. My best regards to Lesley.

John

February 3, 1984

Dear Lesley:

Thanks for yours of November 18. Herb Gentry, who is in town, was also glad for your response. We're all deeply sorry about Chester's condition. We know how tough it must be on you. Are your plans simply to remain there or what?

We were also pleased to know that at least there are some moneys coming in and that you are managing. Hope, though, that all the legal business gets straightened out, as I am sure that would help to put your mind at ease.

There are many people here who are concerned with Chester, so if you could keep us posted, we can get the progress report around. I am in regular touch with Ishmael Reed too, so our West Coast friends know something about what's going on.

Winter has been a mixed blessing, sometimes mild and at other times bitterly cold—nothing constant, the way it used to be over a period of time. I understand the weather has been unusual in Europe as well this winter.

Since there's nothing new here, I'll close and wish you the best possible New Year. Please stay in touch. Lori sends love.

Sincerely,
John

November 28, 1984

Dear Lesley:

We heard and read. We extend our deepest condolences. Serious health problems, suddenly discovered, have been the cause of our delayed contact following the announcements of Chester's death. We are sorry, but we also believe with you that this was what he wanted after such a long and lingering illness. Of course, the tributes will come now, and the reissuance of his books. I wish it had been otherwise. When Chester was Chester I loved him. We wish you well and hope that from time to time we may hear from you. (Our trip to Europe did not go all that well, which was why you didn't hear from us.)

Our best/Our sympathies,
John

January 9, 1985

Dear Lesley:

By now you've probably settled into some kind of routine. I hope that
all's going well and that you can start to see some daylight again. I would
have thought that Herb Gentry would have been in touch with you early
on—that is, if he was in Europe. He does spend a lot of time here, although
I haven't seen him since last spring.

There has been some talk, not much of it consistent, about having a
memorial for Chester. Nothing more than talk, however.

What are your plans? Will you go to England or stay there to clear up
business? If you came to the U.S., would that be a permanent move or just a
visit?

I think Howard University did a nice job with *A Case of Rape;* I only
hope they handle the business end as prettily as they produced the book.

We are all well. Some problems with aged parents, but who doesn't have
those? We're also looking over colleges for Adam, just to show you how time
really does fly. The literary scene continues to be extremely depressing, but
we all press on because what we do is write. Take care of yourself, and let us
know if and when you'll make it this way.

John

March 29, 1985

Dear Lesley:

We hope all's going well with you.

You may not have seen the enclosed, so here it is. Nothing developing
in the way of a memorial, although this piece indicates that he is thought of.
Something may yet come of a memorial, which would be late, as usual, but
perhaps better than never.

We're all well here, in the throes of rummaging around for a college for Adam, and our own killing kinds of work. But we survive.

As ever,
John

-§-

Moraira (Spain)

6 March 1987

Dear John,

I have just had a very pleasant two-week visit of Michel Fabre and his wife. We have been going through all the letters, papers, etc., and we hope Michel will be able to start work soon on Chester's biography. It will take two to three years, but he is not in a rush.

I would like to ask you whether you would be willing to lend us some of Chester's letters to you? We would, naturally, edit anything you think should be edited. We do have quite a few, but not all of them. I am also looking to other friends to whom he wrote frequently. And I hope they will answer me positively.

It seems so long since I wrote to you, but Christmas was rather a rush for me because I had an emergency operation just two days before departure for England.

Do you have Melvin Van Peebles's address? I was told by Michel that he is working as a stock broker or some such thing. Can it be true? Maybe Gentry will see him in the Chelsea Hotel (where maybe he now lives) sometime.

Please give my fondest regards to Lori and the rest of the family. Are you all well?

Much love,
Lesley

JOHN A. WILLIAMS AND CHESTER HIMES, WEST 92ND STREET, NEW YORK, 1967

Lesley Himes, Chester Himes, and Lori Williams, West 92nd Street, New York, 1967

LORI, JOHN A., AND ADAM WILLIAMS, WEST 92ND STREET, NEW YORK, 1968

JOHN A. WILLIAMS, WEST 92ND
STREET, NEW YORK, 1969

LORI WILLIAMS, 1968

CHESTER HIMES, ALICANTE,
SPAIN, MAY 1969

LESLEY HIMES, ALICANTE, SPAIN,
MAY 1969

CHESTER HIMES AND JOHN A. WILLIAMS, ALICANTE, SPAIN, MAY 1969

CHESTER HIMES AND
JOHN A. WILLIAMS AT THE
BLACK ACADEMY OF ARTS
AND LETTERS INDUCTION,
SEPTEMBER 20, 1970

Ossie Davis (*far left*), Chester Himes, John A. Williams, and Ruby Dee (*at the podium*)
at the Black Academy of Arts and Letters induction, September 20, 1970

Chester Himes with cat Griot, Alicante, Spain, Casa Griot, 1972

CHESTER AND LESLEY HIMES IN ROSLYN TARG'S APARTMENT, NEW YORK, 1973

CHESTER HIMES (*seated*) WITH ADMIRERS: (*from left*) ISHMAEL REED, CLARENCE MAJOR, STEVE CANNON, AND JOE JOHNSON, PARK LANE HOTEL, NEW YORK, 1973

Afterword

Afterword

I remember those two cats, Griot and Chester. In a favorite closeup photograph, Griot sits on his master's shoulder, both looking remarkably alike, both grinning those Cheshire-cat smiles. When Chester was Chester, he often smiled and laughed. He was fun, loving, often downright hilarious. When he wasn't Chester, he wasn't fun to be around. He possessed a temper that was often unpredictable. And like the Cheshire cat, he too could unpredictably disappear, sometimes for months, sometimes for years, as he shuffled with that old limp between Paris and Biot, Amsterdam and Berlin, Alicante and Sisal, Mexico. Wherever he was, I was always certain of one thing—that he was writing. When he would reappear in my life, quite often unpredictably, he would turn on his considerable charm and I'd feel a closer bond between us. Regardless, he was never far away, not really. All I had to do was look around my office and there would be Chester, lining the bookshelves, smiling from a framed photograph.

At the time of his death, he was seventy-five, a man old not so much in years but in experiences and in the *sameness* of those experiences. His was a hard life; he worked hard, worried hard, drank hard, and, most significantly, wrote hard. But if he had lived for another century, he could not have written all the books that were in him. He simply knew too much about people, places, and things. He saw stories in the lives of those about him, some of which required no elaboration, while others did, bringing out the creative touch he was forever sharpening, forever pushing to the center of whatever matter he was creating, and the more unusual, the better. Even today it's sometimes a mean task to have a book published, let alone eighteen novels, numerous short stories, and a two-volume autobiography, all written with an enviable degree of versatility. And more often than not, we tend to cry about the state of the American novel, yet we manage to kill off—literally and figurative-ly—novelists whose works are representative of America, although, perhaps, not the America we like to believe we live in.

He was a naturalist writer. And why shouldn't he have been? Turmoil sur-rounded him. His mother looked down on his father, basically because she had much lighter skin than he. Furthermore, job opportunities for a "professor of black-smithing" were dwindling as the automobile gradually replaced the horse. Children who witness parents screaming at and battling one another tend to become battlers and screamers themselves. Chester was not left unmarked by the experiences of his childhood. Later in life, his fall down an elevator shaft left him with more than severely broken bones. A somewhat gimpy gait was also attributable to the fall, as was a slight lisp that sometimes clouded his speech. But his hurts were beyond the physical hurts he received in that fall, hurts that plagued him his entire life. But what a life he lived.

If Chester liked you, he'd tell you what happened. He would tell you because he was a natural raconteur, with a thousand digressions from the main story. He would, perhaps, tell you in his rugged little duplex on the Chateau de Bourbon, which you would reach only after climbing an endless flight of stairs and only after stepping over a couple of *clochards*. He would tell you with murder in his laughter and between deep draughts of *vin ordinaire* or whiskey, if it had been a good month. Once when I was visiting him in Paris, he asked Lesley to go for some of that *vin ordinaire*, which she agreed to do, down and then later back up those very same steep stairs. When she returned, slightly out of breath, he then asked sweetly in that honeyed voice, "My dear, would you go get us some cigarettes?" If looks could kill! But that too was Chester.

It is interesting to think about his earliest work, written and published while in prison, and first appearing in *Esquire* magazine, perhaps the most prestigious publication for male readers at that time. His first story in "*Eskie*," "Crazy in the Stir" (1934), was soon followed by several other stories in different publications. Himes was one of the first, if not *the* first, black author to publish in *Esquire*. It probably paid more than *Negro Story*, the NAACP's *Crisis*, or the *Pittsburgh Courier*, *Chicago Defender*, and other black papers and magazines in which Himes frequently appeared. These publications, of course, were more interested in the social advance-ment of African Americans than in crime and sex tales. But Himes wrote for them prodigiously, and no doubt the writing was a psychological escape from prison life. Shortly after his release he met Langston Hughes, then later worked as a butler for Louis Bromfield at Malabar Farm. From his letters Chester tells us that Bromfield "read my prison manuscript [*Cast the First Stone*] and promised to help me get it published or made into a film . . . he talked my book up and sent me to see some people. A few Hollywood people knew of me from *Esquire*—which was then the Hollywood Bible—but no one suspected I was black. When they saw my face, I was finished, period." More hurt and disappointment, but he continued. *Cast the First Stone* was published, but not until 1942. And down through the aching, frustrating years that followed, the writing continued, and other novels saw print: *If He Hollers Let Him Go* (1945), *Lonely Crusade* (1947), *The Third Generation* (1954), and *The Primitive* (1955). Those books showed little trace of the satiric or macabre. But *The Primitive* marked a turn. He sat down in Mallorca with a kind of I-don't-give-a-damn attitude and wrote. From then on, his creative vision was often comical but also dark and violent.

In 1953 he put this land behind him. He would return occasionally to New York to see his old friend Carl Van Vechten or to work on some deal or another. But he was a nervous, wretched man. Once you are out of New York, you can almost see from which direction the pressures are coming; when you are in the city, in America, you expect them to come from any direction, at any time. And you can't see them. It was almost inevitable, then, that incident with the taxi driver. Chester was a shaken man when he got to his hotel, shaken with anger. We drank until the next day dawned, cold and gray. Some months later, I had to appear as a witnesses at the Hack Bureau. They took away the cabbie's license for two weeks or so. I was glad Chester wasn't there.

The now-famous black detectives Grave Digger Jones and Coffin Ed Johnson were born in Paris and were overnight sensations. To some readers they seem to have been let loose to provide a low level of mystery and a high level of black slapstick for French readership, but the series was quickly translated into English and other languages. Back at the ranch in New York, writers who had known Chester were sneering, "He's writing detective books now." But what detective books! In every age someone has to provide the setting from which readers can taste, and perhaps even confirm, their fantasies of places and people they've only heard or read about—like Harlem, and the black cops who often kill both black *and* white bad guys there. For many readers, Chester Himes provided that setting, and he could do so easily, often in a marathon of writing and in a storm of paper flying from the typewriter, laughing as he wrote. At the same time, his imagination danced, even frolicked, with the characters and situations into which he placed them.

In Paris, Chester also became a close friend of another novelist, Richard Wright, who had moved there in 1948 after the publication of *Uncle Tom's Children* (1938), *Native Son* (1940), and *Black Boy* (1945). In that post–World War II period, Jim Crow America forced several black American artists and writers to relocate to France, but few, if any, were more prestigious than Wright and Himes. Yet that scene too became tired as it gradually lost some of its vitality. There were, in fact, too many "brothers" in Paris, Chester frequently complained when back in New York.

He was the only teller of jokes I knew who could not finish a joke without first falling out and letting loose a hurricane of laughter. I still hear that explosive laughter and that slightly slurred speech when listening to the audiotape of the interview for *Amistad 1*. The wine we shared that day helped to improve our mood and perhaps enhanced the slurring of words. Certainly, the laughter came more easily because of it.

In the later years, his temper was shorter; he saw doctors more often; his sullen moods were longer, his laughter wilder. He would freeze someone out one month and lavish champagne on the same person the next; he could draw up almost like a serpent with some and then behave like Jesus himself (almost) toward others. But beyond his problems, he left us a monumental legacy with his writings. He topped a lot of fine writing with *Pinktoes,* and I for one never cared how much murder there was in his laughter, as long as he kept on writing. He was, in the end, one of America's great mirrors reflecting the absurdity surrounding African American life for more than half a century.

Since my last letter to Chester in 1983, my life and the lives of my family have changed considerably. Lori and I are still married, and even though she is now retired from publishing, she still supervises everything and everyone. Eldest son, Greg, and his wife, Lucia, at this writing twenty-five years later have a son, John Gregory, now twenty-eight, and a daughter, Nancy, age twenty-three. Next son, Dennis, and his wife, Millicent, have a twenty-nine-year-old daughter, Margo, and a son, David, who is twenty-two. Greg and Dennis teach at Temple University and Georgetown University, respectively. Thirty-nine-year-old Adam, his blond curls now dark, graduated from Berklee College of Music in 1992, was a member of the rock band Powerman 5000 for thirteen years, and is now a music producer.

I retired from Rutgers in 1994. Chester would be pleased to know, I think, that since my last letter, the writing continues. The Pryor book, *If I Stop I'll Die,* was published in 1991, and three novels have also been released: *The Berhama Account* (1985), *Jacob's Ladder* (1987), and *Clifford's Blues* (1999). *Safari West* (1998), a collection of poetry, garnered an American Book Award, and in 1999 a collaboration with composer Leslie Burrs produced *Vanqui,* an opera that opened in a six-day run and has had several concert performances. I've continued to write essays, while coauthoring and editing six books of nonfiction, including *Street Guide to African Americans in Paris* (1996) with Michel Fabre and four college textbooks with Gil Muller. A novel, "Colleagues," remains unpublished as I work on another novel and more poetry, as well as a memoir.

Lori and I still hear from Lesley, now retired and gardening under the Spanish sun in Alicante. Her bookshelves are filled with memories, with books by or about Chester and by others, writer friends and admirers. She lives alone but for the two griot spirits that forever shadow her steps, Griot the cat and the old griot himself, my friend, Chester Bomar Himes.

John A. Williams

Appendix
My Man Himes: An Interview with Chester Himes

Most young, newly rabid readers of black literature don't know who Chester Himes is, which is unfortunate. People who know him consider him to be a novelist, but Himes still writes articles for European papers and magazines and got his start in the United States publishing short stories and articles, many of which appeared in the now defunct Abbot's Monthly.

As a writer identified only by a prison number, he published in Esquire *six short stories from 1934 to 1936. When he was released from the Ohio State Penitentiary and appeared at the* Esquire *offices (obviously a black man), his publishing days, there at least, were over. But he went on to publish articles in the* Journal of the NAACP *and the* Journal of the Urban League.

This interview that I did with Himes in 1969 requires no headnote. I include it here, with his kind permission, because I feel that young writers, particularly young black writers, can derive much from Himes's raps about writing as it ties into everyday living. No other writer that I know of, black or white, has ever spoken so candidly about his profession.

As the interview was going to press for the first issue of Amistad, *from which it is taken, I received a special delivery letter from Himes. He asked me to delete the names of certain people about whom he'd been openly and angrily critical when the interview was taped. He felt, after seeing the typed interview, that he'd been too harsh. As it developed, those same people he'd tried to protect continued their practices that had made him criti-cal in the first place, and Himes was forced to seek legal redress—which is almost nonex-istent for writers.*

The interview itself was long, and we often got off the track. Lori spent most of that summer transcribing the tapes at the same time I was editing the material into block sec-tions and headings that would make sense in the reading. Without a doubt this was my most satisfying interview, and I was grateful for the tape recorder. Sometimes I've used that instrument and come away feeling that it hadn't really captured anything.

I couldn't think of a better way to end than to include Himes's interview, after which nothing more can be said about the position of the black writer in the United States today.

New York was chilly that Friday, disappointing after a couple of days of hot weather. Then spring had beat a hasty retreat. London the next day was London: chilly, gray, and somber at Heathrow. Then we boarded a Trident, as tight and crowded a plane as the Caravelle, and split with a full passenger list, mostly British except us, to Spain and Chester Himes.

Lori brightened considerably when we crossed the Pyrenees. (Once we had driven through them, back and forth from the Spanish to the French borders, paus-ing now and again to picnic in the hot green areas between the snow-filled slopes.) Not long after, the Mediterranean flowed out beneath us as the coast of eastern Spain bent to the west, and we prepared to land in Alicante.

It was clear, bright, and warm there, and going down the ramp I was conscious once more of the strange sweetness that lingers in the Spanish air, as though the entire nation had been freshly dipped in sherry or cognac. Down on the tarmac we saw Chester and Lesley waving, and I felt great relief. For Himes is sixty-one now and is not well, although he takes extremely good care of himself, mostly under Lesley's guidance. He smokes a great deal less, drinks mostly wine, and adheres to a strict diet. Himes' life has been filled with so many disasters, large and small, that I lived in dread that one of these would carry him away so that I would no longer have the chance to see or talk to him.

I suppose it is known that I admire the man and his work. This began late in 1945, when I was a boy of twenty. I was then on Guam in the Mariana Islands with my outfit, the 17th Special Naval Construction Battalion, waiting to be shipped home. There was not much to do. The war was over; we were all waiting.

I was a hospital corpsman, and we held two sick calls a day; otherwise we slept, swam, or read. Mostly I read and tried to write the kind of jive poetry a twenty-year-old will write. I don't remember how the novel came into my hands, but I never forgot it. It was *If He Hollers Let Him Go.* The author was Chester B. Himes. Years later, long after it was published, I read *Third Generation.* Until 1962 that was the extent of my Himes.

That year I met Himes in Carl Van Vechten's apartment in the San Remo on Central Park West. I had met "Carlo" when *Night Song* was published in 1961. Van Vechten met, photographed, knew, and corresponded with every black writer who ever came down the pike; now that I look back, perhaps he anticipated their importance in and to American letters fifty years before anyone else.

If anything, Himes was even more handsome than his photographs. Not terribly big, about five-nine or ten. One remembers his eyes mostly; they sit in that incredible face upon which ravages show—but which they have been unable to destroy—and at certain angles the long-lashed eyes are soft, *soft,* as though clinging to some teen-aged dream of love and goodness and justice. The eyes have remained that way, although today, at certain other angles they clearly reveal the pain of life as a black man and artist.

Himes is perhaps the single greatest naturalistic American writer living today. Of course, no one in the literary establishment is going to admit that; they haven't, and they won't. Reviews of his books generally wind up in the last half of the *Sunday New York Times Book Review,* if they are reviewed at all. Himes will tell you that he doesn't care, that all his career he has been shuffled under the table. Perhaps this is, after all, the smallest of hurts he has suffered. He is a fiercely independent man and has been known to terminate friendships and conversations alike with two well-chosen, one-syllable words. Worse than the words is his silence. I swear I have felt him glowering at me across the Atlantic from Paris at times.

Soon after I met Himes for the first time, Van Vechten told me, "Chester doesn't like many people. He likes you."

Well, I liked him. We corresponded regularly after our meeting; we exchanged books, and he gave me a quote for *Sissie;* as I recall, it wasn't used. Himes was still publishing in France in the Gallimard Série Noire. Although he had won the Grand Prix for detective novels for *La reine des pommes* (*For Love of Immabelle,* it was called here) he was still living pretty much from hand to mouth. I managed to see him once in Paris, but most often I saw him here after he arrived on the *France.* He stays at the Hotel Albert on 10th Street and University Place when he comes. In Europe I missed him often enough, for he would move frequently to avoid having his work disturbed by other expatriate brothers. Then he would undergo periodic fits of disgust with the Parisians and go to Scandinavia or Holland. Sometimes, through Daniel Guérin ("the French expert on the brother," Himes says), he went to La Ciotat near the Riviera to be isolated and to work. (La Ciotat, Himes says with the pride of association, is where André Schwarz-Bart wrote *The Last of the Just.*)

Chester Himes finally got a piece of what he deserves through the American publication of *Pinktoes.* He was back with an American publisher after almost a decade away from them. His detectives, Grave Digger Jones and Coffin Ed Smith, came back to America in hardcover after titillating (one of Himes' favorite words in describing the effect black people have on white people) the French for several years. The early novels of their adventures had been spirited away, more or less, by soft-cover publishers—often without Himes' knowing they were being published in America. He would write and ask me to confirm their presence, for word would have been brought to him by visitors to the Continent. That he was being paid little or no money for these rights only supported his contention that publishing was a brutal business and brutal businesses always take advantage of black people.

In both 1965 and 1966 we missed Himes in Europe; he had reserved a hotel for us in Paris and we were to have dinner, but he had fled France, leaving his flat to Melvin Van Peebles, the filmmaker. We were to visit him in La Ciotat, but he'd packed up and taken off again. The next time we saw him was in 1967, when he and Lesley and their Siamese cat, Griot, flew to New York. That was when he started working on a film treatment of *Cotton Comes to Harlem* for Sam Goldwyn, Jr. (I read the screenplay by Ossie Davis and Arnold Perl while in Alicante and thought that if Davis as director could put on film what he has put on paper, the movie would be a very special thing.)

So, it was almost two years to the day when we saw them again in Alicante. Lesley had reserved a room for us in a hotel around the corner from their small apartment. Lori and I unpacked, grabbed a couple hours of sleep, then went around the corner to pick them up for dinner. Chester and Lesley lived on the ninth floor of number 2 Calle Duque du Zaragoza, a step off Rambla Mendez Muñoz, four short blocks from the Promenade and the port.

With some writers you get the feeling that you are interrupting their work, that they wish you to be gone, out of their homes, out of their lives. I've never had that feeling with Himes; he has always made me feel welcome, whether it was in the Albert, in the Quarter in Paris (I repaid the hospitality that time by falling asleep in front of the fire and holding up dinner), or in Alicante. Besides, Himes deserved a break away from his typewriter. He is always at it. If not books, then letters; he has always been a compulsive letter writer. (He once wrote a letter to President Roosevelt.) So I was, I think, a welcome interruption.

While Lori and Lesley shopped (Lori has a thing about Spanish sunglasses, which never fit once we are back home) Himes and I talked endlessly in the room he uses as a study, in the living room with its balcony that overlooks the city and the port, and on walks down to and along the Promenade. There was never a time when I dared to be without the recorder, for out of Himes pours so much, at any time and at any place.

He's slower getting about than he used to be, but intellectually he is as sharp as ever and his opinions as blunt and honest as always. I am always impressed by how well he has kept up with what's going on in the United States. Most expatriate blacks I know tend not to care. Not so Chester Himes; his information is as fresh as the morning paper. Another thing: over the years he has repeated many anecdotes to me. What amazes me is that they are always the same. They are never embroidered or exaggerated. They are exactly the same. Most of us, with the passage of time, tend to embellish.

Last fall Chester and Lesley moved into their new home near Javea, still in Spain, still in the province of Alicante. We were to have seen it one day, but something came up so we were unable to make the trip.

It gave me the greatest pleasure to be able to see Himes again, to see him at a time when a kind of physical comfort was coming his way at last; to see him still producing long, articulate and sensitive works. He let me read the first volume of his autobiography, *The Quality of Hurt* (394 pages, ending in 1955). It is a fantastic, masculine work whose pages are haunted by vistas of France and Spain, of family life in the United States, of his first marriage, of Richard Wright and Robert Graves and others. American male writers don't produce manly books. Himes' autobiography is that of a man. So we talked, and the sound of bronze church bells filled the background, and the sweet smell of Spain blocked up our nostrils, and my man Himes rapped. . . .

This Publishing Business

Williams: How do you feel about the double standard of payment, say, advances—this amount for black writers and that amount for white writers?

Himes: It's pitiful, you know, it's really pitiful, pitiful. You know, the double standard of advances is so pitiful. Even friends took advantage. . . . I got a thousand-dollar advance for each of my last three books.

Williams: Really?

Himes: Yes. And they resold them to Dell for a fifteen-thousand-dollar reprint.

Williams: Each?

Himes: Yeah, and then in the end they didn't want *Blind Man* [*Blind Man with a Pistol*], and I thought—

Williams: Goddamn! Are you kidding me?

Himes: I'm telling you the truth. You know, I have never been paid anything in advance. I'm the lowest-paid writer on the face of the earth. So . . .

Williams: Now wait a minute, Chester, people have known you since the forties.

They know everything that you produced, and they offered you a thousand-dollar advance for each of these three books?

Himes: Oh, yes, that's what they paid, a thousand-dollar advance.

Williams: Goddamn!

Himes: You talk about double standards. I find this quite annoying. Y'know, I have been in desperate circumstances financially, which everybody has known, and they've just taken advantage of this—friends and enemies and everybody alike. I remember in *The Third Generation,* I was paid a two-thousand-dollar advance, and they resold the reprint rights to Victor Weybright of NAL for ten thousand dollars, and that's the money I came to Europe on. But then when I got broke in Europe and I had to spend a year's time helping ———, the woman I was living with at the time, write a book of her own, which never made a cent . . .

Williams: That was the book you said was much better than the Caldwell-type books—*The Silver Chalice*?

Himes: *The Silver Altar.* I have it in my autobiography. You can read it if you like.

Williams: Can I take it and read it tonight?

Himes: Sure, you can read it tonight, or you can take it back to New York as far as I'm concerned. [Laughter.] I have two copies. I think if you want to do any background on me, some of the things you should know you'll find in it. But going back to the payment, you see. Now, I couldn't find a publisher for *The Primitive.* I was very broke and desperate for some money, and I finally thought that I would send it to Weybright because they had begun to publish originals. So I sent it to Weybright, and Weybright wrote me this long letter about how we'll pay you a thousand-dollar advance on this because we feel it's best for the author to have a small advance and have substantial accruals. [Laughter.] I'll never forget that phrase. I never got any accruals, substantial or otherwise, from that book [laughter], until five or six years later they brought out a new edition for which they paid a fifteen-hundred-dollar advance. That's why I began writing these detective stories, as a matter of fact. Marcel Duhamel, the editor of the Série Noire, had translated *If He Hollers Let Him Go.* The Série Noire was the best-paid series in France. So they started off paying me a thousand-dollar advance, which was the same as the Americans were paying, and they went up to fifteen hundred dollars, which was more.

Double standards are so pitiful. Well, as I said, the American system toward the Negro writer is to take great advantage of the fact that the black writer in America is always in a state of need, and they take great advantage of that need. They take advantage just willy-nilly. Then one or two will get through. Not one or two—I mean, the American system works like this: *Time* magazine and a few other sources and the *New York Times* and all feel that they'd like to be king-makers of a writer, and they put him in a position so that he can earn some money, like Baldwin. Now Baldwin got into a position where he could command sizeable advances and royalties. But the average black writer is never paid in comparison to the white writer.

Williams: What is the most you ever made on an advance of a book?

Himes: Morrow, I suppose. Morrow paid four thousand five hundred advance, which was just for *Blind Man with a Pistol.* . . . No—that's right, Putnam paid a ten-thousand-dollar advance for *Pinktoes.* Walter Minton was buying up Girodias's [Olympia Press] books. He had been successful with *Lolita* and *Candy,* and he was anxious to get *Pinktoes.* Stein & Day had offered me seventy-five hundred, so Minton upped it twenty-five hundred. And then Stein & Day and Putnam started a lawsuit against one another, and that's why they published it jointly. They figured it'd be more expensive to go to court, so they just decided that they would work out a system, a very elaborate one, so elaborate that I ran into difficulties with Stein & Day because—Putnam kept the trade book edition, they were responsible for that and for collecting my royalties—Stein & Day were responsible for the subsidiary rights and the reprint and foreign rights and so forth. And finally Stein & Day began rejecting various offers from foreign countries. The last one—the one that really made me angry—was that they had an offer from a German publisher to bring out a German edition of *Pinktoes,* and Stein & Day rejected that, and I went to the Author's Guild and to the lawyers to see what I could do. And they said that that was the most complicated contract they had ever seen. Even now, even a couple of weeks ago I wrote to Walter Minton to find out what happened to my royalties because Corgi Books brought out a paperback edition in England, which has seemingly been very successful. I know that they have reprinted the jacket design, so I figure they must have sold quite a number in the first design to have brought out a different one.

Williams: Well, you know the younger black writers back home always say that Chester Himes has given away more books than most people have ever written.

Himes: Yeah, that's right, I must tell you the truth. You know that the younger generation of black writers are getting paid far more than I'm getting paid, even now. Even now I get paid so little. I just got disgusted with the whole business.

Actually, I have a good agent now. Roslyn [Targ] for me is a very good agent because she will fight for whatever she can get, you know. And she tries everything she can.

Williams: How about some of the experiences, other than royalties, that you've had with publishers? You once wrote me something about an award you were supposed to get at Doubleday when Buck Moon was your editor.

Himes: Yes, well you know, *If He Hollers* sold I think it was eight thousand copies before publication. That was Doubleday. Well, then *If He Hollers* hit the bestseller list. Then I received a number of letters from all over the country. I'd been in Los Angeles and San Francisco—one brother was living in Cincinnati; one was down in Durham, North Carolina, teaching at the North Carolina College—and I received letters from all of these people and other people whom I'd forgotten, that they'd been in stores to buy copies of *If He Hollers* and they had been told that book stores had sold out and had ordered copies, and the orders were not being filled.

Williams: That's something that happens to me all the time, too.

Himes: So I went to Doubleday and complained and said the same thing and showed them the letters, and at that time Doubleday was being run by five vice presidents. I think about a month afterward Ken McCormick was promoted to editor-in-chief, and he was in control of Doubleday. He became the top vice president, or maybe he was the president. So I talked to him. He said my complaint didn't make any sense because if they published a book they were going to sell it. I couldn't argue with this. But it got to be rather dirty. Doubleday was in the *Time* and *Life* building on 49th Street at that time, and I was going up in the elevator with Hilda Simms and her husband and a joker who was doing freelance promoting for Doubleday, and I was telling them that the book orders weren't being filled and this joker rushed in and told Ken McCormick that I was complaining about Doubleday. So I got in Ken's office, and we had some bad words, you know. I said to Ken McCormick, "You know that you got this black corner here. . . ." He said, "No, we haven't. It's not a black corner," and I said, "You got Bucklin Moon, he's the head of the black department in Doubleday." So then I didn't get any more information from Doubleday concerning anything. So, I think seven years later when I was living with Vandi [Haygood], Buck stopped by one day and Vandi was in the kitchen making some drinks, and Buck said that I was right about the whole thing, but he had felt it would do me more harm to tell me the truth than to let me remain in ignorance. That what had happened was Doubleday was giving an award called the George Washington Carver Memorial Award of twenty-five hundred dollars each year for the best book. And that year Doubleday had *If He Hollers,* the outstanding book on the black theme that they had published. But there was one white woman editor whose name was never told to me, who said that *If He Hollers* made her disgusted and it made her sick and nauseated and if *If He Hollers* was selected for this memorial award that she would resign. They gave the award to a book called *Mrs. Palmer's Honey,* written by some white woman. It was about a Negro maid in St. Louis.

When Doubleday advertised *Mrs. Palmer's Honey* in the *Saturday Review,* they said this book has a nice story that will appeal to a lot of people, and it was not like some other books that they had published, and they referred, but not by actual name, to *If He Hollers Let Him Go* and called it a "series of epithets punctuated by spit." This was their own advertisement. I complained about this, too. But what had actually happened to *If He Hollers* was that this woman editor—Doubleday was printing their own books in Garden City—had telephoned to their printing department in Garden City and ordered them to stop the printing. So they just arbitrarily stopped the printing of *If He Hollers* for a couple of weeks or so during the time when it would have been a solid bestseller.

Williams: You were at Knopf too, for a while. *Lonely Crusade* was a Knopf book, wasn't it?

Himes: Yes, well, that's why I went to Knopf. I went to Knopf because of this. I was talking to Van Vechten, whom I had met, and . . .

Williams: You met Van Vechten after *If He Hollers* came out, which would be late
'45 or '46.

Himes: That's right. Richard Wright had taken me over to meet him. Dick was
going over to get his picture taken. And when Van Vechten was taking
his picture he acted so pompous I got hysterical, and I was sitting there
laughing away and Van Vechten was peeping at me and . . . So he was
intrigued with me and we became quite good friends because of that.
But Dick was a real friend despite his eccentricities. He had reviewed *If
He Hollers Let Him Go* in *PM,* a good review, and took me over to the
Book of the Month Club. Well, *If He Hollers* was being distributed by
the Book of the Month Club. So when I told Van Vechten that I was
unhappy at Doubleday he said that he would talk to Blanche Knopf and
she would buy my contract from Doubleday. So she bought the contract ultimately. It wasn't a very large sum because Doubleday had only
given me a thousand-dollar advance for my next book, and then I went
on and wrote *Lonely Crusade,* which she liked very much indeed. I'd say
she liked that book as much as any book she ever published. She gave it
a very good printing, very nice—you've seen copies of the book, haven't
you?

Williams: Oh, sure, sure.

Himes: Very nice book, and she lined up a lot of radio appearances for me.
I don't remember all of them now—Mary Margaret McBride, CBS
book shows—and I was to talk to the book department at Macy's and
Bloomingdale's on the day of publication. So I sent for my father to
come to New York from Cleveland, and I went out early that morning
to go to Macy's, and this joker down at Macy's—the head of the book
department—was looking guilty and said, "Well, we're going to stop
this procedure of having authors speak to the book sellers because they
would show favoritism since we couldn't do it for all the authors." So
they canceled the whole thing. So then I went over to Bloomingdale's,
and at Bloomingdale's there were no books, no *Lonely Crusade* on dis-
play whatsoever. So I realized that something had happened. The director of Bloomingdale's books department didn't want to talk to me at
all. So then I rushed home to get my wife and go to the Mary McBride
radio program, but she said she'd been trying to get in touch with me
because they had received a telegram from the radio that I'd been canceled off that program. And then before the day was over, they canceled
me off the CBS program. Then I learned that the Communist Party had

launched a real assault on the book.

It had some of the most terrible reviews, one of the most vicious reviews I ever read. The *Daily Worker* had a picture of a black man walking across the page carrying a white flag—catch the caption: "Himes Carries a White Flag." In some of the passages they had they compared the book to the "foul words that came from the cankerous mouth of Bilbo" [Sen., D., Miss.], and so forth.

Williams: Didn't you tell me once that Jimmy Baldwin did a review too?

Himes: Jimmy Baldwin did a review for the Socialist newspaper, *New Leader* I believe, under the heading "History as a Nightmare." I don't remember the gist of the review. But all of the reviews I remember seeing were extremely critical, each for a different reason: *Atlantic Monthly, Newsweek, Commentary, New Masses*—the white press, the black press, the Jewish press, reactionary press—*all*. Willard Motley, whom I had met at a party given for the publication of *Knock on Any Door* at Carl Van Vechten's house, wrote an extremely spiteful review for the Marshall Field newspaper in Chicago.

Williams: Was that the only book that Knopf did for you?

Himes: Yes. Knopf had given me an advance for another book, but then they . . . I had trouble with Knopf too. I tried to have some kind of dialogue with Blanche to discuss some of these reactions. I said, "Now, you have all of these reviews from *Atlantic Monthly, Commentary, New Masses,* the *New York Times,* the *Herald Tribune,* and *Ebony,* the black press. All of these reviews have different complaints about this book, different ways of condemning it. Well, this doesn't make any sense, and these reviews should all be published in an advertisement showing that all of these people from the left, the right, the blacks, the whites, that if all of these people dislike the book there must be some reason. It would stimulate interest; people would want to know why. Because I never found out why everybody disliked this book."

But I know why the black people disliked the book—because they're doing the same thing now that I said at that time was necessary. I had the black protagonist, Lee Gordon, a CIO organizer, say that the black man in America needed more than just a superficial state of equality; he needed special consideration because he was so far behind. That you can't just throw him out there and say, "Give Negroes rights," because it wouldn't work that way. And so this is what most of the black writers had against it; in saying that, of course, by pleading for special privileges for the black people I was calling them inferior.

Williams: And now that's the route that everyone is going.

Himes: Yes.

Williams: Except that they're not saying it. I think a few years ago they were saying it, but now it seems to me that what the kids are saying on the campuses is . . .

Himes: Yes, that's what they're saying; that's what I'm saying. It's the same theme because it's obvious, you know, that the black man in America must have, for an interim period of time, special consideration.

Williams: What about your experiences with editors?

Himes: Well, as a rule, the whole of my experiences has been bad. Over a long period of years the editor whom I got along with best as an editor was Marcel Duhamel, the editor of Série Noire, because he was a friend, but more than being a friend he was an honest man, which is very rare among editors. He was honest and straightforward, although he was surrounded by a bunch of dubious people at Gallimard. But he did as much as he could. A journalist from *Combat* once said, "You know, Marcel is a good man, but Marcel is a three-legged duck as far as Gallimard is concerned." I always remembered that. They never really included him until later years. Série Noire became so successful that he became a capitalist.

Williams: You know, over the years in many conversations we've had I get the impression that, well, it's more than an impression now, you never found much difference between American and French publishers and editors.

Himes: No, no, I didn't, because the only difference—it goes like this: the French don't have the difficulty that Americans do because most black people that come to France realize that they are from the undeveloped countries and they keep their place.

   And very few of them feel any injustice when they're not given the same accord as the French writer. They don't feel that this is unjust.

   The American black man is very different from all those black men in the history of the world because the American black has even an unconscious feeling that he wants equality. Whereas most of the blacks of the world don't particularly insist on having equality in the white community. But the American black doesn't have any other community. America, which wants to be a white community, is their community, and there is not the fact that they can go home to their own community and be the chief and sons of chiefs or what not.

Williams: That old lie again, huh?

Himes: [Laughter.] Yeah. The American black man has to make it or lose it in America; he has no choice. That's why I wrote *Cotton Comes to Harlem.* In Garvey's time the "Back to Africa" movement had an appeal and probably made some sense. But it doesn't make any sense now. It probably didn't make sense even then, but it's even *less* logical now, because the black people of America aren't Africans anymore, and the Africans don't want them.

Williams: Yes, I found this to be true.

Himes: Yes, they wouldn't have him in their world, so he has to make it in America.

Williams: You were saying that New American Library once gave you a contract with sixteen pages.

Himes: Yes. Well, I was in Paris, and like George Orwell's book I was down and out in Paris and I had submitted this book, *The Primitive,* to Gallimard. But I was in a hurry and Gallimard was taking their time, so I sent it to NAL. So NAL took it and at the same time they took all of the rights, took every right worth considering, and they sent me a sixteen-page contract to sign. So Gallimard had to buy the book from NAL. What they paid for it I never discovered. I don't remember if anyone ever paid me for that. So at that time I realized that contracts were getting much more intricate than they had been previously, much more detailed. Publishers stipulated their rights. Of course, then publishing was getting to be a big business. The artists who could command a lot of money—and who could command a lot of attention, I should say, from publishers—were also getting more rights, so they could keep their subsidiary rights, even their paperback rights.

Williams: I think there's a move in the direction to recapture these rights for the writers once more. It's going kind of slowly. There're some writers whom I've heard about who manage to keep their subsidiary rights, or most of them, like the reprint rights. I understand Robbins is one of these guys.

Himes: Yes, that's right. The first one who I heard of who was able to keep his subsidiary rights (I heard about but probably a lot of them did before) was Wouk, when he wrote *Marjorie Morningstar*. Well, you see, that's a considerable amount of money. You take a writer like Jean Le Carré. I don't know what Putnam paid him for the advance for the book rights, although Putnam did very well with the book, but Putnam sold the reprint rights for I think twenty-five or thirty thousand dollars, and then Dell, on the first three months of publication of *The Spy Who Came in from the Cold* made three million dollars. So that's a considerable amount of money involved.

Williams: I recall that Lillian Ross story about Ernest Hemingway that appeared in the *New Yorker,* where he got a twenty-five-thousand-dollar advance from Scribner's. And now these guys are getting like a quarter of a million. What do you think about that? People like Roth and . . .

Himes: Yes, I read that piece. Well, the industry has gotten to the place where they make considerably more money out of, say, Roth's book [*Portnoy's Complaint*]. They'll make more money out of Roth's book probably than the American publishers have out of all of Hemingway, because the industry is so much bigger. The whole process of circulation of books. There's so much advance. You know, America is a very big book market, and I wonder if these people read these books. I suppose they do. But anyway, as long as they get something that will titillate them, they will read them.

I remember when the book industry was very much afraid of television. They thought that television would do damage to the book industry. It didn't make any difference whatsoever. As a matter of fact, the book industry is very healthy now from the point of view of profit systems.

Williams: Well, I think it's healthier now than it was ten years ago.

Himes: Yes, it's healthier now than it ever was.

Williams: Who's your favorite American publisher in terms of what it does for blacks, producing good books?

Himes: Well, I couldn't say. I don't know enough about American publishers to have an opinion. As far as publishers are concerned, in talking to other people, all publishers, Morrow has a very good reputation as a publisher with other publishers. Has a better reputation, I think, than Putnam. But as far as publishers are concerned, that is very difficult to say.

Williams: What was the print order for *Blind Man with a Pistol*?

Himes: I don't know. Once upon a time you could get the figures. I couldn't get these from Morrow. As a matter of fact, I haven't been in close contact with them at all.

Personal Worksheet

Williams: Well, how would you place yourself in American letters? [Himes laughs.] You're sixty-one years old now, you've been writing long before *If He Hollers* came out—you've been writing now for thirty-four years.

Himes: Yes, I've been writing since 1934. Let's see, how long is that? My first story in a national magazine was published in *Esquire* in 1934. That's thirty-five years. Well, I don't know where to place myself actually on the American scene of letters because America has a highly organized system of reputation-making which I'm afraid would place me in the bottom echelon. The American communications media are very well organized about what they intend to do and how they intend to show that this person is of great importance and that person is chickenshit.

So they work this out and they make reputations. Not only do they make reputations of writers, which is insignificant, but they take people like Roosevelt and they will set out systematically to break his place in history. They'll spend millions of dollars to do so if they wish. And the same thing happens with the literary scene. That's why I never contemplate it, because I realize the Americans will sit down and they will take a white writer—he will be one that appeals to their fancy, one that has been abroad and clowned around, like Hemingway—and they will set him up and they will make him one of the most famous writers on the face of the earth. And not because of anything he has written, because his work is not that important, but because they wish to have an American up there at the top of the world literature. Anyone reading him will realize that Hemingway is a great imitator of the styles of Ford Madox Ford, James Joyce, and D. H. Lawrence. As a matter of fact, if you have read the works of these four writers, you can see the lines; you can see the exact imitation. So there's nothing creative about even Hemingway's form. This was borrowed, as Gertrude Stein says.

But the Americans set out and they made him a legend. Now, it's very difficult for me to evaluate any of the people on the American scene, because if I take my information from the American white communications media then, of course, it is slanted to whatever way they wish to slant it to. So one can't form any opinion, unfortunately.

Williams: Do you foresee the time when you'll ever quit writing?

Himes: Well, no, no I don't foresee it. I mean writing is like . . . I remember I have a line in a book—I've forgotten now what book it was where I quote [Max] Schmeling. He said a fighter fights, and I went on to say ". . . and a writer writes." That's what I do, that's all I *do,* and I don't foresee that I will quit, as long as I'm able to write. No. I do foresee the fact that age will deteriorate my writing, as it does everyone else's writing. I don't foresee the fact that because age will deteriorate my writing, and that I will realize that I can't do what I could do when I was young (I know damn well that I can't do what I could do when I was young), that I am going to blow out my brains like Hemingway did when he discovered that.

Williams: It seemed to me when I started reading the first couple of pages of your autobiography, *The Quality of Hurt,* that you were sort of preparing yourself for the time when you wouldn't write anymore. But then I also noticed that this is volume 1, the carbon that I have. How many volumes do you foresee in this autobiography?

Himes: I imagine there will just be another volume in which I will write about the change in my writing habits or change in my attitudes toward the entire American scene, and my change from pessimism to optimism. I became much less subject to the inroads of the various attitudes of people that I didn't particularly respect. I know that I will write another volume that will concern my beginning to write detective stories, and then my beginning to write the last ten or twelve books that I have written.

Williams: In one of your letters you said—and you've mentioned it since I've been here—that you were working on the bloodiest book that you have ever worked on, that you'd ever conceived, but you didn't expect (you said in this letter) to have it published in America, that it would be difficult to have published. Do you remember that?

Himes: Well, yes, because I can see what a black revolution would be like. Now, first of all, in order for a revolution to be effective, one of the things that it has to be is violent; it has to be massively violent; it has to be as violent as the war in Vietnam. Of course, in any form of uprising, the major objective is to kill as many people as you can, by whatever means you can kill them, because the very fact of killing them and killing them in sufficient number is supposed to help you gain your objectives. It's the only reason why you do so.

Now, when you have resorted to these means, this is the last resort. Well, then, all dialogue ceases, all forms of petitions and other god-damned things are finished. All you do then is you kill as many people as you can, the black people kill as many of the people of the white community as they can kill. That means children, women, grown men, industrialists, street sweepers, or whatever they are, as long as they're white. And this is the fact that gains its objective—there's no discussion—no point in doing anything else and no reason to give it any thought.

Now a soldier, if he would have to think about the morality of going out and killing the enemy, or if he had to consider his feelings about killing people, he would be finished. To do so, he would get court-martialed or shot on the scene. A soldier just goes out and kills; no one thinks anything about it; that's his objective. The objective for a foot soldier is to kill the enemy, and that's all. It's very simple. There's nothing else to be added to it or subtracted from it.

Well, that's what a revolution by the black people in America will be; that's their only objective. Their objective is not to stand up and talk to the white man and to stand him in front of a gun and say, "Now you did so and so to me"; the only objective is to blow out his brains without a word, you see. So I am trying to show how this follows, how the violence would be if the blacks resorted to this. Even individually, if you give one black one high-powered repeating rifle and he wanted to shoot it into a mob of twenty thousand or more white people, there are a number of people he could destroy. Now, in my book all of these blacks who shoot are destroyed. They not only are destroyed, they're blown apart; even the buildings they're shooting from are destroyed, and quite often the white community suffers fifty or more deaths itself by destroying this one black man. What I'm trying to do is depict the violence that is necessary so that the white community will also give it a little thought, because you know, they're going around playing these games. They haven't given any thought to what would happen if the black people would *seriously* uprise.

The white community gets very much upset about the riots, while the black people haven't seriously undertaken in advance to commit any great amount of violence; it's just been forced on them. What little violence they have done has actually been for protection; it's been defensive, you know. So what I would hope is to call to mind what *would* happen, what *should* happen, when the black people have an armed uprising, what white people should expect. It seems that the whites don't understand this.

Because one thing is sure—I have said this and I keep on saying it over and over again—the black man can bring America down, he can destroy America. The black man can destroy the United States. Now, there are sensible people in America who realize this, regardless of what they might think about the black man. The black man can destroy America completely, destroy it as a nation of any consequence. It can just fritter away in the world. It can be destroyed completely. Now I realize of course that the black man has no money, he has very little equipment to do this, he has very little fire power, he has lots of things against him, he hasn't been trained particularly. Even a Southern white cracker colonel . . . I remember a Southern white cracker colonel in the army in the Second World War got up and he made this famous speech about the black people, saying, "You have never been taught to use violence and you have never been taught to be courageous, but war calls for these things and you must learn them." Well, he's right. That's the most right thing he ever said.

Williams: Do you think the publishers will be . . .

Himes: I don't think . . . I don't know what the American publishers will do about this book. But one thing I do know, Johnny: they will hesitate, and it will cause them a great amount of revulsion, because the scenes that I have described will be revolting scenes. There are very few war books written that have ever described actual scenes of war, 'cause in war people are killed and blown to pieces and all. Even when they just say "blown to pieces," that doesn't describe what they *look* like blown to pieces. When a shell hits a man in a war, bits of him fly around, half of his liver is flying through the air, and his brains are dribbling off. These are actual scenes, no one states these outright.

Williams: How do you think the majority of white readers react to your books and other books by black writers?

Himes: The white readers read into a book what they wish, and in any book concerning the black people in the world, the majority of white readers are just looking for the exotic episodes. They're looking for things that will amuse or titillate them. The rest of it they skip over and pay no attention to. That was one of the remarkable things about Richard Wright's autobiography—that the white community was willing to read his suffering and poverty as a black man. But it didn't move them, didn't move them one bit. They read it and said, "Tsk, tsk, isn't it awful?"

Williams: Well, you know, I sometimes have the feeling that when they read books like that, they say to themselves, "Boy, ain't we a bitch! Look what we're doing to them people."

Himes: [Laughs.] Yeah, something like that. They're thinking along those lines; certainly they're not thinking in the ways you'd like for them to think. That's one of the saddest parts about the black man in America—that he is being used to titillate the emotions of the white community in various aspects. Now I couldn't say exactly how he titillates them, but in any case it's titillation in a way that's not serious. America is a masochistic society anyway, so they probably just like being given a little whipping, enough to get a feeling out of it, a sensation, but not enough for them to be moved. I want these people just to take me seriously. I don't care if they think I'm a barbarian, a savage, or what they think; just think I'm a serious savage.

Williams: There's a rash of books, I hear (I haven't read them)—detective books in which there are black detectives, and of course one of these books was made into a movie with Poitier, *In the Heat of the Night.* Do you feel that these people are sort of swiping your ideas?

Himes: No, no. It's a wonder to me why they haven't written about black detectives many years ago. It's a form, you know, and it's a particularly American form. My French editor says, the Americans have a style of writing detective stories that no one has been able to imitate, and that's why he has made his Série Noire successful, by using American detective story writers. There's no reason why the black American, who is also an American, like all other Americans, and brought up in this sphere of violence, which is the main sphere of American detective stories, there's

197

no reason why he shouldn't write them. It's just plain and simple violence in narrative form, you know. 'Cause no one, *no one,* writes about violence the way that Americans do.

As a matter of fact, for the simple reason that no one understands violence or experiences violence like the American civilians do. The only other people in the white community who are violent enough for it are the armed forces of all the countries. But of course they don't write about it because if the atrocities were written about the armies of the English and the French in Africa, they would make among the most grisly stories in the history of the world. But they're not going to write about them. These things are secret; they'll never state them.

American violence is public life; it's a public way of life; it became a form, a detective story form. So I would think that any number of black writers should go into the detective story form. As a matter of fact, I feel that they could be very competent. Anyway, I would like to see a lot of them do so. They would not be imitating me because when I went into it, into the detective story field, I was just imitating all the other American detective story writers, other than the fact that I introduced various new angles which were my own. But on the whole, I mean the detective story originally in the plain narrative form—straightforward-violence—is an American product. So I haven't created anything whatsoever; I just made the faces black, that's all.

Williams: You know, I'm always amazed when I read your books. Here you've been out of the country for twenty years, but I'm always amazed at your memory of things and how accurate you are in details, like the guns that the cops use. In rereading the screenplay last night, there was the business of the drop slot in the car. How do you come by all this knowledge?

Himes: Well, some of it comes from memory; and then I began writing these series because I realized that I was a black American, and there's no way of escaping forty some odd years of experience, so I would put it to use in writing, which I have been doing anyway. I had always thought that the major mistake in Richard Wright's life was to become a world writer on world events. I thought that he should have stuck to the black scene in America because he wouldn't have had to live there—he had the memory, so he was still there, but it was subconsciously, which he discovered when he went back to write *The Long Dream* and the sequel (which was never published, I don't think).

Well, then, I went back—as a matter of fact, it's like a sort of pure homesickness—I went back, I was very happy, I was living there, and it's true. I began creating also all the black scenes of my memory and my actual knowledge. I was very happy writing these detective stories, especially the first one, when I began it. I wrote those stories with more pleasure than I wrote any of the other stories. And then when I got to the end and started my detective shooting at some white people, I was the happiest.

Harlem Renaissance

Williams: Chester, how about the Harlem Renaissance? You were just arriving in New York when it was . . .

Himes: It was on the wane when I got there. I knew a lot of people involved in it. There was Bud Fisher.

Williams: He was a doctor or a radiologist, wasn't he?

Himes: I don't know what Bud Fisher was. I only know he was a writer. And there was a young man whose name I should know; I think he wrote *The Blacker the Berry, the Sweeter the Juice.*

Williams: Was that Braithwaite?

Himes: No, Wallace Thurman, I think. He went to Hollywood, and he was one of the most successful black people writing out in Hollywood. He did very well on the Hollywood scene at that time.

Williams: How would you evaluate the Harlem Renaissance?

Himes: Well, I think it was one of the greatest movements among black writers that existed up to then.

Williams: But then Hollywood wasn't interested.

Himes: No, Hollywood had no interest in the black writer, but the black writers like Claude McKay and Countee Cullen and all produced things of substantial consequence, and so as a group the writers of the Black Renaissance produced works that were encouraging; it encouraged all black writers.

Now, the way I look at it, the next movement of any consequence was when Richard Wright hit the scene. Nothing happened between the end of the Renaissance and the time Richard Wright came on the scene. I always had a great respect for Richard Wright because of the fact that I believe that his first works, *Uncle Tom's Children, Native Son,* and *Black Boy,* opened up certain fields in the publishing industry for the black writer, more so than anything else that had happened. The Black Renaissance was an inward movement; it encouraged people who were familiar with it, who knew about it and were in contact with it, but the legend of Richard Wright reached people all over.

Williams: Well, he hit it about the same time you did.

Himes: Yes, that's quite true, but his name was taken to the masses, and that is what is important.

Williams: I somehow had got the impression from something that you had said that they didn't think that much of him.

Himes: No, I didn't say they didn't think much of him. I said that Wright's works themselves did not make any great impression on the white community, although they read them. As a writer, he made an impression on the publishing world. Although the white community read his works and gave a performance of being moved and touched and so forth, it didn't mean a damn thing to them—they just shed it. It's unfortunate but it's quite true.

   A few white people around were considerably shocked by some of it, but I remember in Cleveland—I think it was with *Uncle Tom's Children;* no, it was *Native Son,* which was published about 1939 or early 1940—I remember various white people expressing amazement at being told that black people hated them. But these people were people of no consequence. I'd like to talk a little bit about Langston Hughes. When I came out of prison I met Langston. He was in Cleveland; he didn't live too far from where I was; he was living with his aunt. He was writing plays for Karamou House. As a matter of fact, it was through Langston that I met the Jellifes; through the Jellifes I met Louis Bromfield, and that's how I went to Hollywood. But most of his plays were produced first at Karamou before they were produced in New York. And Langston stayed there a great deal. He lived there, as a matter of fact, and only visited New York. It was some time before he moved to New York.

Williams: Well, he's gone now. Tell me, when did you first meet Carl Van Vechten?

Himes: The year that *If He Hollers* was published. I knew very little about him, other than the legend. He was only connected in my mind (until I met him) with *Nigger Heaven,* which I think was his most successful book. Although when he published *Nigger Heaven* he was on very good terms with most of the writers of the Black Renaissance, but after he wrote it they practically never spoke to him again. He told me, "Countee Cullen never said another word to me."

George Schuyler was also in this group. I knew him, and Philippa Schuyler [killed in a helicopter crash in Vietnam in 1967] when she was a little girl. She used to go down to Van Vechten's.

Williams: But Schuyler became terribly, terribly right-wing.

Himes: Yes, well Schuyler was a man whose life was plotted like Pegler's. He is a man who wants to say strong things, individual things and all, and he makes some statements which are contradictory, which Pegler did all his life. Pegler contradicted himself so much that he wound up, I suppose in an insane asylum, or wherever he is now . . . [Editor's note: Westbrook Pegler died in June 1969.]

Hollywood

Williams: Hoyt Fuller [Editor, *Negro Digest*] mentioned your *Cotton Comes to Harlem.* How do you feel about that? With Ossie Davis directing the film and all. Are you pleased with it?

Himes: Well, I was talking with Sam Goldwyn, Jr., and he agreed with me that he wanted Ossie Davis in it whether he directed it or not. He had this Arnold Perl, a Hollywood screenwriter, write the first version of it. First he had a young man, whose name I've forgotten, who did a version. Then I wrote a version, a quickie, about a hundred and thirty pages, which he paid me practically nothing for. Sam Goldwyn, Jr., is a nice man to talk to, but he doesn't say anything about money.

Williams: You were working on it, then, the last time we saw you in New York.

Himes: Yes, that's right. Then Goldwyn couldn't use it, which I knew would be the case, because I'm not a screenwriter. But I told him that in advance. I said, "Now listen, you need to get a professional." He said he had sounded out LeRoi Jones, for whom he had great admiration as a playwright. As a matter of fact, he had extreme admiration for him as an artist, for his sharp scenes. He said that he had taken many screenwriters and producers to see LeRoi's plays when they were showing in Los Angeles, and he contacted LeRoi. LeRoi said it was a matter of money; what LeRoi wanted was for Goldwyn to pay him in advance (I don't know how much it was). Anyway, he would undertake to write the screenplay and he would do as many revisions as were required, and then he would get a second payment. And Goldwyn said it didn't work that way—which was a damned lie.

Williams: Of course it is.

Himes: Anyway, the reason he didn't get along with LeRoi was because LeRoi wanted to be paid like the Hollywood writers—

Williams: Like the white writers.

Himes: —and Goldwyn didn't want to do that, so that was that.

Williams: Are you pleased with the present screenplay of *Cotton Comes to Harlem*?

Himes: Well, no one could be pleased with that. But I don't know enough about screenplays to know what it'll be like when it's finished.

Williams: That's true. But in terms of what you see on the paper . . .

Himes: Well, it's not as bad as it was. It's much improved. Ossie Davis improved it considerably over the Perl version. . . . And he has some good things in it.

Williams: He's updated it a little, with the militants and . . .

Himes: Yes, he has a black orientation, which I like. That's what I told Sam Goldwyn, Jr. That's what I like best about Ossie Davis' treatment of it. He took the Perl treatment, which had some stuff in there that was really offensive. The treatment of the blacks in there was so offensive. . . . You know, some of the Jewish writers, because of the fact that they belong to a minority too, can get more offensive than other writers do.

Williams: They mistake closeness for familiarity.

Himes: What I dislike most about the screenplay—and I told Goldwyn—it's a good story, but it's a story about Deke, and the main purpose of Gold-wyn is to make a series of movies of Coffin Ed Smith and Grave Digger Jones; he wants to keep them alive. But if this is the purpose of the first movie, they are dead because they are of no consequence in the movie. He has to bring them out stronger if he wants to keep them. What you have now is a movie of a swindler, which is a good movie. But it's about Deke; Deke is the character in this movie. As a matter of fact, in Ossie Davis' treatment he comes through very fine; he comes through as a real solid character.

Williams: I started reading it. I got about a quarter of the way through just since we left you, and it recalled the book for me, which I guess is good. As you say, the difference between the printed page and what they put on the film can be—

Himes: Oh, yes, I will give them credit; they have stayed closer to the book than the usual Hollywood treatment of a book, because as a rule Hollywood lets it go altogether. It was to Hollywood's advantage to keep the story in this book because they couldn't improve on it. If they're going to depart from the story altogether, then it would deteriorate; and I'm not a big enough name to carry it. Like Hollywood buys a lot of name writers, and they do what they want to because the name of the writer is sufficient. The treatment of the book doesn't make any difference. But Hollywood is a strange business; don't get me talking about Hollywood.

Williams: Well, talk about it.

Himes: I went out to Hollywood because I had been working on Louis Brom-field's farm in Malabar, and he read my first version of my prison story. He became excited about it and said he'd like to see it get submitted to the movies. So Bromfield was going to Hollywood to work on a screen adaptation of Hemingway's *For Whom the Bell Tolls*. They paid him five thousand dollars a week, but finally they just threw his version away, and they got a screenwriter to write the movie version. But he took my book out there and he gave it to some producers, and I followed him. I was trying to get work. And then I went to the shipyards in San Fran-cisco.

Williams: Were you aware at this time—or did you have the feeling—that your work would probably outlast Bromfield's?

Himes: No, it never occurred to me at all. But I didn't think that Bromfield's work was substantial enough to last. It didn't occur to me that Bromfield had been very successful then with *The Rains Came.* He was making quite a bit of money at that time. This was in the late thirties or 1940, and writers like Bromfield were getting that large money from the serialization in magazines. They were not so much concerned with things like book clubs or reprints and so forth. But the magazine serializations: *Cosmopolitan* was paying Bromfield seventy-five thousand dollars for the serialization of the book. Anyway, I went out to Hollywood—Los Angeles—where I met Hall Johnson and a number of other black people on the fringes of the movie industry. As a matter of fact, Langston Hughes gave me a list of names of people to see when I went out there. Most of them were connected with the Communist Party. I saw these people, and then I got involved also with the communists out there. Politically, I was never intrigued by communism. Communism was very strong in the States, in Hollywood particularly. ——— was out there; he was the dean of the communists. Great numbers of stars and producers and directors were fellow travelers, at least. There were two young men, black men, who had been in the Abraham Lincoln Brigade in Spain. ——— was the one I knew. I forgot the other's name, but his brother had been wounded, and he was quite a celebrity among the Communist Party there. But anyway, the Communist Party was collecting old clothes, which they sold and then sent the proceeds to a refugee camp for Spaniards from the Spanish Civil War in Mexico. I would go around with ——— in his truck to pick up these clothes and various stuff. And we would drive up to many, many big Hollywood estates, of producers and various people (I wish I could recall the names), and they'd come out and set us up a few drinks in the kitchen.

Williams: In the kitchen! But you were supposed to be a part of them, right?

Himes: Yes, but this was their home; it didn't mean we got out of the kitchen! [Laughter.] I swear to God, my material for writing *Lonely Crusade* came from these experiences. I met these people. And the CIO union there was beginning to print a newspaper. At the same time I had been considered for a place on the staff. But, you see, the communists were also playing a game. They wanted people like me to help break the color line. I was a tool; they wanted to send me to thousands of places that had no intention of employing blacks at that time because Los Angeles was a very prejudiced place and the only jobs black people had were in the kitchens in Hollywood and Beverly Hills.

Williams:	But they liked them; that was a status job.
Himes:	Yes, but the point of it was the Negro ghetto at that time was not Watts but Central Avenue from 12th to about 40th, I guess. And you know, they didn't open those night clubs and restaurants on Central Avenue until Thursday.
Williams:	Maid's day off.
Himes:	Yeah, they were closed. Because, you know, some of Raymond Chandler's crap out there, he writes in *Farewell, My Lovely,* he has this joker ride about in the Central Avenue section. Some of that's very authentic—it was like that. A black man in Los Angeles, he was a servant. So there was nothing I could do out there, and that's why I went to work in the shipyards. And then someone told me to come back to Los Angeles because they were filming *Cabin in the Sky.*
Williams:	Oh, yes, the great all-Negro epic. [Laughter.]
Himes:	That's right. And Hall Johnson was the technical director, getting twenty-five thousand dollars. They used his music, anyway. I don't know what he was—musical consultant or something. Anyway, he was being paid quite well. And I went back to Los Angeles, to MGM, because I had been told (I don't remember who had told me) to go there and see a joker named Wheelwright, who was head of the publicity department, and I could probably get an assignment doing publicity. So I went out to get a job doing publicity for the Negro press, but they had already hired a young black man named Phil Carter. Well, when you go into MGM, just to the right of the entrance was the publicity department. And then you go in a little more and you come to what they called "Old Dressing Room Row"—a long string of old dressing rooms. Well, they had this young man named Carter to do the publicity for the black press in America. They gave him, for an office, one of the old dressing rooms, at the very end, as far as they could get from the publicity office.
I got on fairly good terms with the editors of *Collier's.* I felt I could get an assignment from them to do a *Collier's* profile on Lena Horne. But then one of *Collier's* white writers, Kyle Crichton, decided he would do the story. It was one of Lena's first big publicity breaks.
Williams:	You'd said something once about the black people in the cast—no matter how high up they were—and the extras . . .

Himes: Being Jim-Crowed in the "commissary"—the public diner. Yes, what had happened was that I had been out to MGM several times. But first, let me tell you this: One time Marc Connelly, who wrote *Green Pastures,* had a number of screen-writers, so-called intellectuals, and various others whom he had invited to a conference to discuss a film on George Washington Carver, along with two black faces for color, me and Arna Bontemps, I think.

Williams: The story of Stepin Fetchit. [Laughter.]

Himes: Marc Connelly was sitting at the head of the table with about twenty people sitting around, and he said, "Well, now I know how we're going to start this film; I know that much about it, and then we can go on from there. Well, you see, Dr. Carver was a very humble man, and he always ironed his own shirts. So when we start this film on Dr. Carver, he goes into the kitchen and irons his shirt." So at that point I left.

At that time, they had black people out there for decor. They almost always had some black face out there. I was reading something recently in the paper about black technicians and various people who are beginning to break through out there, making it seem like a real advance, when actually so few, if any, technicians are employed by studios. But to get back to my story, later I made my efforts to get work in Hollywood. I met the head of the reading department, I suppose they call it, you know, where they have people read the novels and write a one-page synopsis, which is all producers ever read; they don't have time to read a book. So I was tried out by the young man who was head of this department at Warner Brothers. It was a job of no consequence. They were only offering something like forty-seven dollars a week to start, whereas you could make eighty-seven a week as a laborer. Anyway, he offered me the job, and I was going to take it. I wrote the synopsis for *The Magic Bow,* a well-known book about Paganini, and submitted it. He said it was a good job and that they would employ me. And then—this is what *he* said: he was walking across the lot one day and he ran into Jack Warner and told him, "I have a new man, Mr. Warner, and I think he's going to work out very well indeed." Warner said, "That's fine, boy," and so forth. "Who is he?" And he said, "He's a young black man." And Warner said, "I don't want no niggers on this lot." [Laughter.]

But what I was going to tell you about *Cabin in the Sky* . . . Well, in the commissary they had a sort of reserved section for people like producers and the like. Everybody ate at the commissary, and if people had a guest they would just bring them to the commissary. When they were making *Cabin in the Sky* they had this entire black personnel, and they wouldn't serve the blacks in the commissary at all. They couldn't go in there and get a piece of *bread*. And so, Lena Horne stopped Louis B. Mayer on the lot one day and told him that none of the cast of *Cabin in the Sky* were permitted to eat in the commissary; they had to bring their lunch. And then he made out like he was amazed. [Laughter.]

When you think about how things happen, then you get very discouraged about what the white community is doing.

Black on White

Williams: What about today's racial scene?

Himes: Nowadays, since twenty-five years have passed, my opinions have changed; because I don't believe the whites have any desire, any intention whatsoever, of accepting the Negro as an equal. I think the only way a Negro will ever get accepted as an equal is if he kills whites; to launch a violent uprising to the point where the people will become absolutely sickened, disgusted; to the place where they will realize that they have to do something. It's a calculated risk, you know, whether they would turn and try to exterminate the black man, which I don't think that they could do.

Williams: You don't think so?

Himes: I don't think the Americans have the capability, like the Germans, of exterminating six million. I don't think the American white man could. Morally, I don't think that he could do this; I don't think he has the capacity. Even to kill a hundred thousand blacks I think would disrupt America, actually ruin the country.

Williams: You're saying that *morally* the white man in America is unable to do what the Germans did?

Himes: Yes, he's unable to do it because it would destroy America. He doesn't want America to be destroyed, you see. I think that if he has to take the choice between giving the black man his rights or destroying the entire economic system in America, he'll give the black man equality. But that's the only reason he would do it now. Appeal to him—doesn't mean a thing. I think that he just has to be given a choice, because America is very vulnerable, you know. Armed uprisings by millions of blacks will destroy America. There's no question about it. There's not any question in the fact that the Americans can release enough power to destroy the blacks. Obviously the Americans could destroy North Vietnam and the whole people physically. It's not a question of whether they could destroy the blacks physically; it's the fact that they can't do it morally— and exist in the world. Because America exists in the world by a certain balance . . .

Williams: A sort of jive morality.

Himes: Yeah, a certain balance in more than just morality. It's just a certain balance in its relationship with other nations in the world, so that it cannot do this. It cannot destroy the black man. The black man in America doesn't realize this, or probably he doesn't act because he doesn't want to get killed; of course, life is precious. I can see why no one wants to get killed. But other countries realize the fact that the blacks have the power to destroy this necessary balance. When Israel first got its independence, you realized that Britain couldn't kill all the Jews that were in Israel, and the Jews were damn few in number compared to the blacks. Israel realized they couldn't kill them all, so Britain gave them independence.

Williams: Yes, but weren't those different times, though? Everyone was feeling guilty because of what had happened to the Jews in the camps?

Himes: Different times, but the conditions now are the same—even more sensitive. Even America cannot afford to fall out, not only on account of the economic balance of the world, which is so sensitive; it cannot even afford to form any enmity with all the nations with whom it collaborates, even the small nations in South America. It's just an absolute fact that if the blacks in America were to mount a revolution in force, with organized violence to the saturation point, that the entire black problem would be solved. But that is the only way the black man can solve it. So the point is, that the white people are jiving the blacks in America by putting on this pretense of wanting the blacks to suggest how *they* can do this without submitting the white race to violence; whites want the blacks to find a solution where the blacks will keep themselves in a secondary state, which would satisfy the whites perfectly, because the whites themselves haven't been able to devise any way acceptable to the blacks.

Williams: It's quite a theory, and it's one I've not heard anyone discuss. I find that younger kids are all for insurrection and rebellion and rioting on an indiscriminate, unplanned, unorganized kind of thing. I discourage it.

Himes: Yes, well, I discourage that too because what that does—by means of the white communications media, the press, and television and radio—is divide one group of the black race against the other group, and thus damage the progress the blacks are making.

Williams: How big a role do you think that book publishing has in all of this?

Himes: Well, the book publishers, first of all, are trying to exploit the black consciousness to sell books. As long as it titillates the whites, they will do so to sell books.

Williams: Except that there are some books that frighten them, like your book [*Lonely Crusade*] that they pulled off the stands.

Himes: Very few. And when they do, the white press kills them. White people in America, it seems to me, are titillated by the problem of the black people, more than taking it seriously. I want to see them take it seriously, good and goddamn seriously, and the only way that I think of to make them take it seriously is with violence. I don't think there's any other way. I see it on the faces of the whites around the world—the smirks, the sneaking grins, and all this stuff; I realize they're not taking the blacks seriously. There are certain segments that are beginning to take them seriously, but they are so isolated and so unrelated to the entire problem. Like the uprisings in the colleges and the elementary schools. Of course, the white people realized the uprisings in the elementary schools [school decentralization] in New York created an extraordinary amount of resistance and enmity and animosity. But since that was in one small section they felt that they could contain it, put it down with force. But if the conflict had been enlarged to the place where every black man was out on the street popping down white people right and left, this might have achieved the black goals, as in the African countries. Africans killed the colonials and burned their flags. I remember the time in London when they thought of Kenyatta as being a black murderer of the most depraved kind. Well, then the Mau Mau killed enough of these Englishmen over there so that there was nothing else they could do but give Kenya independence.

Williams: That's kind of remarkable, because I think in total the Mau Mau killed maybe fifty-four or a hundred fifty-four whites and just hundreds of blacks, so that if you can kill a small number of whites, then the effect is . . .

Himes: Yes, now in black uprisings in America, blacks would have to kill considerable numbers of other blacks in order for it to move, because the whites will employ some of those blacks to speak up against uprisings. In addition to this, the white press will find enough blacks to publicize. When they do, they know, of course, that they are weakening the position of the black leaders. Take Stokely Carmichael, for instance. They give him enough publicity to realize that they are weakening his position so that in a period of time that will make him absolutely valueless.

Williams: In the black community.

Himes: Yes, in the black community. So they give him publicity to the saturation point, where his value in the black community is just dissipated. They devised that technique from handling Malcolm X. They figured that they would give Malcolm X the saturation of publicity so that eventually his effectiveness in the black community would be weakened. Of course, when you sit and look at it from a distance you realize exactly what they're doing, and I think part of the reason my relationship with the white community in America is so bad is the fact that they know that I know this. My relationship with the white community in America is as bad as a black man's could be. But what saves me is I'm not important.

Williams: Would you then agree that the amount of publicity that they gave Martin Luther King created the same reaction?

Himes: Yes, yes. Of course, absolutely.

Williams: Now, you knew Malcolm pretty well.

Himes: Well, I knew him, not very well. I met him in 1962, I guess. He told me he had read *If He Hollers Let Him Go.*

Williams: He used to visit you when you were on rue Bourbon; well, how do you feel about his death? Most people feel that the government killed him.

Himes: Yes, well, personally I believe—and I will always believe this—that the

CIA organized it and black gunmen shot him. Because it would take an organization, the way it was so perfectly planned and executed with certain methods that blacks don't generally use. It's the first time that I ever read of black gunmen employing gangster techniques from Chicago of the 1920s. And we know the CIA has employed these techniques before. So the way that it was so perfectly organized—that with all of the bodyguards that he had they were able to rise up there in that place and shoot, gun him down, it had their trademark on it. And then the fact that the Black Muslims had already threatened him gave the CIA a perfect, ready-made alibi. They were doing this in many countries until lately. They were doing this in the East, in Morocco and North Africa, all over. If one studied their techniques, one would realize that this very easily could have been done by the CIA. And since I'm the type of person who believes it *was* done by them, I do believe it was done by them. Nothing will change that. They can say what they want to; I believe it.

Williams: How do you feel about the kind of mythology that has grown up around Malcolm? Last night we were talking about the movie that they're making now.

Himes: Yes, well, I think the reason why they became frightened about Malcolm X is, as I've always said, as long as the white press and the white community keep throwing it out that the black man hates white people, he's safe. It doesn't do a damn thing to him; he can walk around wherever he wishes to. Look at LeRoi Jones, who stands up there and tells those white people whatever he wants to tell them. Stokely Carmichael, Rap Brown, anybody—they're safe. They might find something to put them away, but most of the time they don't do a damn thing to them. But then, you know, when the black man enlarges this philosophy and includes a greater scope of people in it who will understand . . .

Williams: He'd opened his own mind.

Himes: Malcolm X had developed a philosophy in which he included all the people of the world, and people were listening to him. And then he became dangerous. Now as long as he was staying in America and just hating the white man he wasn't dangerous. But then when he involved others, they figured that if he kept on—since they themselves had brought him to the attention of the world—that he could use this; that they had set up for him to bring in masses of other people, masses of whites, masses of North Africans, masses of yellow people, all that would make him dangerous. So the only thing to do with him was kill him. Because that's the way white Americans solve every problem. You know, I have never even thought for a moment that the Black Muslims organized his assassination on their own. It never even occurred to me. First of all, there are a few Black Muslims who are rehabilitated from prisons and drug addiction and various things; there are a few that are personally dangerous to each other. But when a person gets the stature of Malcolm X at the time that he was executed, I think that he is absolutely safe from the Black Muslims. It would take an organization which is used to toppling kings and heads of states and big politicians to organize his assassination. I think he was absolutely untouchable by the Black Muslims.

Anyway, you know, there is no way that one can evaluate the American scene and avoid violence, because any country that was born in violence and has lived in violence always knows about violence. Anything can be initiated, enforced, contained or destroyed on the American scene through violence. That's the only thing that's ever made any change, because they have an inheritance of violence; it comes right straight from the days of slavery, from the first colonialists who landed on the American shores, the first slaves, through the Revolutionary War, the Civil War, the Indian wars, and gunslingers killing one another over fences and sheep and one goddamned thing or another; they grew up on violence. And not only that, it's gotten to be so much a part of the country that they are at the place where they are refining the history of their violence. They don't refer to the massacres of the Chinese during the last century out on the West Coast in California.

Williams: But not until they'd helped put the railroads in.

Himes: Yeah, that's right. They got all the labor that they could out of them before they killed them. Yes, they grew up on violence, and this is the only thing that they're going to listen to, the only thing that will move them. The only people that the white community in America has tried to teach that it is Christian to turn the other cheek and to live peacefully are the black people. They're the only people they have said bounce back. They have never even suggested it to anyone else. That is why the whole legend of Martin Luther King is such a powerful legend—because his was the teaching of nonviolence.

Williams: Right. He was a godsend to the American white people.

Himes: Absolutely. There's no question about it.

Black Writers

Williams: What happens, Chester, to young black writers who go over to Europe? It seems to me they're not producing like you and Wright and Harrington and Gardner produced. You were talking about Lomax [S. P.], who started out to be a writer. William Melvin Kelley was in Paris for a while and I think he got disgusted with it and now he's in Jamaica. What's happening to these younger guys who go over there?

Himes: Well, I don't know. I never met Kelley. Some of them continue to write, you know; some of them work very hard at it. But it's just the fact that there is a great resistance among American publishers against expatriate blacks, so that they have a much better opportunity of getting their work published in America if they're living there. Because if they are living abroad, the American publisher, as a rule, will just reject their works out of hand. Now this I know for a fact because I sent a number of manuscripts, recommended them, to American publishers myself, which have been turned down flat. Now the American publishers feel that the blacks should live in America and they have a sort of spiteful attitude toward blacks who escape from getting a head-beating in America.

Williams: They don't want them to get away.

Himes: Yes, that's another thing. That's part of the scene that makes magazines like *Time* have such a great and hard and relentless fury against Richard Wright, because Wright got away and *Time* never forgave him for that. And they continued to pick at him in one way or another. They thought, "Now, we helped this black man to become famous and so forth, and here he is escaping us." So they set out to punish him. Well, Dick was suffering under these various things—being the black writer who was best known in the world—he was the one that the white communications media could pick on. He was the only one who was vulnerable enough, being famous as he was. They could conceivably pick on me, but there wasn't any point 'cause nobody knew me. [Laughs.] When people began finding out who I was, they did begin picking. Until then they just left me alone entirely.

Williams: So your advice would be for them to stay in the States?

Himes: My advice to the black American writer would not be to stay in America, but just to continue to write. Not to be concerned about the attitudes in any place they are because one thing is for sure: there are great segments of the world who will be opposed to them, and this opposition, if they let it hurt them, will destroy them. That will happen anywhere they are. But there's no particular reason why—if they are young, have great vitality and a great love of life—why they just simply shouldn't stay in the States and write there. There's nothing they can learn here, that's for sure. There's nothing they can learn about their craft or anything else from going to places like Paris. The only reason for going to Paris is just to have a certain amount of freedom of movement for a limited period of time. But they won't even get any inspiration from being in France. *I* don't think they will.

Williams: Let me ask you kind of a cliché question. Two questions, really. What is the function of the American black writer now, and what do you think his role will be in another ten years?

Himes: Well, I think the *only* function of the black writer in America now is just to produce works of literature about whatever he wants to write about, without any form of repression or any hesitation about what he wishes to write about, without any restraint whatever. He should just produce his work as best he can, as long as it comes out, and put it on the American market to be published, and I believe now it will be (which it wouldn't have been ten years ago). All right, now, what will come out of this ten years from now? No one knows. But at least the world will be more informed about the black Americans' subconscious. And it is conceivable, since black people are creative people, that they might form on the strength of these creations an entirely new literature that will be more valuable than the output of the white community. Because we are a creative people, as everyone knows, and if we lend ourselves to the creation of literature like we did to the creation of jazz and dancing and so forth, there's no telling what the impact will be.

Williams: Can we do this? Can we make this impact without owning our own publishing companies?

Himes: I suppose so. Look, I have talked to black sharecroppers and convicts and various black people who could tell, without stopping, better stories than Faulkner could write. And they would have the same alliteration, the same wording. Some of them couldn't even read and write, but they had the same genius for telling stories that Faulkner had, and they could tell continuous stories, too. The narrative would go on and on, and they would never lose it. But then these people couldn't write, you see. So I believe that the black man certainly has a creativity that is comparable to the highest type of creativity in America because he has the same background. And probably even greater. And then the blacks of the northern ghetto have an absolutely unlimited source to draw their material from.

Somebody else comes up—like Upton Sinclair—and draws a little from this material, and builds a great reputation. Well, look at the black man now in the slums in Chicago; look what he can do. If Richard Wright had kept writing about Chicago he could have written forever.

Williams: But isn't there a kind of censorship that goes on if you don't have your own publishing outfit?

Himes: Yes, that is very true. You say "censorship"; the American publishers have what is called a conspiracy of censorship, where they don't even need to be in contact with one another to know what they are going to censor; there are certain things that they just automatically know they are going to censor, and they all will work in the same way. Yes, it's true that this automatic and unspoken conspiracy of censorship among white publishers works against the black man. He has an absolute wall against him, but in the course of time this will break down. In literature, it seems as if it's already breaking down, and it will if black writers particularly find that they need their own publishers very badly. Then white publishers, faced with competition, will have to change. That is one of the unfortunate parts of the entire American scene, that the black—well, I wouldn't say industrialists—but the black heads of firms who have sufficient money to do these things won't do them. And one doesn't know why, because it's possible for everybody else. One doesn't know why a black publisher wouldn't come up and tap this source of wealth of the black community of writers, because it seems to me it would be unlimited wealth. One wonders why one of them doesn't do so, since the white publishers realize it is rich and they are tapping it as best they can, even with their standards of censorship.

Williams: There's another young black writer on the scene. His name is James Alan McPherson. He's just published a collection of short stories called *Hue and Cry,* and most of the stories are pretty damn good. Ralph Ellison has a blurb on the back of the book in which he says that this kid is great, this is real writing. The implication is that a lot of black writers whom he considers "obscenely second-rate" use their blackness as a crutch, as an excuse for not learning their craft. What do you say?

Himes: Well, I don't know what to say about that. If Ralph means that the black writers are writing about their experiences of being black in the world—what else can they write about? Now, that reminds me of this famous conversation between James Baldwin and Richard Wright that various people have written about, this confrontation they had in Paris. Baldwin said to him, "You have written my story." He meant, of course, that when Dick wrote *Black Boy* he had written the story of all black boys. Anyway, the point I'm trying to make is what else can a black writer write about but being black? And it's very difficult to hide. It's not insurmountable, but it's difficult. And then, any beginning writer will always write about his experiences.

Well, you know, I think that Ralph is rather a little bit hipped on the business of learning his craft. I remember when he was imitating Richard Wright to the point where there was a confrontation and Wright accused him of it. Dick told me that Ralph said to him, "Who else can I imitate if I don't imitate you, Dick?" So I think he's gotten a little bit pompous in making the statements about the craftsmanship of the young black writers of the world. *Invisible Man* was a very good book, but that didn't make Ralph an authority. It didn't mean to me that Ralph was a particularly outstanding craftsman in relationship to other black writers. I think that particular remark is uncalled for; it's not a particularly beneficial type of criticism. It seems that a remark like that appeals more to the white community than the black community.

Williams: What advice do you have for all these young black writers who are growing up and getting on the scene?

Himes: Well, I was reading that book *Yellow Back Radio Broke-Down* by Ishmael Reed out there, and I agree that there's no reason why every black writer shouldn't produce a style of his own. If he has the talent. No particular purpose is served by imitation in writing, you know. You take a writer like Joyce. He had to produce his own narrative style, which any black writer can—I don't say that they can produce what Joyce produced, but they can produce a style of their own whatever it might be. Like Ishmael Reed. And I think that's what they should do. And then in the course of time this will make an impact. They will have their style. I find that hard to do myself. I can give that advice, but people are creatures of habit. I would like to produce a definite style. Of course, I won't be able to do that now, that's for sure. But I have always wanted to produce an entirely different approach to the novel form.

Williams: Than what you now use?

Himes: Yes.

Williams: What do you find lacking in the form you now use?

Himes: Well, I would like to see produced a novel that just drains a person's subconscious of all his attitudes and reactions to everything. Because, obviously, if one person has a number of thoughts concerning anything, there is a cohesion. There has to be because they belong to one man. Just let it come out as it is, let it come out as the words generate in the mind, let it come out in the phrasing of the subconscious and let it become a novel in that form. Of course this has been done, but not purely; there's always been an artificial strain. Since the black American is subject to having millions of thoughts concerning everything, millions of reactions, and his reactions and thoughts will obviously be different from that of the white community, this should create an entirely different structure of the novel. Of course, that requires youth. . . . I remember when I used to be able to write creatively thirty-five or forty pages a day. When I first began writing I was doing much better in introducing a story than I was doing in later years, because I would put down anything. I would be going along in a narrative form and listening to jazz and then a trumpet solo, say, would take my mind off for a second, I would follow it and write about it, and then go back to the narrative, and that would become part of the narrative. But of course this was always rejected by the editor.

Williams: You know, we once had a conversation about *The Primitive,* and I told you I'd been reading it on the subway and I missed my stop. Remember? And I told you I thought it was a brutal book, I think a great book, and I remember that you apologized for its being a brutal book. But I hadn't said that it was brutal in the sense that an apology was necessary. If you're talking about attacking the sensitivities on all levels, this is what I mean; this is what *The Primitive* did.

Himes: Yes, but that was what I was able to achieve in Mallorca because I didn't have any distractions with *The Primitive.* I wrote that out of a complete-

An Interview with Chester Himes

ly free state of mind from beginning to end; where I saw all the nuances of every word I put down, so *The Primitive* is my favorite book.

Williams: Yeah, that's a fantastic book. It's my favorite, too. But you once said *The Third Generation* was your most dishonest book. Do you remember?

Himes: Yes, yes. I had read a number of pages of a manuscript that my mother had written about her family. Her family was one of these slave families that had been interbred into the Southern white slave owners until the time of the Civil War. My mother's grandfather (I think it was) was the half-brother of his master; they were about the same age and they looked a great deal alike. When his master went away to the war, this half-white slave of his went with him as his body servant.

Well, she had produced this novel in detail, and I thought that that should have been part of the book. The reason I didn't use it was that— I needed for it to be published and I thought that would be offensive to the publishers and would make it difficult for publication at that time. That was some time ago. Nowadays, the black man has got over that thinking. They do have the freedom to write, more or less, what they want. Many books I read now by black writers would not have been published fifteen years ago under any circumstances. And there are a number of themes that won't be published now, and that's why I want to write a book and break through a certain reticence on the part of the publishers.

I read *The Godfather* [Mario Puzo], and the author has experienced a certain hesitation on the part of the publishers to publish a book that relates all the gruesomeness and the power of assassination, of ruling by this power; that relates the effect that a group of people can have by controlling—by simply shooting other people in the head. Shooting people in the head generates power. This is what I think black writers should write about. I remember Sartre made a statement which was recorded in the French press (I never had any use for Sartre since) that in writing his play *The Respectful Prostitute* he recognized the fact that a black man could not assault a white person in America. That's one of the reasons I began writing the detective stories. I wanted to introduce the idea of violence. After all, Americans live by violence, and violence achieves—regardless of what anyone says, regardless of the distaste of the white community—its own ends. *The Godfather* is not only a successful book, but it's a successful book about a successful organization that rules by violence. And not only do they rule by violence, but the American community has never been able to do anything about them.

Williams: Well, I think this is largely because people who control the American community are in cahoots either directly or indirectly with the Mafia.

Himes: Yes, that was the same thing during all the days of Prohibition, when everybody realized that the gangsters and the politicians worked side by side, close together. As a matter of fact, the gangsters were only servants of the politicians, the servants of the rich. That's why the gangsters in America were almost an untouchable breed during that time.

White Writers

Williams: What about your experiences with white expatriate writers?

Himes: I don't have any experiences with white expatriate writers.

Williams: Remember once you told me a story about how James Jones used to hold this soirée every Sunday at his place, and he said he'd like to meet you and you should come over, and you said, "What the hell do I want to see James Jones for?"

Himes: Yeah, that's probably true. I never met James Jones all the time I was in Paris. I actually don't know if I'd know him if I saw him. Lesley's pointed him out once or twice, but I don't remember what he looks like. I have nothing to say to James Jones, absolutely nothing to say to him whatsoever. And from what I've heard about his career and so forth, I don't *want* to know anything about him.

The thing about white writers . . . it's very pitiful you know. Take white writers like Hemingway, for instance. Now Hemingway became one of the great writers of the world, but as far as I know Hemingway never, one time, in one book or one story, had any message or statement to make about anything other than what he called courage or bravery and so forth, which I think is simpleminded. And that is all. But then, you see, to a black writer they say, "Well, what statement is he making?" He could write a book, one of the most fabulous stories in the world, and they'll say, "That's a good book, but what is the statement? What is he saying about the conditions of the black people in America?" Well, most black writers have something to say about this because most black writers from America—what else can they say, what else can they write about, what else do they think about? So that is why it becomes an absolute part of their writing, because it's part of their thinking. But I don't think that it's all done deliberately—just to sit down and make a statement; it's subconscious. Of course, most writers of any consequence are against various forms of social injustice. Take them all—even go back to old Russian writers like Dostoyevsky, old English writers, Dickens and so forth, and the new English writers, Joyce and all. Because this is part of the human emotion, you know, to protest against various forms of social injustice. And all the rest of them who are famous throughout the world. So the black writer does so because as a writer this is part of his trade. But to sit down and deliberately do so, results in a tract which quite often gets away from the author.

Williams: Are there any white writers that you admire? Not necessarily contemporary. You mentioned Dostoyevsky . . .

Himes: Yes, I mention Dostoyevsky so much because I've always admired him to a great degree because by reading him I understand his process of writing. There was a man who wrote very rapidly and very brilliantly all the time, and the reason that he did so was that he needed money all the time. He'd need it all the time, and as soon as he'd get money he'd throw it away. Also, being epileptic he had this extraordinary perception that most epileptics have.

But then I also like Faulkner because when Faulkner was writing his stories, his imaginative stories about the South, he was inventing the situations on sound ground—but still inventive. He was inventing them so fast that if you breeze through Faulkner you can find any number of mistakes. Faulkner would forget characters. You can read certain books, especially *Light in August,* and Faulkner has forgotten the names that he attaches to certain characters, then he goes on and he gives them other names.

Williams: I've noticed this, but I always figured it was something I had misread.

Himes: No, no, he was writing so fast he forgot. I do that myself. I remember years ago when I was starting to write short stories I had a joker shot in the arm but later I forgot he was shot in the arm. [Laughter.] Yes, you know this happens quite often, especially in the movies. Not that they forget it; they just pass it over.

Williams: You know, Chester, there seem to be more white guys who are writing about black people today than ever before. There have always been some, but now they seem to be crawling out of the woodwork.

Himes: Oh, yes, everywhere, everywhere. This has been happening about the past five or six or seven years. And you know why this is? Because at the beginning of the black uprisings in America, when the blacks were seemingly going to use violence to the point where it would have some meaning, well then they had world coverage. They had the greatest coverage of any story—more than even the assassination of Kennedy or the politics in Russia. Total saturation in the world press made the white writers eager to cash in on what they figure will have the greatest appeal, so as you said before, they came up with the idea. On the whole, the white writers are better trained than the black writers, because they've had more facilities for education in many of the techniques and crafts of the trade. So a white writer can sit down and he can write some of the goddamndest, most extraordinary bullshit about the blacks, but he will successfully project his story since he's not interested in having any authenticity. All he's concerned about is reaching the largest audience and what he can do with it. Like this joker who wrote the book *The Man*.

Williams: Oh, Irving Wallace, yeah.

Himes: He didn't give a damn about whether this story was possible or whether it had plausibility; the main thing was to write a story that would titillate the greatest number of whites and make them buy the book. It wouldn't even make them think; it would be a diversion. It is true that the white writers of the world have a much better chance of learning their craft.

Then, the white writers in America conduct writing as a major business, which it is. Harold Robbins has more writers working for him than Shakespeare had. All he has to do is just sketch out the plot and put his writers to work and knock out his books.

Williams: I didn't know he used other writers.

Himes: The way I found out, I was in New York talking to Bucklin Moon, who had become, after some hard times, the editor-in-chief of Pocket Books. And I found that in addition to working as editor-in-chief, he was also working on Harold Robbins' *The Adventurers*. Yes, he was a competent writer, so he was writing some of the passages. Harold Robbins didn't have time to write. [Laughter.] After all, it was a million-dollar project. He could afford to pay Bucklin Moon probably better than Pocket Books was paying him as editor-in-chief.

Williams: Did you read the Styron book *The Confessions of Nat Turner*? You know the big stink about it?

Himes: I didn't read very much of it, just off and on. I read in an English paper that Styron was employing a gimmick there. He figured that he could write about Nat Turner as long as he made him a homosexual, lusting after white women. That was the only way the story of Nat Turner could be acceptable, because Nat Turner was one of the only black slaves who had the right idea: the only thing to do with a white slave owner was to kill him. But Styron couldn't have him just kill him outright because he wanted to be free; he had to make him a homicidal homosexual lusting after white women. Which I find very . . . [laughter] funny. It was a cute gimmick, you know, and it went down very well.

Williams: Yes, it was an immediate bestseller.

Himes: Yeah, obviously. Black homosexuals and black eunuchs have always been profitable in white literature. The profit incentive has corrupted American writing, but that's what writers write for anyway—white writers as well as black writers; they write for profit. The only thing is black writers get such very little profit. In the last ten or fifteen years it's become very big business. Now, whether this is true or not, I heard that when Martin Luther King was assassinated, no serious money-making publisher was particularly interested until they realized the world was not only incensed but extremely interested in the life of a black Christian who had been assassinated, and that it was a very big story, a tremendous story. So the publishers began bidding for the biography of Martin Luther King which was to be written by his widow. I don't know who told me this, but probably my editor, that the publishers bid for this book, unwritten of course, but it didn't make any difference whether she could write or not because they would supply any number of writers to write it. But anyway, McGraw-Hill won it on a bid of a contract to pay her a $500,000 advance.

Williams: I heard it was $450,000, but who the hell is going to quibble about $50,000 when you're talking about that kind of money.

Himes: Yeah, well, there you are—half a million dollars.

Williams: That's a lot of money involved in that book.

Himes: Yes, because anything which will hold the public interest, for the next ten years anyway, will be popular. King was a much greater man in the world and a much more significant personality in the world and touched more people in the world after he was killed than before. That's when most of the people in the world even got to know who he was. But everybody knows who he is now—even the people walking down the street here, and most of the people who live in Spain.

Williams: So you say that for the next ten years he'll be a viable subject?

Himes: Yes, that's the way I feel. It might be longer than that, but I think certainly ten years.

Williams: The piece that you have in here [*Beyond the Angry Black,* 1966] I see quoted pretty frequently: "Chester Himes says . . ." And you told me that you did that piece in 1940 . . .

Himes: I guess I must have done that when I was at Yaddo [a writer's colony], and that was in 1948. Horace Cayton, who was the director of the South Parkway Community Center, and the woman who was teaching creative writing out at the University of Chicago got together and decided that they would bring me to Chicago to read a paper on the Dilemma of the Negro Writer. When I finished reading that paper nobody moved, nobody applauded, nobody ever said anything else to me. I was shocked. I stayed in Chicago a few days drinking, and then I was half-drunk all the rest of the time I was in Yaddo. That was the time I started getting blackouts, I was drinking so much. I would get up in the morning and go into town, which you weren't supposed to do, and by eleven o'clock, I was dead drunk.

Williams: Into Saratoga . . .

Himes: Yes. I lived across the hall from Patricia Highsmith, who wrote *Strangers on a Train,* which Hitchcock bought for practically nothing but made a classic out of. He bought the full movie rights for five thousand dollars. Hitchcock doesn't believe in paying writers either, you know.

Williams: Who else was up there in Yaddo when you were there?

Himes: Well, part of the time, there was Truman Capote. I think he had already published *Other Voices, Other Rooms.*

Williams:	He's done very well.
Himes:	Yeah. I don't remember any other people who were there. I think Katherine Anne Porter, who wrote *Ship of Fools,* was also there most of the time, but I didn't see her. She spent almost all her days when she was in America up at Yaddo. She had a special room up there in the big house in a tower.
Williams:	What did you think of *Ship of Fools* as an example of an American book that's supposed to be long awaited, with the great writer?
Himes:	I found it innocent enough, but I didn't think it was a serious book that had any particular meaning other than the fact that I could see her up there typing away. It wasn't worth waiting twenty years for it. I would think that the book that ———— and I wrote, called *The Silver Altar,* was certainly as good as *Ship of Fools.*

Black Anti-Semitism

Williams:	What does the "B" in your name stand for?
Himes:	That was my mother's family name, Bomar.
Williams:	Because when I first read *If He Hollers* . . .
Himes:	Yes, I was using the "B" then.
Williams:	Chester, let me ask you, do you know what your name "Himes" is derived from? Is it English or . .
Himes:	It's Jewish, like "Chaim," "Jaime" . . .
Williams:	Spanish Jewish?
Himes:	I don't know. It came down from "Heinz." Anyway, my father's grandfather's owner was "Himes." I don't know, maybe it was his father's—my grandfather's—owner. He was a slave blacksmith; that's how my father got into that. It was a trade that came down from father to son. My father was able to go to college and learn a few other things, like wheelwrighting and various skills. But the trade of blacksmithing was a hereditary business. It came out of slavery, and the owner of our

family was named in a certain variety of "Heinz," but it was a Jewish name. My forebears just took the name "Himes"—that's the way it was pronounced by the slaves. It was a literal translation, whether it was "Chaim" or "Jaime" or "Heinz." I don't know. But the "Bomar" of my mother's family's slave name is Irish, of course. I should call myself Chester X.

Williams: That's interesting. That's interesting. Let me ask you one final question, and we'll quit for the day. I see you sitting there getting kind of wilted. I'm getting pretty tired myself. I don't know whether you've been reading about it or not, but there appears to be growing animosity, at least in New York City, between blacks and Jews (though one can't really trust the press). Do you think this is a result of the closeness, as I said earlier, whereby familiarity breeds contempt?

Himes: No. You know, I have a very long discussion of this in *Lonely Crusade*. That whole business between the black people and the Jews in America is part of the book, and that's the part the Jews disliked so much. As a matter of fact, I have a copy of the French Jewish magazine, which has a photo of me on the cover. They ran an eighteen-page interview on my discussion of the relationship of blacks and Jews in *Lonely Crusade*. It was obvious, even when I was a little boy in the South that the only stores black people could go to, like hardware and department stores, were owned by Jews. When you went to non-Jewish stores you couldn't get in the door. So, where the black man and the Jew are concerned, the Jew has always taken the black man as a customer. Because the Jew has always been in business, and he found out that in a basically anti-Semitic country like America the most available market for a poor Jew on the lower rung of business was the black man. That was his market. He could rent them houses and he could sell them food.

Well, because the blacks were ignorant and the descendants of slaves, the Jewish merchants and landlords misused them. Where blacks might have been creative in other ways, in the ways of the commercial world they were babes in the woods. They were pigeons; anyone could take advantage of them who wanted to, so the Jewish merchants did—and the Jewish landowners (the ghettos were owned by Jews). It's very seldom any other name than a Jewish one appears as a landlord or proprietor in any ghetto in any city of America. All businesses in the ghettos were owned by Jews, and then a few of the blacks were eventually able to buy some of them. Then, of course, the black majority developed an unspoken anti-Semitism, even though they were doing business every day with the Jew around the corner. The black had an ingrown suspicion and resentment of the Jew. He realized that he was being used in certain ways by all Jewish landlords and merchants. Even today a Jew will make a fortune out of the race problem, and this builds up a subconscious resentment—although most of the white people I do business with, who help me, whom I love and respect, are Jews. But that doesn't negate the fact that the Jews are the ones who had contact with the blacks and took advantage of them. Now the gentiles had enslaved the blacks and worked them as beasts, but when they were freed, the gentiles didn't want to have a damn thing to do with them. They left the blacks without food or shelter. They worked them for a pittance and that was all. Whereas the Jew realized that to house and feed the freed black man was a business, a business that paid off. This paid off better than any other business because where else could Jews, who were in a ghetto themselves, open up any kind of a business and have customers, other than in the black ghetto?

Williams: Well then, why is there such a great reaction—as in New York to the fact that, particularly in the school system, the black teachers want their thing, the black people in the community want their thing? The Jews are saying this is anti-Semitism—which to a large degree it is—but it's also, as you seem to imply, an awakening to the fact that they have been used.

Himes: Yes, that's right. You see, the way it is in the city school system in New York, a quarter of a century ago the only white teachers who would teach in black communities were Jews.

Williams: That's where the Irish sent them.

Himes: Yes, they're the only ones who would go there. So, over a period of time they got entrenched, and now that the black people are rising up, they're resentful of the kind of uncommitted teachers, more so than the fact that they're Jewish teachers. It just so happens that most of them are Jewish teachers and that they are guilty. The blacks claim they're guilty of: giving kids bad education, ignoring them on certain points. These teachers on the whole are Jewish, but they have been entrenched in the school system because this is where the gentiles sent them. It's an unfortunate situation but it's inevitable, because as the blacks begin to have any kind of protest, it's a spontaneous protest against the first individuals whom they have had direct contact with—who they know are guilty.

They have not looked back far enough to realize that the Jewish school teachers are no more guilty of actually misusing black students than the white gentiles who exiled them there in the first place. No one is looking at it that way, because no one ever does. The younger Jews, I read, seriously are trying to get the older Jews, who are people of great habit too, to see that there is a different side . . .

Williams: Yeah, this is something that I've noticed too.

Himes: Well, this whole problem in America, as I see it, developed from the fact that the slaves were freed and that there was no legislation of any sort to make it possible for them to live. So this is what has built up to such a tremendous problem that now . . .

Williams: Right. They felt that freedom was enough by itself.

Himes: Yeah, what is it that they have in heaven—milk and honey? That some poor nigger could go and live on nothing. Just to proclaim emancipation was not enough. You can't eat it; it doesn't keep the cold weather out.

Wright

Williams: What was Paris like, with you and Wright, Harrington, William Gardner Smith, and Melvin Van Peebles? It must have been a pretty great scene.

Himes: Well, we always met at the Café Tournon. In fact Dick Wright wasn't in it as much as Ollie Harrington, who was actually the center; and Melvin wasn't there then. Ollie was the center of the American community on the Left Bank in Paris, white and black, and he was the greatest Lothario in the history of the whole Latin Quarter. And he was a fabulous raconteur too. He used to keep people spellbound for hours. So they collected there because of Ollie. Then the rest of us came. Dick was a good friend of Ollie's; as a matter of fact, he used to telephone Ollie every morning. Dick was a compulsive conversationalist in the early hours of the morning. When he woke up he had to telephone somebody and have a long conversation. When Ollie wasn't there he had to find someone else—Daniel Guerin or even Jean-Paul Sartre. But they got tired of these conversations, so he chose Ollie. As long as Ollie was in town Dick would telephone him as soon as he woke up in the morning, whether Ollie was awake or not (it didn't make any difference) and have long conversations about the CIA and the race problem and all. You know, that kind of conversation doesn't go down too well at seven thirty in the morning.

Williams: What did you decide about the CIA in Paris? I know that Wright had some pretty positive ideas about what they were doing.

Himes: I don't know really. You see, I can't make any definite statement about the CIA in Paris because I didn't have any knowledge or even any thoughts about their operation. I realized that the FBI had a dossier on me going back to my childhood anyway, so it didn't make any difference to me one way or the other. And when I got my passport from the State Department I had to go and send my certificate for the restoration of my citizenship.

Williams: What's the restoration certificate?

Himes: Well, you know, when you've been to prison they take your citizenship away. And then the governor of the state returns your citizenship after a period of time. And my citizenship had been returned to me by a governor named Burton, who later became a Supreme Court justice. He was a Supreme Court justice at the time I applied for my passport. So I realized that the CIA knew everything they wanted to know about me already. They weren't interested in me anyway. The CIA was only interested in Richard Wright, and only because of the fact that they thought that he might have had information concerning the communist affiliations of people in high places in government, and that he might conceivably be having a dialogue, not a conspiracy or anything, but just a dialogue with people that they considered dangerous such as Nkrumah or Frantz Fanon. The only other person I know they were seriously interested in was Malcolm X. And of course everyone knows the CIA was interested in Fanon. They went to Fanon's assistance in the last years of his life to show that they had goodwill. Took him over to America and put him under medical treatment. By the way, he wrote a long article on my "Treatment of Violence," which his wife still has, and which I've thought I might get and have published. Because he had the same feeling, of course, that I have.

Williams: How long is the piece?

Himes:	I don't know. Julia Wright told me that she had read it and that his wife has it.
Williams:	You know, Julia is in New York. No . . . it's Rachel.
Himes:	Yes, Rachel. Well, Rachel never got along with her mother. Rachel was Papa's daughter all her life. 'Cause she was a little blonde daughter, you know, and Dick was devoted to her. But Julia looks just like her father.

When Dick died Ellen was in London, and then she didn't know what to do. When she came back she wanted to have a private funeral. Ellen and I personally had a furious argument about this. I told her she couldn't do that. When Dick died Lesley and I were spending the winter in St. Tropez and our landlady asked us if we knew a man named Richard Wright. And she said he had died; it had just come over the radio. So we got into our little car and rushed up to Paris, and when we got up there we found that Ellen had said that she was going to have a closed funeral, and that no one was going to be admitted, and that Dick's body was going to be cremated.

Well, we were staying with Ollie Harrington. As a matter of fact, he had just moved into this apartment, so we were sleeping on a mattress on the floor. So Ollie didn't say anything—he didn't want to cross Ellen. Ollie was a great diplomat. But anyway, I telephoned Ellen and told her she couldn't possibly have a closed funeral for Dick. So she decided after Dick had been dead three or four days and the funeral was rapidly approaching that she would open it. Which meant that a great number of people were not there who would have been if they had known earlier that it was to be an open funeral. But as it was, Dick had been on the outs with great numbers of people by that time. The head of Présence Africaine, Alioune Diop, was one of the people who gave the funeral oration. But at that time, before Dick's death, Dick and Diop weren't speaking. It was a relatively small funeral and he was suddenly cremated. After his cremation a very strong rumor started in Paris that he had been poisoned.

Williams:	I remember hearing about it at the time.
Himes:	Yes. Now, Ollie was supposed to have more testimony; he had more evidence than anyone because Dick had sent Ollie a telegram, which I saw when I was in Ollie's house, which said something like "Come to see me right away." And Ollie hadn't gone because, as I said, Dick was always telephoning him early every morning and he was sort of pissed

off with him, so he didn't go. Well, the next Ollie heard of Dick, he was dead. He did die suddenly. Everyone knows the circumstances of his death—the fact that he was being released and was in supposedly good health. And then supposedly a mysterious woman had come to see him. Whether this is true or not, I couldn't say; this is the essence of the rumor. And the rumor still persists. Personally, that is one death I do not connect with the CIA, although of course with these things one never knows because the CIA was interested in many, many things. . . . And Dick realized that he was a sick man and he might have had some revelation to make and decided to make it, and people might have decided he was better off dead. This is all guesswork on my part.

Williams: Had he made a public talk in the American Church two or three weeks before this, in which he was running down the CIA activities of people connected with the arts? Connie mentions it in her book.

Himes: Yes, well, everyone was doing that too, you know. And whether that has any relation to his death or not I couldn't say. I wasn't there anyway. I had been away from Paris for some time, moving around. I wasn't close enough to the scene to have any definite information until I arrived back and talked to Ellen, mostly just about the funeral.

Ellen and I never got along, as you already know. We got along very well once upon a time, but then we fell out just around the time Richard Wright was writing *The Long Dream,* because she didn't want him to write it. She didn't want him to go back into his Mississippi childhood and write about the black oppression in America, because he had written a number of books on the world scene. And I felt just the opposite. I felt that he should go back to the roots, the sources of his information, and write about the American scene. As a matter of fact, I was doing the same thing myself at the time. And Dick had come and talked to me at great lengths before he began writing this book.

Then Ellen stopped me on the street one day and said that I shouldn't encourage Dick. And I said, "Well, you know, I can't encourage Dick to do anything." And she said, "Yes, you're encouraging him to go back and write this book, and he's a big man now and he should not do this." So that made me so angry that I said some very impolite things, and we were shouting at one another on the Boulevard St. Germain. After that Ellen and I never got along. I see her now, I kiss her and embrace her because we've known one another many years. But it's just the fact that I know without a doubt that she wants certain information about Richard Wright's life not to be revealed. If Dick hadn't had his sexual relationships, if he hadn't seen the people that he had, if he hadn't had that certain type of curiosity that he had, he wouldn't have been Richard Wright. So there's no point in trying to hide the character of a man. But Richard Wright also reached a point, after he had been in France for four or five years, where he was well entrenched, had a really splendid apartment equipped in the American fashion, was a real celebrity to the press and everybody else. As my translator said, he was such a celebrity that if he had called a press conference at the foot of the stairs leading up to the Sacré Coeur and said, "Gentlemen, I want you to run up these stairs," they would have done so. But anyway, after a time, Dick became ashamed of his own image. The French continued to think of Dick as "Black Boy," and Dick was beginning to think of himself as a world figure, which he was. But at the same time, he was still Black Boy. The French were subject to thinking of him as Black Boy exclusively and excluded the fact that he was a world personality. Also, the French liked to believe that he belonged to them.

Williams: Why did they turn on him?

Himes: Well, they turned on him primarily because just that—the fact that he began writing on the world political scene. The French are very sensitive to any world figure in France who writes on the world political scene, especially if he's a black man. They are very sensitive about it. And then what the French do, they just take him out of the press. And to take Dick out of the press, since he had been such an extraordinary celebrity . . . he was plagued by it—this sort of comedown bothered him. So eventually this sort of corroded him and he decided he was going to move from France and go and live in England. But then he discovered England wouldn't give him the—racism in England had tightened up to the point where they wouldn't even consider having Dick living there.

Williams: I remember Ollie's description about when Wright went in to see about his passport, his permanent visa. He wanted an explanation from this official, who threw his passport at his feet and said, "I don't have to explain a goddamned thing to you."

Himes: Horace [Cayton] actually knew quite a bit about Richard Wright from the time of the publication of *Native Son* until Dick left for France. He was quite close to him. He'd have Dick up to the South Side Community House in Chicago, where he was director. Dick was very naive, you know, and Horace used to get embarrassed because he was such a slick cat himself, and he'd have some of these white chicks over from the University of Chicago, and Dick would get excited and wouldn't know how to behave. Dick was a strange man anyway. He was not only a genius but an astute political tactician—but in some ways he was very naive too.

Index